A HISTORY OF AFRICA
1840–1914

Michael Tidy
with
Donald Leeming

Volume One 1840–1880

**AFRICANA
PUBLISHING
COMPANY**
A division of Holmes & Meier Publishers, Inc.
30 Irving Place, New York, N.Y. 10003

TO

my wife Anastasia Obuya
(whose loving spirit and
practical assistance have
sustained me in the writing
of this book, and who has
given my life a new dimension)

M.T.

British Library Cataloguing in Publication Data

Tidy, Michael
  A history of Africa, 1840–1914.
  Vol. 1
  1. Africa – History
  I. Title   II. Leeming, Donald
  960'.2   DT22

ISBN 0 340 24419 4

First published 1980
Copyright © 1980 M. Tidy and D. Leeming
Maps copyright © 1980 Hodder and Stoughton Ltd

Represented in East and Central Africa by
K. W. Martin, P.O. Box 30583, Nairobi, Kenya.
Represented in West Africa by Nigeria Publishers Services Ltd,
P.O. Box 62, Ibadan, Nigeria.

Printed in Great Britain for Hodder and Stoughton Educational,
a division of Hodder and Stoughton Ltd, Mill Road, Dunton
Green, Sevenoaks, Kent, by Richard Clay (The Chaucer Press) Ltd,
Bungay, Suffolk

Contents

List of Maps

Preface

This two volume history aims to supply a need for a readily available survey of the whole African continent during the critical periods before, during and immediately after the European Partition. The writing of the book owes an immense debt to the work of innumerable historians of Africa. However, much of their work has been unavailable to the general reader while other material has been published in regional, national or local histories. *A History of Africa 1840–1914* attempts to bring together much of this material in one history and to make it more readily accessible. Inevitably a history such as this has to be selective, but it is believed that the selections of material will give the reader a good overall picture of Africa between 1840 and 1914.

Volume 1 covers the period from about 1840 to the beginning of the Scramble. It examines the considerable African achievement in the pre-colonial era by looking at a number of diverse societies, and surveys their response to European penetration throughout the continent. The increasing European interest of the nineteenth century, including the work of traders, missionaries and explorers, is dealt with. The Volume ends at the point where the European powers are poised for the Scramble. Volume 2 will deal with the period of the Scramble and the African response to the loss of independence.

We are both deeply grateful to our Kenyan students, fellow-teachers, historians and other friends and colleagues, all of whom have made our work in Kenya so meaningful and our lives there so enjoyable.

M.T./D.L.
October, 1979

I
Pre-colonial Africa:
A general survey

Enlargement of scale

The nineteenth century in Africa was a period of tremendous change which affected political, economic and social systems. Part of this change was a great enlargement of scale. This enlargement involved far more than mere growth in size. In the political sphere, states of increased size developed, and in many areas a more efficient system of government arose than had existed before, with centralized administrations and military forces. In economic affairs production of goods certainly increased, but there was also enlargement in the sense that Africa became more and more a part of the world economy, influenced by economic developments outside Africa. In social affairs there was the same sort of development. Alien cultures impinged upon and influenced Africa more than in the past. Christianity and Islam spread more widely and began to undermine traditional religions. North of the Sahara and in parts of West and East Africa Islam had long been significant. It was now challenged more widely by Christianity than ever before. As the two religions expanded, Africa became more important for them as a continent in which to spread their faiths.

An African 'partition' of Africa took place between 1800 and 1885, as huge and well-administered empires arose from Zululand to Egypt and from the Ethiopian highlands to the Mandinka forests. There had been earlier large states in Africa, but the nineteenth century saw a greater enlargement of scale than ever before.

Economies also underwent an enlargement of scale. The cultivation of new crops, like vegetable oils in West Africa, and the expansion of production of iron goods in Bantu Africa led to a remarkable growth in long-distance trade. Dyula traders of the Mandinka lands were to be found on the west coast at Freetown and deep into the Sahara. Nyamwezi traders from central Tanzania took their goods to the Indian Ocean, Zanzibar and to the Atlantic ports of Angola.

There was enlargement of scale in religious culture, as Africans increasingly adopted the world religions, Islam and Christianity, and adapted their traditional religions to a rapidly changing world by developing new, trans-ethnic cults.

Enlargement of political scale

The period from 1800 to 1840 saw the formation of more multi-ethnic states than had occurred at one time since the sixteenth century. In West Africa the Islamic jihad of Usman dan Fodio resulted in the foundation of the Caliphate of Sokoto in northern Nigeria between 1804 and 1809. Ahmad Lobbo reformed and enlarged the Kingdom of Macina west of the great north bend of the Niger. After 1819 the same process of state-formation or enlargement occurred in southern Africa where Shaka created the Zulu empire about 1820. Shaka also helped to set in motion the *Mfecane*: the forced migrations which led to the rise of many new states in Central and East Africa. This period was also marked by the consolidation and extension of their authority by rulers such as Muhammad Ali in Egypt (1805–48), Seyyid Said in Zanzibar (1808–56), Kimweri ye Nyumbai in Usambara (after 1803) and Al-Kanemi in Bornu (1808–37).

The period 1840–85 saw an acceleration in the growth of larger political units. In the western and central Sudan this growth was closely tied up with the rise of the militant Muslim brotherhood, the *Tijaniyya*. It was a growth spearheaded by the jihad of Al-Hajj Umar, who created the Tokolor Empire. Other great state-builders, included Samori Toure of the Mandinka and Mahmadou Lamine of the Sarrakole. In South, Central and East Africa the migratory hordes of the Mfecane generally settled down in the 1840s and then began to build centralized states. In the north the 1840s saw the rise of Kasa, later Emperor Tewodros II of Ethiopia, the first of the great modernizers and reunifiers of his country. Egypt under Muhammad Ali had conquered northern and central Sudan in the 1820s and continued this enlargement in the 1840s, after the southern Sudan had been opened to the forces of Egyptian expansion. States like Dahomey, Benin and Buganda continued to expand their authority further afield, and to consolidate the process of centralization.

In some areas Europeans were consolidating their positions. In the south, the Great Trek of the Boers ended in the late 1830s; in the 1840s they consolidated their republics on the High Veld. On the coast the British, in response to Zulu and Boer activity, established the colony of Natal. In Algeria, the French finally defeated the nationalist hero Abdul Qadir who was sent into exile in 1847. In the 1850s France expanded three hundred miles inland in Senegal.

The 1870s and the early 1880s, the eve of the European Partition, saw the apogee of the enlargement of political scale in Africa before the colonial period, with the revival of ancient Bunyoro under its modern Omukamas, Kamurasi and Kabalega, the rise of the new Nyamwezi states of Urambo and Ukimbu, the creation of a Swahili dominion in the eastern Zaire Basin, the emergence of Ibadan on the ashes of Old Oyo, the growth of Samori's Mandinka empire, the more effective reunification of Ethiopia by Yohannis IV, and the phenomenon of the Mahdiyya in the Sudan. This African partition of Africa, though violent in its execution, brought about a larger measure of political stability to a politically fragmented continent.

The new African states of the nineteenth century were better organized internally than their predecessors. There was more administration, and it was more centralized. In the great states of the Sudan, from the Atlantic to the Red Sea, in Zanzibar, and even in traditionalist Asante, literate Muslims were employed in the developing civil services. Even in non-literate states more efficient systems of administration began to develop. Nyungu-ya-Mawe, ruler of Ukimbu in Tanzania, evolved a system of district officers with well-defined functions; a system that the Germans used as the basis of their rule later. Dahomey, with its many departments of government and its elaborate financial organization and system of inspection was one of the best organized states on the continent. Ministers were selected for their ability and were responsible for a particular department. Regular censuses of both people and livestock were held. All citizens were taxed.

An interesting feature of the nineteenth century African administrative revolution was the use of men of commoner and slave origin to enhance both royal power and efficiency. Many rulers increased their central power and weakened that of the hereditary provincial aristocracy by appointing to key posts in the administration and the army men of no traditional social standing, who had proved their ability and who, owing their elevation to the ruler, were loyal to him. Samori Toure in West Africa, Kabalega in East Africa and the Ndebele ruler, Mzilikazi, are just a few examples of the many rulers who improved their government in this way. There was, of course, the danger that disputes would break out between the hereditary aristocracy, who had seen their position undermined, and the newly promoted men. In the Niger delta Jaja, a man of slave origin, became so powerful that he was able to secede from Bonny and found the new state of Opobo.

Closely connected with the development of centralized administration was military reform, especially the creation of standing armies and of regiments that cut across local and ethnic loyalties. Military reform also involved the use of new weapons. Some of them were modern, such as the guns imported from Europe. But some were traditional weapons which were adapted to different uses. One of the more famous is the short stabbing spear introduced by Shaka. These weapons were often more useful than guns, which required sophisticated maintenance and ammunition. In the long run, however, Africa's lack of western military technology was to prove to be her downfall. The spear, however effectively used, was no match for the Gatling gun and the Maxim gun.

Large parts of Africa experienced major political consolidation in the half-century or so before the European invasion of the 1880s. However there were certain political weaknesses which made Africa vulnerable to European invasion. Many millions of Africa's peoples were organized in small political units. For example, in most of Igbo country and in most of what became Kenya, political organization existed only at the village level. These societies did not even have chiefs, let alone kings. Often intricate and complex, they were perfectly adequate entities in the pre-colonial era, but were extremely vulnerable to European political invasion. Not only did village 'states' lack western military technology; they also lacked experience in co-operation with neighbours against foreign invasion and often had no inclination to co-operate until it was too late.

A further weakness was that even large states were not always effectively centralized. Both the Sokoto and Tokolor empires tolerated considerable local autonomy. When faced with European invasion this local particularism made united effective resistance very difficult.

The massive changes in Africa did not always bring the enlargement of states. The Rozwi state was destroyed by the Ngoni, part of it later being occupied by the Ndebele. A large state was here succeeded by a number of smaller ones. In many ways the Rozwi empire was more sophisticated and advanced than the Ndebele state which succeeded it in its former south-western territories. It had developed a highly complex system of chieftainship which involved a large element of consultation between rulers and subjects. It was closely related to an advanced African religious system, based largely on the Mwari high god cult. In general, however, new African states of the nineteenth century replaced many small ones, and contributed to a process of political unification not destruction.

Enlargement of scale in the economy

Throughout the period 1800–85, Africa's economy as a whole experienced considerable growth, especially after 1840. Just as the 1840s mark a turning point in the enlargement of political scale, so these years show a similar speeding-up of the process of enlargement of scale in the economy.

In agriculture, there was a veritable revolution with increased production, the spread of new crops, and the use of new methods. Increasing production was a feature of almost all parts of the continent. In the West African forest zone, the production of vegetable oils for export rose dramatically. Palm-oil production roughly doubled between 1830 and 1840, doubled again by 1855, and continued to increase up to the early 1880s. Groundnut oil production developed rapidly from the 1850s. Increased production in east central Africa was due largely to the introduction of new crops such as cloves at the coast and a whole range of food crops in the interior. Plantation agriculture, dominated by the Swahili-Arabs on the east coast, was extended into the interior, especially the eastern Zaire basin. In West Africa there was the development in the Mandara Uplands on the present Nigeria/Cameroon border, of a system of intensive agriculture which included soil conservation, the use of fertilizers, crop rotation and afforestation.

In manufacturing there were new advances, such as the manufacture of copper crosses for currency in Katanga and, in the same region, the development of wire-drawing and the skill of repairing guns. In East and Central Africa generally there was a tremendous expansion of hoe and spear manufacturing. Clearly though, Africa was not in this period progressing towards an industrial revolution. Industry continued to be organized, as in pre-industrial Europe, on a house-hold or guild basis.

Trade expanded considerably between 1800 and 1885. In West Africa, the Saharan trade actually increased after 1840, and reached its peak around 1875, before it began to decline. There was a rapid expansion of the savannah trade in cattle, horses and kola nuts. At the coast, vegetable oil exports and imports of European manufactured goods—now much cheaper after the European Industrial Revolution—reached unprecedented levels of quantity and value. In West, East and Central Africa, the oceanic slave trades reached new peaks, in spite of abolition treaties between European and African states. On the west coast, largely due to expansion of the Angolan-Brazilian slave trade, trade across the Atlantic reached a peak in the 1830s.

The east coast slave trade was at its height in the 1870s. Some European governments and traders, however, refused to abandon the struggle against the 'illegitimate' trade in humans. Eventually, the oceanic slave trades were effectively suppressed by British naval intervention, in the west in the 1850s and 1860s, and in the east in the 1870s. The effect, however, was merely to encourage the expansion of the internal slave trade in the interior of the continent, and this new trade was not effectively tackled until European occupation of the interior in the 1890s and 1900s.

The east coast experienced, especially after 1840, the rise of an extensive trade in ivory, cloves and rubber. The peoples of the eastern and central African interior not only participated in the expanding coastal trade, but also greatly expanded their long-established long-distance internal trade, in salt, iron ore and iron goods, and copper ore and copper goods.

As trade grew, so did towns. There was a minor urban revolution in Africa from the 1840s. In East and Central Africa, the coastal ports expanded, and in the interior new towns arose as capitals of new or expanded states; Mengo in Buganda, Urambo, Tabora and Ujiji in present Tanzania. In West Africa, many towns expanded. The most spectacular example was Ibadan in Yorubaland. A new town in 1830, Ibadan became the centre of palm oil production and the political capital of a new empire. Already, by 1890, with 100,000 people, it was the most populous city in tropical Africa, a position it still holds today.

In the European colonies, the Cape, Natal, the Boer republics in the extreme south and Algeria in the extreme north, white settlers contributed to enlargement of economic scale by transplanting European techniques and utilizing European capital.

The enlargement of economic scale had two important—but contradictory—political effects. Firstly, as traders or rulers used wealth to buy guns or iron spears, they were able to impose or expand their authority, and thus either create new states or enlarge existing ones. In many areas, too, the spread of new food crops along trade routes increased food production, and therefore it became easier for rulers to support non-productive specialists, such as administrators and soldiers. The second political effect was the stimulation of European economic imperialism which wished to take advantage of the new economic opportunities. This economic imperialism was one of the factors which led to the European partition of Africa and the destruction of African states, both old and new.

There was, therefore, economic *growth* in Africa between 1800 and 1885. However, Africa became increasingly *underdeveloped* in this period in comparison with the industrialized areas of the world. The pattern of trade between Africa and the industrializing world in the nineteenth century—a pattern that still exists today—was one which contributed to underdevelopment. Europe robbed Africa of her surplus products to feed its own economy, obtaining African exports at low prices and using them to boost its own industrialization, thus steadily widening the gap between itself and Africa. Colonialism after 1885 intensified this economic imperialism as well as introducing political and cultural domination.

Enlargement of scale in religious culture

From 1800 to 1885, there was an enlargement of scale in religious culture. By this we mean that while in some areas traditional ethnic religions began to give way to Islam and Christianity more than ever before, in other areas ethnic cults spread widely beyond their area of origin. However, a sense of proportion must be kept. Islam had made considerable inroads into West Africa and the coast of East Africa long before 1840; North Africa had been largely Muslim for over a thousand years. But the early nineteenth century saw considerable Islamic expansion: Usman dan Fodio began his jihad in the early years of the century and revolutionized Sokoto, and in 1840, Al-Hajj Umar began his preaching tour among the Tokolor people. In West Africa, Islam was to make greater progress during the period of colonial rule than it did in the thousand years preceding it.

   Although some attempts at Christian missionary activity had been made in black Africa before the nineteenth century, they were almost entirely unsuccessful. In the period before colonial rule missionary activity became more pronounced, with some areas such as Yorubaland and Buganda receiving a disproportionate amount of attention. However, the impact of Christianity was small in this period. It has been estimated that there were only about 50,000 Christians in West Africa on the eve of colonial rule. In many areas Christianity had little impact except on those who were outcasts from traditional society. The Bombay Africans of the Kenya coast (see Chapter 8) and the Mfengu (refugees from Shaka's wars) of South Africa are two such examples.

   Even where missionaries seemed to be welcomed in the precolonial period, they were largely used by African rulers for their own ends. In Buganda, the Kabakas hoped to use them as a counter-weight to Egyptian expansion. In Yorubaland they became part of the political balance in the rivalry in the area. In the 1830s Moshweshwe of the Basuto welcomed French missionaries. They could act as intermediaries between himself and the white man; and they were positioned on the outskirts of his territory to discourage attack. Mirambo of the Wanyamwezi hoped to use Southon of the London Missionary Society to improve his standing with Sir John Kirk on Zanzibar.

   At the onset of colonial rule the southern two-thirds of the continent was, and still remains even today, largely 'pagan', following neither Islam nor Christianity. Traditional religions remained strong and often adapted themselves to new situations. They were far from being static. There is growing evidence of African cults transcending ethnic barriers. One such cult which expanded was the Mwari cult in

Central Africa. This cult, with its institution of a High God, spread from the Shona to the Ndebele invaders thus becoming a territorial cult related to a particular area rather than to one ethnic group. Ultimately this cult was to be one of the factors in Ndebele resistance to European invasion. Some cults were, however, so closely related to the political system that they declined once the political system began to disintegrate. The Mbona cult of the Manganja was eclipsed during the mid-nineteenth century upheavals in Malawi.

The themes of enlargement outlined in this opening survey will be developed in the next few chapters of our study.

2
Military States and Peoples: the Mfecane and Difaqane

Overview

The *Mfecane* is a term that is inevitably linked with Shaka, the Zulu king who carried out a revolution in military techniques. Mfecane is an Nguni word to describe the 'forced migration' of various Nguni-speaking and Sotho-Tswana-speaking communities from the south-eastern part of southern Africa to other parts of southern, central and east Africa from about 1810 to 1860. *Difaqane* is the Sotho-Tswana word for the same event. (Nguni is the name for a

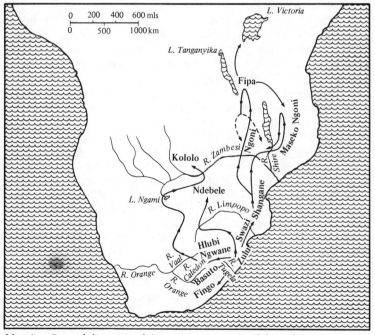

Map 1.   General direction of the main movements of the Mfecane.

language group which includes the Xhosa, Zulu, Swazi and Ndebele peoples.)

The general causes of the Mfecane are still a subject of debate for historians. Until recently it was commonly assumed that overpopulation and pressure of land among the Nguni living between the Drakensberg and the Indian Ocean was the most important single factor accounting for the rise of the Zulu kingdom under Shaka; the Nguni invasions southwards, westwards and northwards were supposed to have been in search of new lands for themselves and their cattle. However, some historians now believe that the complete lack of statistical information on Nguni populations and their rate of growth in this period provides no basis for this theory. It seems likely that the Mfecane was caused by the evolution of age-grade military systems into age-regiments, dedicated to professional warfare as their reason for existence. Shaka's role in these events has also been played down in recent years. He was only one of many great Nguni and Sotho leaders who exploited the age-sets and turned them into powerful military forces which were used to conquer neighbouring communities and create larger states. Thulare, the leader of the Sotho-speaking Bapedi in the north-eastern Transvaal, Moshweshwe in Lesotho, and Shaka's predecessors as kings of the northern Nguni, Zwide and Dingiswayo, all began the process of state-formation after first distinguishing themselves as age-grade leaders.

The most obvious of the Mfecane's results was the spread of the Zulu type of military system over vast regions of Africa south of Lake Victoria. The short stabbing spear was used instead of the long throwing spear. This introduced a new method of close hand-to-hand fighting, which was devastatingly effective. New tactics were also developed. These included the bull's horn formation first to probe and then to encircle the enemy, surprise night attacks, and the organization of soldiers into disciplined age-regiments and a regular standing army. This new military system was carried northwards by such groups as the Ngoni, Ndebele and Kololo.

The Mfecane had many negative consequences. There were many wars of aggression. Many people were killed and a considerable amount of property was destroyed. There was an increase in slave-trading, because the Ndebele and Ngoni took prisoners as slaves. Ngoni raids around Lake Malawi also weakened many communities who were then more easily raided by east coast slave-traders. In some areas there was a decline in cultivation and in population, especially on the High Veld of South Africa and between Lake Malawi and the Indian Ocean, though in the latter area Swahili, Yao and Chikunda slave-raiding was as equally damaging as the activities of the Nguni. Some trade routes suffered. The Ngoni raided Swahili caravans between Kilwa and Lake Malawi, and between Tabora and Ujiji. The devastation of the High Veld created great empty spaces which were soon filled by the ox-wagons of the

Boers. The Great Trek, as John Omer-Cooper puts it in his book, *The Zulu Aftermath*, 'was as much the work of Shaka and Moshesh as of Pretorius and Retief'.

Some large states such as the Rozwi empire of Zimbabwe, the Lozi kingdom of Zambia and the Undi empire of Malawi were destroyed, but many new ones were created. A number arose from Nguni imperialism including the Zulu nation itself, Gaza in Mozambique founded by Soshangane, the Ndebele state in Zimbabwe under Mzilikazi, and the separate Ngoni kingdoms in Zambia, Malawi and Tanzania. The Sotho state in Bulozi was founded by the Kololo. Defensive nation-states were built by the Basuto under Moshweshwe and the Swazi under Sobhuza. In many cases these new states were multi-clan and in some multi-ethnic. The Mfecane clearly contributed to the growth of larger states.

Another sign of positive progress in the Mfecane was the increase of strong central government. The use of age-regiments which cut across local loyalties enhanced the growth of loyalty to central government under a strong king. The new Nguni and Sotho kings appointed commoners to important positions as military indunas and provincial administrators. Their position depended entirely on the king, a factor which ensured their loyalty. It would not always be correct to equate this increased centralization with a growth in despotism, although some rulers, like Shaka and Mzilikazi, *were* despots—military dictators of a ruthless kind. However, the need for strong leadership and more organized government was often met without recourse to absolute monarchy. Men like Moshweshwe and Sobhuza tended to govern by the rules of the traditional Nguni and Sotho-Tswana political systems they were trying to defend. Consultation and consensus were important in their systems. A new social unity was also created by the Mfecane; people absorbed into the various migrating groups came to regard themselves as full members of the conquering group. A united social and political group was created. The use of a common language helped to increase the feeling of unity: for instance, the Ndebele adopted the Khumalo dialect. Intermarriage was both a result of the increasing unity and a cementation of that unity.

The Mfecane thus brought turmoil and violence to much of Bantu Africa, but also considerable military, political and social development.

Nguni imperialism: the Zulu nation

Shaka and Dingane

Shaka, the first Zulu king, carved out an empire from the border with Mozambique in the north to the vicinity of the later city of Durban in the south, and from the Drakensberg Mountains (or Khalamba) in the west to the sea. He conquered many small Nguni polities and developed a highly centralized despotism which made him, in Leonard Thompson's words, 'the senior executive, the ultimate court of appeal, the sole source of laws, the commander-in-chief, and the high priest' (*The Oxford History of South Africa*). The state also controlled food production and external trade, the latter becoming a monopoly of the king.

The concentration of political, military and economic power round the central monarch instead of the local territorial rulers reduced the possibility of territorial rulers breaking away from the kingdom. However, it did not remove altogether the danger of disunity. Dissatisfaction could be expressed by the transfer of loyalty from the king to another member of the royal family. This happened in 1828, when Shaka was assassinated, partly because the army wanted a rest from constant campaigning and partly because the nation was tired of Shaka's despotism. It happened again in 1839–40, when most of the army deserted Shaka's successor, his younger brother Dingane, for another brother, Mpande. Dingane was generally disliked for his arbitrary rule, his dislike of war, his preference for feasting and dancing and the company of women, and for his failure to cope with the invasion of Trekboers into Natal. Mpande became king when, at the climax of the first Zulu civil war, he defeated Dingane at the Battle of Magongo on January 29, 1840. Dingane managed to escape from his former subjects, but was killed by the Swazis among whom he vainly sought refuge.

Mpande

Mpande's reign (1840–72) showed that the strength of the Zulu nation relied no less on the person and the personality of the king than on the nature of its institutions. A peaceful man who hated war, Mpande, like Dingane, preferred the pleasures of his vast harem to leading his armies into battle. Indolent and grossly obese, he had to be carried around in a cart. His sole campaign was an almost bloodless cattle raid against the Swazi. Mpande gave the Zulu a breathing space from war, and the population steadily increased. However, he failed to grapple with the problem of the succession, and allowed his sons Cetshwayo and Mbuyazi to fight a civil war over the claim to be heir. The second Zulu civil war ended at the Battle of Ndondakusuka in 1856, with a great victory for Cetshwayo in which Mbuyazi was killed and his army of 7,000 was annihilated. In the immediate aftermath of the battle, the dependants of Mbuyazi and his followers, 23,000 defenceless women and children, were slain.

Cetshwayo

Cetshwayo (1872–9), the son of Mpande and the nephew of Shaka, more closely resembled his uncle than his father. Tall, handsome, physically fit, intelligent and forceful, he wanted to revive the vanished glories of the days of Shaka. As the effective ruler of the country after Ndondakusuka, Cetshwayo re-organized the army. At his accession the Zulu regiments were at a peak of efficiency. They were able, a few years later, to inflict on Britain a humiliating defeat at Isandhlwana.

Yet Cetshwayo did not favour war for its own sake. He wanted to carry out the traditional practice of the 'washing of the spears' of the army of a new king on the blood of an enemy, not for the sake of tradition but out of practical necessity. Whilst he was heir apparent, the expectations of the regiments had been aroused. These expectations had to be fulfilled. Cetshwayo tried to do this with campaigns against the Swazi and Thonga. He studiously ignored the movement of Boers into the northern areas of his country in order to avoid a conflict that might bring destruction to his state. At the same time he prepared for the possibility of war by tightening up conscription into the army, and obtaining firearms through Lourenço Marques.

Cetshwayo also tried to maintain peace with the British. He had two coronations: a 'traditional' Zulu one followed by an extra-ordinary British ceremony where he was crowned by the Natal Secretary for Native Affairs, Theophilus Shepstone, whom Cetshwayo had invited for the purpose. Cetshwayo merely wanted to cement Zulu–British friendship, but Shepstone took advantage of the occasion to proclaim new laws—laws which remained a dead letter—for the Zulu nation, designed to reduce the number of judicial and political executions in Zululand. Cetshwayo maintained his friendship with the British until 1877, and the British supported him in his boundary dispute with the Transvaal.

Britain's annexation of the Transvaal destroyed the basis of Cetshwayo's foreign policy. It was no longer possible to maintain an anti-Boer alliance with the British as the Boer republic no longer existed. Diplomatically and militarily Cetshwayo's position deteriorated until he was forced into war by the British.

Nguni imperialism: the Ndebele

The Ndebele before 1840

Ndebele means *men of the long shields* and is a nickname given them by the Sotho-Tswana people in the Transvaal. Their origin was in the small Nguni-speaking Khumalo clan. Under their leader, Mzilikazi, they rebelled against Shaka in 1821, fleeing first to the Transvaal and then over the Limpopo River into Central Africa, absorbing various Nguni, Sotho and Shona speakers into the clan. In 1837 the Ndebele were defeated by the Boers at Mosega and e-Gobeni. These defeats, coupled with renewed Zulu pressure, caused Mzilikazi to lead his people north of the River Limpopo into the lands of the Rozwi empire.

The Ndebele in Central Africa

In about 1840 Mzilikazi and the Ndebele conquered the Rozwi empire and in its place set up a new Ndebele kingdom with its capital near present Bulawayo. The conquest was comparatively easy because of the superior military methods used by the Ndebele, and because the Rozwi empire was very weak following its ravaging by migrating Ngoni only a few years earlier. The Ndebele conquered and absorbed the weakened and divided south-western Shona sub-groups such as the Kalanga

The boundaries of the Ndebele state in Central Africa were not clearly marked. It could be said that the boundaries were marked by the farthest extent of Ndebele raids for cattle, food crops and people. Areas near the capital were under firmer Ndebele rule than areas farther away. The latter only paid tribute when forced to do so by Ndebele regiments. The central core of the state was under the direct rule of the king, and contained both the Ndebele themselves and scattered Shona villages. Farther away to the north-east were four zones of Shona-speaking peoples; the first, in western Mashonaland nearest the Ndebele, paying regular tribute to them; another in central Mashonaland, paying occasional tribute to Mzilikazi; a third, in eastern Mashonaland, virtually independent, paying tribute on very rare occasions when the Ndebele invaded; and a fourth, on the eastern boundary, and north-eastern Mashonaland, having no contact with the Ndebele at all, except perhaps through long-distance trade. In this latter area the Rozwi rulers still maintained their authority.

Once the Ndebele settled in Rhodesia the internal organization of their state took its final form. Mzilikazi developed a strong central government in which the king made all important decisions, and appointed generals and administrators. Although in its early years the Ndebele kingdom was a military state, organized for war, Mzilikazi in the course of time allowed the administration to become civil rather than military. At first the army and the whole people were grouped together in military towns. Later, however, as the Ndebele kingdom became permanently settled, the regiments became territorial administrative divisions similar to the pre-Mfecane political systems the Ndebele had known in South Africa. The indunas, though still appointed by the King, took on civil as well as military duties as territorial chiefs. Commoners who owed everything to the King were often appointed to high office. The soldiers continued to be organized in age-regiments which cut across ethnic and clan boundaries, but as the Ndebele settled in their new land and regimental encampments became permanent, inevitably new regional loyalties arose.

Mzilikazi attempted to give unity to his empire in various ways. He used marriage to cement national unity and increase loyalty to himself and the central government. He had perhaps four hundred wives from different sections of the nation. Sindebele, based on the Khumalo dialect which all captives had to learn, became the common language of Khumalo, Sotho and Kalanga. Therefore, there was considerable progress towards social unity. Many who were not Khumalo began to think of themselves as Ndebele. However, this process was not completed. Ndebele society remained divided into three castes. The upper caste were the *Zansi*, consisting of the original Nguni warriors and their descendants. They were dominant in the government and had a variety of privileges. The next group in the hierarchy, known as *Enhla*, were those of Sotho and Tswana stock incorporated during the period spent in the Transvaal. At the lowest level were the Shona who were treated virtually as serfs. Marriage between one caste and another was generally forbidden. When faced with European invasion these divisions proved to be a major weakness.

The independent Shona peoples

Although the Rozwi empire collapsed under the impact of the Ndebele invasion, the Shona never came completely under the Ndebele rule. In the 1850s and 1860s the new Rozwi *Mambo* (ruler) Tohwechipi successfully defied Ndebele attempts to expand into central and eastern Mashonaland. He was forced to surrender in 1866, but the struggle went on after his release, right up to the British invasion. In the 1870s and 1880s Shona strength steadily revived, as they bought guns from the east coast and formed alliances with Portuguese adventurers.

The Ndebele and Shona were not constantly at war with each

other. There was considerable peaceful interaction between the two communities. Both groups found peaceful trade to their advantage. Ndebele cattle were exchanged for Shona grain. The old Shona trading system, exporting gold and ivory for cloth, beads and guns imported from the Portuguese-controlled lower Zambesi valley was not disrupted by the Ndebele. The Ndebele even slotted into the pattern of Shona long-distance trade, with ivory exports to the east coast via Mashonaland.

The Shona influenced the Ndebele both in trade and religion. The Shona for centuries had a highly developed religious system, based on the cult of Mwari—the High God, or Creator. The Mwari priests dominated the religious institutions of the Rozwi court. However the Mwari was not only the royal cult of the Rozwi empire, but also a trans-ethnic oracular cult for all men who consulted the oracle. After the Ndebele incursion, the priests moved from the abandoned royal capital into the Matopos Hills, where they not only remained the focus of Shona religious belief, but also had a profound effect on the Ndebele. The invaders adopted the Mwari cult which gave strength and depth to their existing religious beliefs. The Ndebele were deeply impressed by Mwari, a High God who created all men and served all men, who was not allied to the Rozwi kings and could even reject them. Ndebele adoption of Mwari meant that Ndebele political domination of the Shona was countered by a Shona cultural influence over the Ndebele.

Nguni imperialism: Gaza

Gaza was a powerful state founded in the interior of present-day Mozambique by Soshangane and his people, the Shangane. Gaza was named after Soshangane's grandfather.

Soshangane was a general in the army of the Ndwandwe, a group of northern Nguni defeated by Shaka in 1819. Using the Zulu military system and methods, Soshangane led his regiment and followers northwards, conquered the Thonga people of the lower Limpopo valley and destroyed the Portuguese settlements at Delagoa Bay, Inhambane and Sena. They finally settled in the middle Sabi Highlands.

By 1849 Soshangane's Nguni had exacted tribute from twenty-eight out of forty-six Portuguese prazos, or crown estates, in the Zambesi valley, as well as from the towns of Sena and Tete.

A completely united empire was never created by Soshangane. The assimilation of conquered peoples was never so great as in Zululand or even the Ndebele kingdom. Firstly, the area under the direct rule of the Shangane—as distinct from the much larger tribute area—was rather small, and many peoples continued to be virtually independent under their vassal rulers. Even the subservient Thonga were not Nguni-ized. They were too far from the heart of the empire. Many of the newly-incorporated peoples were killed in a massacre when Soshangane came to believe he was bewitched and suspicion fell on the non-Nguni.

The Nguni in Gaza began to fall out among themselves after Soshangane's death (in 1856 or 1859), when a long succession dispute between Mawewe and Mzila ensued, making it easier for the Portuguese to reassert their ancient authority in the Zambesi. With the rise of the Goan adventurer Gouveia in the 1860s many prazos ceased to pay tribute to Gaza. The lack of political and social unity caused the decline of Gaza, and paved the way for colonial conquest in the 1890s.

Nguni imperialism: the Ngoni

The Ngoni invasions

The Ngoni were originally the Nguni followers of Zwangendaba, leader of the Jere clan, which inhabited northern Zululand. After his defeat by Shaka in 1819, Zwangendaba led his Jere people northwards to Ufipa in Tanzania. They came to be known as Ngoni because of their Nguni language.

Initially the Ngoni migrated into southern Mozambique where they were defeated by Soshangane. They then passed through the Rozwi empire—severely weakening it—and crossed the Zambesi in 1835. Between 1835 and 1840 the Ngoni migrated through the lands of the Senga people and then up the Lwanga valley to the west side of Lake Malawi, where they defeated the Chewa people, who were part of the Undi or Malawi empire. Finally, Zwangendaba and his growing host reached the Fipa Plateau, or Ufipa, the lands of the Fipa people, in present Tanzania. Here they stayed for a time, and created the Ngoni kingdom, but after Zwangendaba's death in about 1848 the kingdom split up into five new states which dispersed in different directions.

The Tuta Ngoni migrated northwards from Ufipa, raiding first the Holoholo on the eastern shores of Lake Tanganyika and then the Nyamwezi. They disrupted the trade routes from the interior to the coast, especially between Ujiji and Tabora. After raiding as far as the southern shores of Lake Victoria they finally settled north-west of Tabora. The Gwangara Ngoni migrated eastwards from Ufipa to the Songea area under their leader Zulu-Gama, drove out the Maseko Ngoni, and invaded the lands of the Hehe. However, the Hehe later adopted Zulu tactics and defeated the Gwangara.

Another Ngoni group under Mpezeni conquered the Senga and Chewa around the present Fort Jameson and completed the destruction of the Undi empire. Mombera doubled back on Zwangendaba's route and created another Ngoni kingdom west of Lake Malawi, where he conquered and absorbed many Kamanga, Henga and Tumbuka. When Ciwere, an Ngoni general of Senga origin broke away from Mombera, he settled in the present Dowa district of Malawi and formed his own kingdom.

Results of the Ngoni invasions

The Ngoni brought disaster to large parts of Central and East Africa, destroying the Rozwi empire. On their migrations they were 'like a swarm of locusts forced to continue advancing as it destroys its own livelihood' (Omer-Cooper). Like the Ndebele, the Ngoni despised cultivation and loved war. Peoples in the path of their advance were raided for cattle, food crops and people to be absorbed as soldiers, wives or slaves. The constantly growing host of people and cattle had to keep moving on to find new lands. When they settled, the Ngoni became less dependent on pastoralism but they continued to raid rather than cultivate; and if they now traded, they could not resist selling slaves as well as ivory for the cloth they bought from the Swahili. Agricultural peoples laboured for them.

Yet there was a progressive side to Ngoni imperialism. They assimilated far more people than they killed in war or sold as slaves. The Ngoni united peoples of vastly different cultures—both patrilineal and matrilineal—and languages. These peoples developed a permanent sense of common identity.

The Ngoni themselves created new and larger states in areas where previously the peoples had been politically fragmented. They inspired the growth of new states by various peoples who wanted to resist them effectively, such as that created by the Chewa in central Malawi under the Mwase-Kasungu, which rose on the ruins of the old Undi empire. Other new kingdoms were created by the Holoholo, the Sangu, the Hehe, the Kimbu and by Mrambo in East Africa. The Hehe adopted the Zulu military system to defend themselves from the Gwangara Ngoni to the south of them and ultimately defeated the Gwangara. The thirty small Hehe clan-states were united under their leader Munyigumba, then conquering the weaker Bena and Sagara. Mirambo of Urambo and Nyungu-ya-Mawe of Ukimbu created new states by using Ngoni methods of war, even hiring Ngoni mercenaries. Even Swahili traders armed with guns were forced into state-building by the Ngoni incursion. Jumbe Kisutu, the east coast ivory trader at Kota Kota on the western shores of Lake Malawi, created a little state by receiving Chewa refugees and arming them to resist the Ngoni. He used the refugees to help him defeat the local Chewa rulers, whom he made subordinate to himself, and he employed the Chewa people as ivory hunters and traders or as food-producers.

Thus it was not only the purchase of European-made guns from the east coast that led to the growth of larger political units in the East and Central African interior. An event which was purely African, the military revolution completed by Shaka spread well beyond the Zulu homeland, and it was of fundamental importance in the creation of these larger units.

Ngoni defensive nation-building: the Swazi

Sobhuza, chief of the Dlamini clan of the Ngwane section of the Nguni, ruled his people from about 1815 to about 1836. After a quarrel with the Ndwandwe over land, Sobhuza retreated with his Ngwane to the mountains north of the Pongolo River. He created an army on Zulu lines, and absorbed weak clans and Nguni and Sotho refugees from the Mfecane. Sobuza's son Mswazi who ruled from 1840 to 1868, steadily expanded the state during the long and comparatively peaceful reign of Mpande in Zululand.

The Swazi military system was a mixture of the Zulu system and the traditional Nguni and Sotho systems. There was, as in Zululand, a standing royal army at the capital, but it was made up of only sections of the age-regiments. In peace-time the majority of soldiers in age-regiments remained at home to play a normal role in the community, and only joined up with their age mates in the standing army in wartime. The Swazi standing army was distinguished by another valuable feature: the soldiers regularly laboured on public works as part of their duties. In contrast, the Zulu, Ndebele and Ngoni made use of slaves for this type of work. The Swazi state was not so dominated by the warrior ethos as were the other Nguni states. The Swazi did not evolve the highly centralized and personalized despotisms of the Zulu and Ndebele. It adopted part of the Zulu military system but none of its political system. Swazi political power was not fully centralized round the person of the king, but was divided between the king and the Queen Mother, who was the ritual head of state, and who acted as regent on the death of a king. The king had power to impose or annul the death sentence, to declare war and peace and to control the distribution of land, but his power rested largely on the consent of the clans, through the national council of clan leaders. John Omer-Cooper describes the Swazi state as a 'constitutional monarchy', a valid description even though Mswazi was inevitably more powerful than the pre-Mfecane Swazi rulers.

Sobhuza and Mswazi did not follow a policy of Dlaminiization (whereas Shaka Zuluized his subjects and Mzilikazi Khumaloized his). The identity of absorbed and conquered peoples was not destroyed and their royal dynasties were preserved. The lack of strong centralization left their leaders with a considerable degree of autonomy. The Sotho who were absorbed adopted Nguni language and culture, but voluntarily.

Mswazi's foreign policy was based on alliance with European states—whom he did not see as aggressive—against the Zulus. This policy was justified during his reign, when neither British nor Boers had yet developed imperialist designs on Swaziland. He leased much unoccupied land to Boers in the eastern Transvaal, since he believed they wanted merely to farm it. He even gave the Boers some land in Swaziland itself. He did not imagine that the Boers would take advantage of these grants.

Defensive nation-building: the southern Sotho

The career of Moshweshwe, founder of Lesotho, is in sharp contrast to those of the aggressive nation-builders, Shaka and Mzilikazi. Moshweshwe, like Sobhuza and Mswazi, built a new state for defence. He used traditional Sotho political techniques to gather the communities of Lesotho into one nation. He relied on war as little as possible, and resorted to it only in self-defence or under severe provocation. He once stated: 'Peace is like the rain which makes the grass grow, while war is like the wind which dries it up.' Moshweshwe understood the importance of justice in a ruler and the need for human beings to live in harmony with each other.

Moshweshwe was born in 1786, the son of a village headman in the Caledon valley west of the Khalamba (Drakensberg). During the period from 1822 to 1836, when the Sotho-Tswana lands were ravaged by the Difaqane, Moshweshwe gathered a band of refugees on the mountain fortress of Thaba Bosiu, and created the southern Sotho kingdom in Lesotho. A highly successful defensive general, Moshweshwe defeated assaults on Thaba Bosiu by 'Matiwane's Ngwane horde (1827), the Tlokwa (1829) and Ndebele (1831). Like Shaka, he carried out a revolution in military technology, but he did not copy the Zulu king. The heavy, broad-bladed stabbing spear and large oval shield of the Nguni were ill-adapted to the mountainous conditions of Lesotho, where lighter weapons were needed. Therefore, Moshweshwe had the traditional Sotho knobkerrie replaced by a battle-axe. For plains fighting he developed a cavalry force armed with guns, copied from the Griqua and Korana, the Eurafrican and San pastoral communities of the Orange River valley. Unfortunately, the short supply of ammunition gave Moshweshwe's cavalry extremely limited opportunities for practice, so their marksmanship was poor. They were defeated at the Battle of Berea in 1852 by accurate British rifle and artillery fire.

Moshweshwe was much less of an innovator in the political field. He became the paramount ruler of the southern Sotho largely because he saved most of his cattle from invaders. He was able to loan his cattle out to other chiefs to herd and milk under the *Mafisa* system, whereby he retained the ownership of the cattle. Mafisa was a traditional Sotho custom. Another traditional technique Moshweshwe used to build up his kingdom was by means of diplomatic alliances with other rulers who became his vassals, such as Moletsane of the Taung and Moorosi of the Phuthi. Polygamy was also used to unite the nation. He probably had more than a hundred wives, carefully chosen to represent all communities and factions. Refugee communities who settled among his people were allowed to retain their existing leaders and methods of government. However, although local autonomy was allowed Moshweshwe maintained considerable control by placing his brothers and senior sons in charge of districts.

In contrast to the Zulu and Ndebele kingdoms, Moshweshwe's had no united or uniform administration, no standing army, and not even, in spite of its comparatively small size, uniformity of language. Moshweshwe's state was a federation, held together by consensus. Far from being a dictator, he regularly resorted to the traditional Sotho *pitso*, or public assembly, to resolve disputes over matters of policy. He relied more on his moral influence, personal charisma and powers of argument than on institutions and force to hold the state together. He never touched alcohol in case it dimmed his skill in public speaking. As he once said: 'If I were to drink, I should be talking folly before my people.'

Moshweshwe, for all his use of traditional political techniques, was a radical reformer in social affairs. He allowed Christian Sotho to be buried by Christian rites. He stopped, for a time, the initiation schools for youths, he granted divorces to baptized women, and he refused to countenance the killing of witches. He neither believed in the claims of witches, nor would he allow any of his people to be accused of witchcraft. He believed witchcraft would die out with the spread of common sense. His humanity is further shown by his refusal to impose the death penalty except in rare cases.

To a large extent, Moshweshwe was helped by his enemies in creating his kingdom. During the Difaqane people flocked to him for shelter and protection. Even after the worst was over, by 1840, there was constant war with Sikonyela, the cruel and war-loving leader of the Tlokwa. Moshweshwe finally defeated him in 1853 when in a surprise dawn attack he captured the Tlokwa mountain. Sikonyela fled, to permanent exile in the Cape, but the majority of the Tlokwa accepted Moshweshwe's authority. The incorporation of most of the Tlokwa marked the culmination of the process of incorporation which built the Sotho state. But his people still had to keep together and remain loyal to him if they were to resist a new and more serious threat from the Europeans. Moshweshwe defended Thaba Bosiu from assaults by the British in 1852 and the Boers in 1858 and 1866, but in the long run he knew the disparity in fire-power would tell. We shall see, in Chapter 7, how Moshweshwe's diplomatic skill, though it could not preserve the independence of his nation, nevertheless safeguarded its identity.

Sotho imperialism: the Kololo

The rise and fall of the Kololo kingdom in Bulozi between 1840 and 1864 is an object lesson in the factors that can promote unity and those which can foster disunity in a state.

The old Lozi kingdom in Bulozi in the upper Zambesi valley was created by King Mulambwa who ruled from about 1780 to about 1830. It covered about half of present-day western Zambia. After Mulambwa's death there were succession disputes among the Lozi which greatly weakened the kingdom. Eventually Mubukwanu became king but he had no time to re-unite the Lozi before the Kololo invasion in about 1840.

The Kololo, or Fokeng, were a Sotho-speaking community who originally lived on the High Veld west of the Khalamba. In the 1820s they were forced to migrate as peoples uprooted by Shaka disturbed them, capturing most of their cattle. The Kololo migrated northwards under their leader Sebetwane into Central Africa, to replace their lost herds.

Why did the Kololo decide to settle in Bulozi rather than elsewhere? Firstly, they wanted to avoid the powerful Ndebele and Ngoni who were dominant in areas farther east. Secondly, when the Kololo reached the middle Zambesi they learnt there were large herds of cattle in Bulozi to the west. Thirdly, they understood that traders were selling guns from the west coast in Bulozi. Sebetwane believed guns would guarantee him peace. Fourthly, Bulozi was politically weak due to the succession disputes after Mulambwa's death.

The Kololo were able to conquer the Lozi kingdom fairly easily. The Kololo had learnt not only Zulu war organization and tactics while in southern Africa, but had also, while living for a time in the middle Zambesi valley, learnt how to use canoes and how to use them in war—a skill which enabled them to assert their mastery over Bulozi which lay in the upper Zambesi flood plain.

King Sebetwane, the leader of the Kololo migration and the first Kololo ruler in Bulozi, ruled so well during his reign (1840–51) that the Lozi were loyal to their Kololo conquerors. However, Sebetwane's son and successor Sekeletu (1851–63) ruled so unwisely that the Kololo lost the loyalty of the subject Lozi.

Sebetwane encouraged the Kololo to mix with the local people and not to mistreat them. He married women from the Lozi and encouraged other Kololo men to do the same. He confirmed many local leaders in their positions. He changed the old Lozi kingship where the king was considered to be divine and was hidden from public eye. Instead, in traditional Sotho fashion, Sebetwane made himself readily available in public to his subjects to deal with their problems. The results of Sebetwane's generous policy to the defeated was that the Lozi freely adopted the name Kololo, the Sotho language of the Kololo, and many Kololo customary laws. His success in winning the loyalty of the subject peoples was dramatically illustrated by his devastating defeat of the Ndebele invasion. Mzilikazi sent 2,000 soldiers to conquer the Kololo kingdom. The Ndebele recruited the Batonka, a Zambesi river community subject to Sebetwane, to ferry their own men over the river. However, the Batonka were secretly loyal to Sebetwane and left the Ndebele army on an island in the middle of the river where they starved to death.

When Sebetwane died he had created a large state, which was, with the tribute-paying areas, about 350 miles from west to east, and about 250 miles from north to south.

Sekeletu undid his father's work in bringing the Kololo and Lozi together, by turning them into enemies. He lacked the personal ability and military skills of his father. A leper, he thought he was bewitched by the subject peoples, so he took only Kololo wives and had only Kololo advisers, generally cutting himself off from non-Kololo. Many important Lozi fled into exile for fear of their lives. Sekeletu persecuted even his own people by having possible Kololo rivals executed, thus weakening the Kololo leadership.

Of more threatening significance to Kololo supremacy was their lack of resistance to malaria. This had been absent in their original homeland on the High Veld, but was widespread in the upper Zambesi flood plain. The Kololo died from malaria in their thousands; this decimation of the Kololo made it much more difficult for them to control the subject peoples.

Sekeletu's reign is distinguished by one major achievement: the opening-up of a new long-distance trading route to Angola on the west coast, although even this development had been foreshadowed in the reign of his father. In the late 1850s and early 1860s many Kololo trading expeditions travelled the whole distance to Luanda, thus avoiding trade through middlemen.

It is probable that if Sekeletu had lived much longer than he did there would have been a Lozi revolt against him. As it was, the Kololo were overthrown a year after his death in 1863. In 1864 the Lozi took advantage of a succession dispute among the Kololo to carry out a successful rebellion which set up a new Lozi kingdom. Sipopa, an exiled Lozi leader who had led the rebellion now became king. The Kololo men were killed and their women were made Lozi wives. However, the Sotho language and some of the customs and military organization of the Kololo were retained by the Lozi, as was the Kololo external trading system.

The new Lozi kingdom

Sipopa reigned from 1864 to 1876. He failed to solve the dynastic disputes between the two Lozi groups which had been exiled to the north and west during the period of Kololo rule. He tried too hard to centralize the government and weaken the power of the aristocratic families, who turned against him. Sipopa was assassinated. Mwanawina, Sipopa's successor, reigned for only two years before he was overthrown in 1878 and replaced by Lubosi, who was later called Lewanika.

Until 1886 Lewanika was constantly involved in dealing with wars and rebellions by rival dynastic groups. His attempts to centralize the government by weakening the powers of the aristocratic chiefs or indunas in the style of Sipopa led to the 1884 revolt when Lewanika was actually overthrown for a time and fled into exile. However Lewanika regained the throne in 1885 with the help of Angolan traders and their guns. After this he ruthlessly purged disloyal elements. The king was now able to carry out centralization without too much opposition. He ended the indunas' power over the army by abolishing their private regiments and putting all soldiers under the command of the king. The indunas lost their control over much of the land and all provincial indunas were, in future, to be appointed by the king. The old concept of Lozi divine kingship was revived and royal ceremonial increased. The ancient cult of the royal graves, which claimed that the king was descended from the High God was revived in an attempt to raise the prestige of the monarch.

Lewanika greatly expanded the kingdom eastwards, at the expense of the Ila and Tonga peoples, from whom he obtained ivory, cattle, food crops and slaves as tribute. However, although he expanded trade, especially the ivory trade with Angola, Lewanika did not participate in the slave trade. Certainly he increased slavery in Bulozi by enslaving many conquered peoples, but he did not sell them outside the kingdom. The expansion of the kingdom kept potentially dangerous factions busy with the spoils of war.

Finally, Lewanika welcomed to Bulozi European traders and missionaries, such as Coillard of the Paris Evangelical Society who set up a mission station in 1885. Ultimately Lewanika was to prove himself to be a skilful diplomat in adapting himself to the European **Partition of Africa**.

3
Military states and peoples: East Africa

The Nguni- and Sotho-speaking peoples were not the only ones in eastern and southern Africa who experienced a revolution in military techniques unaffected by trade with the east coast or by imports of guns. The Maasai and Nandi in East Africa were two communities organized in such a way as to make military prowess pre-eminent.

The Maasai

The Maasai, a Nilotic-speaking community, were dominant in the East African Rift Valley plain from the Uasin Gishu Plateau in the north to the plains around Mount Meru in the south, from about 1750 to the mid-nineteenth century. The Maasai had no political

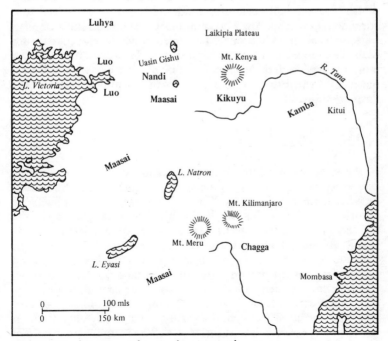

Map 2. Northern East Africa in the nineteenth century.

unity. They were organized in many sub-groups which were independent of each other and grouped loosely around different *laibons*, or religious leaders. This is not to say that the Maasai were not well organized. Their younger men were grouped in efficient and skilful age-regiments for military purposes. These age-regiments developed long before the Ngoni brought their system of age-regiments to East Africa.

Maasai power declined in the nineteenth century, due to continuous civil wars and natural disasters. Between 1850 and 1870, there was a civil war between two different Maasai sub-groups: the pastoral Purko, led by the Laibon Supet, almost completely wiped out the agricultural Uasin Gishu Kwavi. Mbatian, Supet's son, was laibon from 1866–90. From about 1875 the different pastoral groups began to fight each other. After Mbatian's death the Purko split into two warring factions, each supporting a different son of Mbatian as laibon. Eventually Lenana, with British help, defeated his brother Sendeu to become undisputed laibon.

Natural disasters, like a locust invasion which destroyed grass, cholera in 1869, pleuro-pneumonia that wiped out cattle in the 1880s, smallpox and rinderpest, all contributed to the decline of the Maasai.

The history of the Maasai in the nineteenth century contrasts with the general trends in East African history in this period. The Maasai controlled a large area without recourse to guns from the coast and without developing centralized administration—or indeed any administration at all. The Maasai military system and skills were, in the long term, of limited value. They were never developed to form a basis for a more developed political system. However, by exporting religious experts to the neighbouring Nandi (see below), the Maasai indirectly helped the rise of a well-organized military state in the Kenyan highlands.

The Nandi

In the early seventeenth century the Nandi, also a Nilotic people, settled on the highland escarpment west of the Uasin Gishu Plateau in what is now present-day Kenya. They expanded gradually by absorbing various other small Kalenjin-speaking groups. In the eighteenth and early nineteenth centuries they fought defensive wars against the neighbouring Uasin Gishu Maasai.

In the second half of the nineteenth century the Nandi evolved a single state, united not only by common language and common customs, but by their military system and the centralizing personality of a religious leader. The Nandi military organization of age-sets, which ensured that a standing army was always ready, had been developed in defence against the Maasai. The Nandi were experts at night fighting, using surprise as their basic tactic; their soldiers showed great endurance and could march for hundreds of miles. The Nandi were divided into a basic residential unit called the *pororiet*. In military campaigns men from one pororiet fought together. In all there were fifteen *pororosiek* (the plural form of pororiet). Military operations were usually carried out by a single pororiet, but sometimes a few pororosiek combined. Soldiers who went on campaign were volunteers, a factor which helped to keep morale high.

Nandi society was so egalitarian, and the political system so democratic, that the development of a large measure of political and military unity after 1850 is rather surprising. There were no chiefs or even clan heads. Heads of families met in the *koret* (local assembly) to organize collective activities and settle disputes. Representatives of each koret, along with two senior military leaders, met in the pororiet (in this context, a district assembly) to arrange major ceremonial functions, discuss relations with other pororosiek and analyse military matters. Leadership was accorded by consensus, by the weight of public opinion. Each Nandi was a member of a clan, but clans were not localized in particular areas of territory and they had no political functions. This lack of clan organization contributed to national unity because it meant that inter-clan feuding was minimal.

By about 1850 the Nandi felt the need for greater centralization. More co-operation was needed for war against the Uasin Gishu Maasai. The Nandi population was increasing because of comparative freedom from malaria and smallpox on the high escarpment. A society which was formerly totally united, small and homogeneous was growing too big for the existing political system, which was very basic. The Nandi called in a Maasai laibon named Barsabotwo, who became the first Nandi *orkoiyot*, a ritual expert and military and political adviser. Barsabotwo and his successors established a degree of centralization so that by the last quarter of the century the orkoiyot had an agent in each pororiet. Thus there was greater co-operation between pororosiek in war. The emergence of the orkoiyot certainly helped Nandi national unity.

The orkoiyot was not a dictator. He very rarely attended pororiet assemblies, and if he did so it was only as an observer. He did not hold an official post. Indeed, there were usually several *orkoik* (plural form) operating at any one time, though one was normally dominant. If they failed to serve the purpose for which they were employed, they were in serious trouble. In 1890 the orkoiyot Kimnyole, who had sanctioned an unsuccessful cattle raid, was clubbed to death.

The results of Nandi military efficiency and unity were beneficial for the Nandi, but their neighbours suffered for it. The Uasin Gishu Maasai, crushed by the pastoral Purko Maasai in the 1870s were unable to resist Nandi advance into the plateau. The Nandi occupied much of the plateau, because as high altitude land it was ideal both for their cattle and for human settlement. The western neighbours of the Nandi, the Luhya and the Luo, suffered from many Nandi raids for cattle. The Kalenjin of Mount Elgon also suffered similarly and began to live in barricaded caves. The Nandi travelled westwards as far as Uganda, raiding the Bagisu on the western side of Mount Elgon. However, Nandi raids were generally limited in scope and effect, and took place at night. Most communities that were raided were unused to night-fighting, so they offered little resistance to Nandi raids. This minimized loss of life. Moreover, the Nandi did not occupy the lands to the west. They were interested in cattle rather than territory, since the land which they raided was generally lower in altitude, and unsuitable for settlement because of malaria; cattle were susceptible to tse-tse fly. Only small groups of Nandi carried out the raids, and this also reduced their effect.

Nandi relations with their neighbours were not always hostile. Trade between them was common, as it was between the Maasai and their neighbours. Nineteenth century Swahili and European accounts which show the Maasai and Nandi as interested only in fighting are clearly exaggerated.

Nandi power had thus grown without the use of firearms from the coast or the effects of long-distance trade. They had a system of government which, though rudimentary contrasted with that of Buganda, was extremely effective in serving the needs of Nandi society. They had a military system superior to any in the Kenya region, and were able to offer stronger resistance to the British advance than any other East African people.

4
Trading states and peoples: (1) East and Central Africa

Overview; new states and increased trade

New states mushroomed in the interior of East and Central Africa between 1800 and 1885, from the independent prazos of the lower Zambesi in the south to Tippu Tip's dominion on the middle and upper Zaire in the north. Several existing states, like the inter-lacustrine Kingdoms of Buganda and Bunyoro, continued to annex new territory. To some extent this situation arose from a factor that affected many communities not touched by the Mfecane, as well as those who were touched by it: a general enlargement of scale in economic operations, in particular an expansion of long-distance trade.

Long-distance trade expanded because the existing internal long-distance trade was more closely woven into the pattern of the inter-national economy. The development of Zanzibar by Sultan Seyyid Said (1804–56) as a major entrepôt for ivory for the world market and as an export centre for slaves encouraged African traders of the interior to go to the coast and Swahili-Arab coast traders to go to the interior. In the western areas of Central Africa the pattern of inter-national trade had long had considerable impact, but even here the nineteenth century witnessed considerable change.

The ivory trade expanded more than ever before in order to provide Europe with luxuries, and India with bracelets for Hindu brides. Slaves were in increasing demand as cheap labour on the new clove plantations developed on Zanzibar and Pemba islands, and as household slaves in East African coastal towns and Arabia.

Trade was further stimulated by an increase in population and the consequent increase in demand for commodities like iron and salt. Increased agricultural production, that followed the introduction of new food crops such as maize and cassava, led to a greater use of iron tools, especially hoes. The iron and salt trades had existed for centuries in the interior, and expanded with the new conditions of the nineteenth century. Another commodity in increased demand was copper, used widely by East African peoples for manufacturing ornaments, and used both by them and industrialized nations across

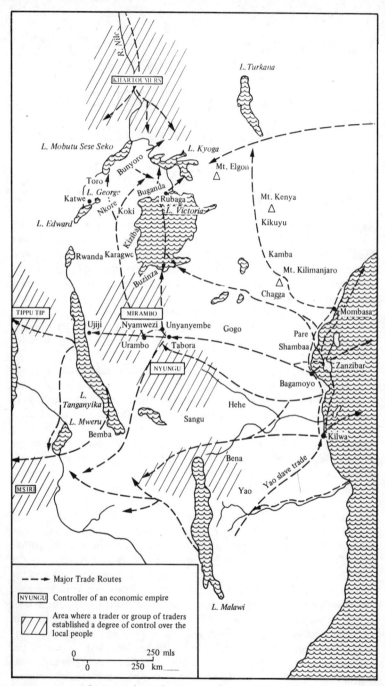

Map 3. East African trade in the nineteenth century.

the seas as currency. If Britain used Shaba copper as a means of exchange, so did the Shaba people themselves.

The results of expanding trade for eastern African political development were remarkable. Some rulers expanded their territory in order to gain control of trade routes and market places, and to obtain political authority over places of production. For example, Kabalega expanded Bunyoro southwards to Katwe, one of the most important salt producing areas. Rulers of small states or chiefdoms, whose power originally depended only on ritual authority, used trade as a new technique to make their power more complete. Rulers could sell slaves and ivory in exchange for guns and cloth with which to arm and reward their soldiers, administrators and traders. In many states the bands of armed followers of the ruler developed into standing armies. The basis of political authority therefore became less ritual or religious, and more military and economic. The old ruling class monopolized long-distance trade in most areas, but raised up a new class of men of commoner origin to serve them in new military, administrative and economic functions.

The growth of trade did not automatically lead to political development. In some cases it resulted in the break-up of political units. To the west, in Shaba, the Cokwe ivory hunters destroyed the Lunda empire and took over much of its trade, but failed to replace it with an alternative centralized political structure. In Tanzania, Usangi in north Upare broke away from the Ugweno kingdom. Not all long-distance trading peoples created centralized government: semi-nomadic ivory-traders like the Kamba of Kenya and the Cokwe of Angola continued to be organized on a segmentary lineage basis, and over large parts of East and Central Africa authority rested with heads of families and not with kings and chiefs.

It has been commonly assumed that the trade in firearms and ammunition had a dramatic effect on East and Central African politics; that the possession of guns was the main factor that enabled a leader to assert or expand political control. The reality, however, is rather different. Guns were more often of ceremonial rather than military value: they were often, like the old flintlocks, of inferior quality; a ruler might face the problem of obtaining compatible ammunition and replacement parts for diverse makes of gun; his soldiers might lack training in gun handling, marksmanship and tactics. He might lack skilled smiths to repair guns. Above all, access to powder and ammunition might be severely restricted. Mirambo, for example, had 20,000 guns but rarely had ammunition for more than a few hundred to be used effectively together. The potentialities of guns were generally ignored, except on a rare occasion such as Tippu Tip's defeat of Nsama. In a 1971 article in *Transafrican Journal of History* Andrew Roberts pinpoints in north-east Zambia the growth of the iron trade as the key to military success and political expansion. He shows that the Bemba in the hey-day of their conquests, from about 1850 to about 1880, were increasingly dependent on iron spears rather than guns. Another example is tht of the Hehe of central Tanzania, who had few if any guns, but in 1880 defeated a Nyamwezi army equipped with guns, repeating this feat in 1891 with a German expedition.

Some communities were able to make effective use of guns, noticeably those at or near the coast who had regular access to supplies of powder and ammunition: for example the Swahili-Arabs, Yao and Shambaa. The Nyamwezi adventurer Msiri, who set up a kingdom in Shaba, relied on guns because of his political authority over smiths skilled in the repair of guns. Msiri also had access to ammunition from the west coast as well as from the east.

As we turn to look more closely at various areas, a view of the East and Central African political map on the eve of the European Partition shows a number of new states like Buganda and Bunyoro that had survived and grown, the remnants of a few large states that had collapsed, and a large number of small village politics. In general, there was much greater political centralization than at the beginning of the century.

The Zanzibari role in eastern Africa, c. 1840 to c. 1890

The economy of Zanzibar

The Sultan of Zanzibar's dominions consisted of the islands of Zanzibar and Pemba and many of the ports along the East African coast from Somalia to Mozambique, together with their immediate hinterlands. The reign of Sultans Seyyid Said (1804–56), Majid (1856–70) and Barghash (1870–88) saw many changes both on Zanzibar and in the role of Zanzibari in East Africa.

Said moved from Oman in Arabia and settled permanently in Zanzibar in 1840, having brought to an end the long conflict between his own family and the Mazrui family of Mombasa. From that time he succeeded in making Zanzibar the entrepôt of a vast trading area stretching from the east coast as far inland as the Zaire River. He brought about an enlargement of scale in production and trade by his encouragement of clove growing on the islands; his commercial treaties with the United States of America and with European states in the 1830s and 1840s; his introduction of a unified customs system, in the form of a five per cent import duty on all goods at all ports; his introduction of a new copper currency; his encouragement of Arab and Indian immigration; and his support for long-distance trade in the interior involving a wide variety of goods. There was a change in the organization of trade, with a decline in barter, more buying on credit and the use of the copper currency.

Although Zanzibar underwent considerable economic growth in this period, it became an example of a country at the periphery of the international capitalist system, exporting primary commodities and importing manufactures. The economy was dependent on international price fluctuations and there was little development of local industry. One major advance was made in the development of clove plantations, to cash in on the enormous international demand for cloves. Zanzibar became the world's leading producer of cloves. The sultans also encouraged Arab settlement and the development of food crop plantations in the country north of Mombasa, particularly in the areas around Malindi and Lamu. These areas had been neglected agriculturally for two hundred years, but were now able to supply Arabia and Iran with large quantities of grain. However, the development of clove and grain plantations led to the creation of a semi-colonial plantation economy in which the Swahili-Arabs of Zanzibar were the masters and the Africans were the slaves.

Seyyid Said actively encouraged Indians to settle in East Africa. In 1840 there were approximately 1,000 Indians at the East African coast, but in 1860 there were about 4,000. The Indians contributed in several major ways to the economic growth of Zanzibar. They managed Zanzibar's important trade with India, exchanging Indian cloth, metal-ware and beads for ivory and slaves. Much of the trade carried on along the coast by European and American firms was conducted through Indian middlemen. The Indian traders were supplied with trade goods by the European firms on credit terms. The distribution of overseas goods in Zanzibar and along the coast was then conducted by Indian firms. Similarly, much of the export trade was channelled through the Indians as they exchanged exports for imports. The Indians were both retailers and wholesalers. They acted as bankers, investing their capital largely in loans and mortgages. They extended credit loans to the sultan and to Swahili-Arab, Indian and European traders. Development loans were made to plantation-owners. The Indian rupee and copper pice currency gradually replaced Austrian Maria Theresa dollars as the principal currency in circulation at the coast. The Indians, therefore, performed many vital economic services in Zanzibar and were ultimately to extend their influence far inland.

Zanzibar's economy underwent drastic change in the 1870s when, due to British pressure, the coastal slave trade was effectively suppressed (see Chapter 9). The hurricane of 1872, which destroyed the clove plantations, and the abolition of the slave trade in Zanzibar in 1873 produced only a short-lived depression. There was steady growth from 1875, largely because of a boom in rubber which overtook ivory to become the most important export. Also, the opening of the Suez Canal in 1869 brought Zanzibar two thousand miles closer to Britain. The new rubber trade increased Zanzibar's dependence on the foreign-dominated international economy, but it did make possible a major adjustment away from the slave trade.

The government of Zanzibar

The Sultanate of Zanzibar's government was rudimentary. There was no civil service of administrative officers, not even a council of ministers or official advisers. Said and his immediate successors dealt with most matters of government themselves, and put little in writing. Said lived in a small palace the size of a house, which was the only government building. He regarded government as largely a matter of resolving disputes between his subjects and of collecting customs revenue, a job he farmed out to an Indian business firm.

The weakness of the sultan's administration is revealed in his limited control of the African Tumbatu and Hadimu communities on Zanzibar island itself. The sultan exercised direct rule only over the city of Zanzibar. The coastal towns stretching from Pate to Kilwa merely paid taxes and customs duties to Zanzibar through the sultan's governors. Otherwise they were self-governing. There was no standing army in Zanzibar until the abolition of the slave trade in 1873, and even then it was under a British commander. No political control was established by the sultanate over any part of the interior, although individual Zanzibaris did have political influence during the nineteenth century.

Zanzibar's role in the interior

The economic achievements of the Swahili-Arabs of Zanzibar in the interior were considerable, but must be placed in perspective. African traders played as great a role in the expansion of long-distance trade as did the Swahili-Arabs. There were always far more Africans going to the coast than there were Swahili-Arabs going to the interior, and the latter used routes pioneered by the former. The coast traders did not take full control of the already flourishing long-distance trade.

The coast traders brought certain economic advantages to the interior. They contributed to the growth of towns, such as Tabora and Ujiji, which developed as bases where coast traders bought goods from Africans and provisioned their caravans. The Swahili-Arabs developed many agricultural plantations at their settlements in the interior, especially in Zaire. However, it must be recognized that there were significant developments in East African trade and agriculture in general.

The activities of the Swahili-Arabs were of little benefit to the interior, and in some ways impaired its economic development. The benefits of the ivory trade were questionable, because the trade proceeded in such a way that elephants (the 'producers' of ivory) were virtually wiped out in many areas. The gun trade was as much a curse as the slave trade it had much in common with. Imports of cheap foreign goods depressed African manufactures.

The East African slave trade outweighed what minor benefits the Swahili-Arab traders brought to the interior. But it is unfair to blame Swahili-Arab and other African slave-traders for it entirely. There can be little doubt that the root cause of the trade is to be found in the foreign demand for slaves, especially from western Asia, and this was allied to the drive of European capitalism to acquire profits from the sale of out-of-date firearms at the East African coast.

It has been estimated that while in 1840 10,000 slaves were reaching the coast annually, the figure had risen to 60,000 a year in the 1860s. The Custom House of Kilwa Kivinje kept exact figures for the number of slaves which passed through it from 1862 to 1867: the total for these five years was 97,203, the annual figure rising from over 18,000 in 1862 to over 22,000 in 1867. Several thousand more must have been smuggled, to avoid the payment of taxes to the Sultan. Thousands were exported from other ports; still more never reached the coast. Livingstone estimated that five times as many Africans were killed resisting capture as were actually captured. In spite of the Moresby Treaty of 1822 and the Hamerton Treaty of 1845 between Britain and Zanzibar which attempted to reduce the slave trade, the trade was at its height in the period immediately before its abolition in 1873.

Sultan Barghash, under British pressure, abolished the slave trade in Zanzibar territory in 1873, and in 1876 issued a proclamation which prohibited the traffic of slaves from the interior to the coast. This resulted in a sharp decline of the slave trade at the coast but a corresponding increase in the slave trade in the interior. The increase in this interior trade after 1875 brought new evils in its wake. Slave labour greatly increased as traders now used slaves to undercut the trade in ivory which was carried by porters. Slaves were used in large numbers to cultivate the estates of the Swahili-Arabs in eastern Zaire, and estates of the Nyamwezi, Gogo and Yao peoples in East Africa.

Swahili-Arab economic activity in the interior had incidental, but nonetheless significant social results. Islam spread widely, notably in the Yao states near Lake Malawi and in Buganda (see below). There was some limited intermarriage and inevitably some cultural interchange. But the spread of Kiswahili as a lingua franca over large areas of East Africa was perhaps the major contribution of the Swahili-Arabs to the development of the region. It was used over a wide area: Tanzania, Kenya, Uganda and eastern Zaire. Although individual Swahili-Arabs had political influence in the interior, Zanzibar did not establish direct rule in the interior of East and Central Africa. Tippu Tip set up a Swahili-Arab state in eastern Zaire, but this was independent of Zanzibar.

The sultans had neither the troops nor a sufficiently developed administrative organization to conquer and rule the interior—even if they had had the inclination. Zanzibar was no stronger than some of the powerful states of the interior, such as Urambo, Ukimbu, Bunyoro and Uhehe. The Swahili-Arab traders had a number of weaknesses: they were very small in numbers and had little chance of waging war successfully against well-organized African societies. They depended on the goodwill of the rulers and communities of the interior for trade and provisions, and so found it a prime necessity to establish good relations with the local peoples. The major exception was, of course, Tippu Tip in Zaire who was able to take advantage of the political weakness of the communities there. If, however, the Swahili-Arabs were not, in general, political imperialists they did manage to exert considerable political influence in four areas: Unyamwezi, Ujiji, Buganda and Lake Malawi.

In the early 1820s Swahili-Arab traders were resident in Unyamwezi, and they founded the town of Kazeh or Tabora in the central Nyamwezi state of Unyanyembe in 1830. The death of Fundikira, ruler of Unyanyembe, in 1858, touched off a long war of succession in which the leading Swahili-Arab trader at Tabora, Muhammad bin Juma, played a major role. The coast traders gave military support to Mnywa Sele (or Msabila) against his half-brother and claimant Mkasiwa (or Kiyungi). Mnywa Sele became the new ruler, but when he began to tax the coast traders they combined with Mkasiwa who became ruler in 1860. In 1878 the Swahili-Arabs helped Isike to succeed his father. At first he seemed subservient to them but he was obviously playing a waiting game. Later in his career he became a determined opponent of both Swahili-Arabs and Europeans.

The political role played in Jiji politics by Mwinyi Kheri, the leader of the Swahili-Arabs at the Lake Tanganyika port town from the 1840s to 1885, was a more peaceful one. Mwinyi Kheri was often called in to mediate in disputes among the Jiji. He regularly paid customs duties to the *Abami*, or overall ruler of the Jiji, and married into local Ha society.

In Buganda the Swahili-Arab arrival contributed to an expansion of Buganda's long-distance trade, which led to an emphasis on trade in ivory, slaves and guns rather than traditional commodities like coffee beans, barkcloth and iron. Yet the most striking aspect of the coast traders' arrival in Buganda was the cultural revolution inspired by Islam, a phenomenon with no parallel in the East African interior. This cultural revolution in turn precipitated a political revolution that was equally unique.

Ahmed bin Ibrahim, who in 1844 was the first east coast trader to enter Buganda, was as keen on spreading Islam as he was on trading with the Ganda. He was encouraged by the willingness of many Ganda to accept new ideas and practices. Islam in Buganda made rapid strides after Kabaka Mutesa adopted the new faith in 1866. Mutesa observed Ramadan continuously for the next ten years, practised religion zealously, learned Arabic, adopted Arab dress and manner, Islamized the Court, and built many mosques. He ordered the execution of many traditionalists who opposed the spread of the new religion. Nevertheless, Islamic practices like circumcision did not become widespread. The Ganda had a traditional distaste of mutilation, and most Ganda Muslims, including Mutesa, remained uncircumcised. Islam certainly spread deeper among the Ganda than among any other community of the East African interior. It also helped to prepare the way for Christianity by opening up the minds of the Ganda to a universal religion.

The political revolution began when the Muslims and Christians were forced to organize themselves into armed political parties to resist the attempt of the Kabaka Mwanga to kill or expel all adherents of foreign religions. This led to the joint Muslim-Christian coup in 1888 which sent Mwanga into exile. The Muslim Ganda divided the Ministries with the Christians, but their uneasy alliance, dominated by mutual fear, led to a purely Muslim coup later in 1888 and the Christians joined Mwanga in exile. The Muslims now had political control of Buganda, but although they were supplied with munitions by the Swahili-Arabs in the capital, they did not take orders from them. They felt their ingrained Ganda nationalism as deeply as their religious faith. The period of Muslim rule in Buganda, from 1888 to 1890, was marked by cruel persecution of Christians which far surpassed the persecution by Mwanga in the mid-1880s. Many Ganda Christians were killed, the European missionaries were expelled, and churches and Bibles were destroyed. The Christians in alliance with Mwanga returned to power in 1890 after a bloody civil war. They then persecuted the Muslims. Nearly all the Swahili-Arabs in Buganda were killed and their political influence died with them. It may be seen from this that the civil wars in Buganda from 1888 to 1890 were the result of traditional factionalism within Buganda, not of foreign interference.

Around Lake Malawi the Swahili-Arab traders managed to establish two small states in the face of strong pressure from the Yao, Ngoni, Portuguese and Chikunda. Mlozi, from his base at Karonga on the north-west shore of the lake, became a prominent ivory and slave trader. With the aid of his armed followers he conquered many of the local Nkonde clans. Jumbe Kisutu at Kota Kota established a flourishing ivory trading business, beginning his rule by giving protection to refugees from the Mfecane (see Chapter 2).

The career of Tippu Tip

Probably one of the best-known of the Swahili–Arab traders was Tippu Tip who was born Hamid bin Muhammed el Murjebi in about 1830. He was the son of Muhammed bin Juma, who became the leading Swahili–Arab trader at Tabora. Muhammed's father was an Arab, but his mother was an African. Hamid's mother was an Arab, but she died when he was young and he was brought up by his stepmother Karunde, a Nyamwezi princess of the Unyanyembe royal family.

As a young man, Tippu Tip (as he came to be nicknamed, either because he blinked a lot, or because of the sound of his guns) gained trading experience by working for his father around Tabora, but he began his own career in earnest in 1867. He set out from Zanzibar at the head of a large and exceptionally well-armed caravan to obtain ivory in Tabwa country in northern Zambia, and entered the territory of the powerful Tabwa ruler, Nsama, who was known to possess a vast store of ivory. Tippu Tip appears to have incited a battle at Nsama's stockade. He won it with the use of his firearms which were far superior to Nsama's spears, and returned to Zanzibar, laden with his loot of thirty tons of ivory, ten tons of copper, and a thousand slaves. Tippu Tip had made his fortune.

In about 1870 Tippu Tip invaded the Manyema country northwest of Lake Tanganyika. He decided that in order to exploit Manyema ivory fully, he would need to establish his own rule. He first obtained territory by guile. He learnt from the Rua, a Zairean community he was trading with, that some time ago they had captured two sisters of Kasongo–Ruchie, a ruler of a small state on the southern border of Manyema. The sisters were then sold as slaves. Tippu Tip visited Kasongo–Ruchie, who was a very old man, and deceived him into believing that he was the grandson of one of the sisters. The old man abdicated in Tippu Tip's favour. This made Tippu Tip the ruler of 30,000 people. From his capital Kasongo in eastern Zaire, he ruled a state which steadily enlarged as he brought more and more political units under his sway by means of alliances or force. From about 1870 to about 1890 he expanded his state northwards until he ruled about a quarter of modern Zaire. He styled himself 'the Sultan of Utetera'. He appointed Swahili–Arab, Nyamwezi and local agents to act for him to maintain order and collect tribute in the form of ivory and slaves. He was able to establish political power in this way because the local populations were small in numbers and politically fragmented; he had plenty of guns (50,000 at one stage) and trained his men in the proper use of them: he knew when to use force and when to use diplomacy. Finally, the navigability of the rivers in his territory greatly facilitated both the extension of his rule and the expansion of his trade.

Tippu Tip was, however, more than a mere conqueror. He and

other Swahili-Arabs developed large plantations of such food crops as rice, sorghum and maize, and constructed large, well-built houses in the Zanzibar style. They were responsible for the adoption of Kiswahili as the lingua franca of eastern Zaire.

Tippu Tip's diplomacy with Mirambo and with Leopold II of the Belgians are further evidence of his political ability. He had friendly relations with Mirambo, in contrast to the Tabora traders who quarrelled with the King of Urambo to the detriment of their trade. He used his close family ties with the Nyamwezi to cement an alliance with Mirambo: Tippu Tip agreed to trade for Mirambo at the coast, while in return Mirambo would protect Tippu Tip's caravans between Ujiji and Tabora from the Tuta Ngoni and other raiders. Tippu Tip did not resist the European Partition of Africa, but became a colonial agent in 1887 when he accepted appointment as Leopold's Governor at Stanley Falls. As we shall see in Volume 2, Tippu Tip's co-operation with the Congo Independent State failed to save his ivory trade, and he retired to Zanzibar in 1892.

The Nyamwezi states

The Nyamwezi people of west-central Tanzania developed long-distance trade in several directions before the coast traders came to their land. They pioneered routes westward to Lake Tanganyika and beyond into the upper Zaire region, southwards to Shaba, northwards to Buganda, and about 1800 they reached the east coast itself. Their strategic position along the central routes from Zanzibar to the interior was a vital factor in Nyamwezi development in the nineteenth century. It enabled them to build on their existing extensive trade in salt, ironwork, copper, grain, livestock, barkgoods and pottery, and enter the international ivory trade. From the 1840s they began to hunt elephants and sell ivory on a large scale. This economic enlargement combined with the new military techniques learned from the Ngoni resulted in the formation of three large states, Unyanyembe, Urambo and Ukimbu, from the large number of small states in the area. These small states were ruled by an *ntemi* (or chief) who sometimes had little more than ritual functions, although in some cases ntemis were more powerful and had political, judicial and military powers. At the beginning of the nineteenth century there were probably about 150 ntemi states amongst the Nyamwezi.

Unyanyembe grew up as the central Nyamwezi kingdom when the coast traders built Tabora near the royal village of Itetemia. Swetu and his successor Fundikira were the first Unyanyembe rulers to use their wealth from trade to strengthen their military forces and use them to exact tribute over neighbouring ntemi states. Unyanyembe declined when a long succession war weakened it after the death of Fundikira in 1858, but after Isike's accession in 1876 the state revived, and began to rival in power the newer states of Urambo and Ukimbu, created by the warlords Mirambo and Nyungu-ya-Mawe, in the 1870s.

Mirambo

Mirambo, or Mbulya Mtelya as his family knew him, was born in the late 1830s the son of a hereditary ntemi ruler, Kasanda of Uyowa (or Ugowe). Uyowa was west of Tabora, and contained only a few thousand people. Mirambo grew up as a warrior; he appears to have gone on long-distance trading expeditions, and may have spent part of his youth among the Tuta Ngoni who invaded Unyamwezi in the 1850s. He used wealth gained from ivory trading to equip a private army of mercenary soldiers or *ruga-ruga*—a motley collection of war captives, deserters from caravans, runaway slaves and refugees. He welded them into a highly disciplined and efficient force using Ngoni weapons and tactics. His personal courage, and the booty he distributed to his followers for their service in war, gained him a large loyal following. In a short space of time, he had by the 1860s created a state of his own called Urambo, annexing to the Uyowa nucleus most of the small states of western Unyamwezi. He expanded westwards as far as Ujiji, northwards almost to Lake Victoria, and southwards to Lake Rukwa. He thus controlled the major trade routes from Tabora to Ujiji, Tabora to Buganda, and Tabora to Shaba, and could exact tolls on all of them. Mirambo had 20,000 guns at one time, but a chronic shortage of ammunition meant they could not be used in war as well as ivory hunting. He relied on spears as weapons for warfare.

Mirambo's relations with the coast traders were variable. His business partnership with Tippu Tip was in sharp contrast to his 1871–5 war against the Swahili-Arabs of Tabora. The Tabora traders refused to pay tolls on routes controlled by Mirambo. Mirambo was equally determined to make them pay. The war was indecisive, but ended when the Tabora traders agreed to pay tolls to Mirambo rather than endure continued disruption of their trade.

Mirambo welcomed those Europeans who he thought would be useful to him, such as the Swiss trader Philippe Broyon, who was a valuable commercial partner, and the British missionary Southon. Southon did not make a single convert in Urambo, but he wrote letters on Mirambo's behalf, and kept him informed on world politics. Mirambo wanted friendly relations with Sir John Kirk, the British consul on Zanzibar. He hoped that British approval would be given to his attempts to enlarge his state. However, the death of two British traders, Frederick Carter and Tom Cadenhead at the hands of some of Mirambo's warriors in 1880 brought to an end all chance of support from Kirk.

Despite his expansion of territory and his personal qualities Mirambo was not a successful modernizer. The state he created was insecurely built on his personal charismatic qualities and did not long survive his death in 1884. He created no centralized administration. When he conquered an area he had the existing local ruler killed, but appointed a new one from the traditional ruling family. This technique of instilling fear and applying generosity, was an interesting blend, but not a judicious one. During Mirambo's lifetime, the new local rulers were loyal to him, but after his death many rebelled to reassert the traditional authority of their family. No real community feeling ever developed. Each component of the state remained basically committed to its own entity. Further, Mirambo's successors lacked his ability, and the personal loyalty of soldiers was not carried over to the new rulers. His brother Mpandashalo succeeded him and ruled from 1885–90. Mpandashalo's unimaginative leadership led to the collapse of the state, and when Mirambo's son Katuga became ntemi in 1890, he inherited little more than Uyowa itself. In contrast, Nyungu-ya-Mawe's state of Ukimbu survived his death because he had abolished traditional local institutions, and created a centralized, if rudimentary, bureaucracy.

Nyungu-ya-Mawe

Nyungu-ya-Mawe means *the pot of stone* or *the pot which does not break*. It symbolizes the man: a ruthless military leader and political dictator, who created what contemporary European missionaries misnamed 'the empire of the ruga-rugas'.

A short man with only one eye, the other having been lost in battle, Nyungu was originally born into the royal family of Unyanyembe. He gained considerable military experience in the long civil war in Unyanyembe after 1858, fighting alongside the ousted ruler Mnywa Sele from 1860 until the latter's death in 1865. He thereafter claimed the Unyanyembe throne for himself. Failing in his attempt to assert his claim in Unyanyembe, Nyungu turned to the south, and between 1875 and 1880 he created a kingdom for himself in Ukimbu and southern Unyamwezi.

In 1875 Nyungu occupied the central Kimbu ntemi unit of Kiwele, using both the claim of his part-Kimbu ancestry, and above all his army of *ruga-ruga*, which was similar in composition to Mirambo's army. It too, was recruited from profits derived from ivory trading. The conquest of Ukimbu was desirable because it lay on caravan routes, and it was facilitated by Kimbu political fragmentation, the recent weakening of Ukimbu by Ngoni and Sangu invasions and the devastating famine that followed. Nyungu conquered most of southern Ukimbu in 1877, the vitally strategic district of Mgunda Mkali east of Tabora on the main coast road in 1878, and Konongo on the Tabora-Shaba route in 1879–80. In 1880 he defeated

Mtinginya, ruler of Usongo north of Tabora, who tried to take Mgunda Mkali from him. Eighteen-eighty marks the end of Nyungu's expansion although in 1883 he managed to defeat a powerful rebellion by Mutitimia, rival claimant to the ntemiship of Kiwele. In 1884 Nyungu died: paralysed, crippled and almost dumb.

Nyungu-ya-Mawe was notorious for his brutality and that of his soldiers who burned and skinned prisoners alive, wore ornaments of human parts such as necklaces of teeth and belts of intestines, and wore caps of human scalps and beards. His company commanders had terrifying praise-names, like 'spitter of blood', 'defecator of men', and 'feeder of vultures'. If Nyungu dropped a cloth, it was a signal for a man to be speared to death at once. If he shook his foot, the victim was merely banished for life. If his soldiers were experiencing casualties in storming a defensive position, he would call for reinforcements with the order, 'Pile on more logs!'.

Yet, ruthless as Nyungu and his army were, there was a positive side to his career. He was a political unifier, who created one state out of Ukimbu and southern Unyamwezi, an area of 20,000 square miles. He achieved a measure of social unity in Ukimbu, and in consequence a lingua franca emerged. This was Ki-luga-luga, the language of the ruga-ruga, a Nyamwezi patois that replaced many separate Kimbu dialects. Above all Nyungu created a centralized administration that kept his state together for ten years after his death, until the German occupation. He left a *mutwale* or district governor to rule over each conquered political unit. Normally the *vatwale* (plural form of mutwale) were commoners, having no ties with either local royal families or even the local area itself. They replaced traditional rulers. Their duties were to settle local disputes, to collect ivory and send it to Kiwele, and to send slaves to Nyungu. The results of this direct rule were that the state survived under Nyungu's successors, his daughter Mgalula (reigned 1884–92) and another woman Msavira (1892–5), because the state functioned regardless of the person of the ruler. The Germans used a similar system of direct rule when they began to rule Ukimbu.

Msiri

Msiri was a Nyamwezi caravan leader who settled with his people, the Yeke, in the Kazembe kingdom in Shaba and created a new state in the area. Msiri took advantage of succession disputes in Kazembe to annex all Kazembe territory west of the Luapula River in the late 1860s. Thereafter he expanded his tributary area to the north, amongst the Luba chiefs, until he ruled a vast area from the Lualaba in the west to Lake Mweru in the east. This area was called Yeke or Garenganze and had Bukenya as its capital.

Like Mirambo and Nyungu-ya-Mawe, Msiri used his wealth from ivory trading to build a military force and create a state by war.

However, unlike them he relied on guns rather than spears. Garen-ganze was centrally placed between the east and west coasts, so he was able to obtain guns, powder and ammunition from both directions, though mainly from Angola. Moreover, Shaban smiths were skilled in repairing guns. A technique which he used to ensure the loyalty of provincial kings was to marry their daughters: a skilful political use of polygamy.

Msiri made a major contribution towards social unity by decreeing that in the interests of nation-building, all his people, regardless of origin, should adopt the facial markings of the Nyamwezi. Significantly, Nyamwezi cicatrices were voluntarily adopted by many peoples outside Msiri's dominions, along the trade routes used by the Yeke, as far as Portuguese Angola.

The Hehe state

Uhehe lies between the Great Ruaha and Kilombero rivers, in the northern part of the southern Highlands of Tanzania. In 1855 the Hehe people were divided into numerous small political units based on clans. The incursions of the Ngoni and the growth of the ivory trade inspired Munyigumba, ruler of the centrally-positioned Hehe clan-state of Ng'uluhe, to build a strong, united state from the scattered Hehe political units. Munyigumba used profits from ivory trading to build up an army along Ngoni lines, and used it successfully to resist Ngoni raids into Uhehe.

When Munyigumba died in 1879 he was succeeded by his able son Mkwawa, but only after Mkwawa had defeated a rival claimant Mwambambe. Having won power, Mkwawa quickly emerged as one of the most powerful rulers of new states in eastern Africa. He continued the Hehe–Ngoni War which had started in 1878, won several battles against the Ngoni, and forced them to make peace in 1881. He organized raids on neighbouring Ubena, Usagara, Ugogo and Usangu, and on Swahili–Arab trading caravans. Raids, trade, and tribute from weak neighbours helped to build up his wealth.

Mkwawa did not hesitate to kill all opponents in Uhehe—even potential opponents—thus creating a general atmosphere of fear. This helped to hold his state together. On the other hand, many people were loyal to him out of gratitude, since they depended on him for their personal position and wealth, and for protection from the Ngoni.

The political organization created by his father was improved upon. Within Uhehe itself Mkwawa made provincial rulers subject to appointment and dismissal by himself as head of state, and thus increased the strength of the central government and the unity within the state. Areas which did not resist his expansion often retained their own rulers, who had to pay regular tribute. Marriage alliances were concluded with as many groups as possible. German rule was eventually to destroy this nascent state.

The Pangani valley states

The Pangani River has its source on Mount Kilimanjaro and its outlet at the Indian Ocean, at the town of Pangani. The Pangani valley provided an easy trade route between the coast and the Shambaa people of the Usambara Mountains, the Chasu-speakers of the Pare Mountains and the Chagga of Kilimanjaro. The influence of the east coast trade was a major factor in state-formation in the valley in the nineteenth century.

The Shambaa kingdom

The Shambaa kingdom was founded by Kimweri ye Nyumbai who ruled from about 1803 until his death in 1868. Paradoxically, before his death the east coast trade which had helped him to build the state was contributing to the state's disintegration. Kimweri inherited a small clan-state struggling to survive against attacks from the Maasai, the Taita and the Kamba from the north, and the coastal Zigua with their guns. He started as a defensive nation-builder, building up an army equipped with guns and driving off the invaders. He next began to expand in order to control part of the Pangani valley caravan route. This eliminated the Zigua middlemen and enabled direct contact with the coast. By the middle of the century Kimweri's empire was composed of all Usambara; Segeju, Digo, and Bondei country between Usambara and the sea; parts of Uzigua to the south and Upare to the north; and even parts of Maasai country to the west.

Kimweri's kingdom was renowned for its efficient system of government. Kimweri was a firm and autocratic ruler, but not a dictator. He ruled by consultation, and regularly summoned the Great Council which was composed of heads of the commoner or non-royal clans. These clan-heads were hereditary and could not be removed by the king. However, Kimweri created a centralized inspectorate under his personal control. The inspectors were sent by the king to inform local governors of his instructions and to ensure they were carried out. Amongst his officials was the Mdoe, a sort of minister of finance, who was responsible for collecting taxes from the districts of the Shambaa kingdom and for conveying and selling trade items to the Swahili–Arab traders at the coast. Kimweri applied direct rule to the centre of the country, but he allowed a good measure of local self-government to the coastal peoples. His rule over the coast was so light that Pangani town, for instance, normally paid tribute only once in every two or three years.

Kimweri was very much open to new influences. He allowed complete freedom of movement to Swahili–Arab traders and encouraged the growth of Islam. Several of his sons were converted and he used a number of Swahili–Arabs as advisers, secretaries and even soldiers at his capital, Vuga. His personal physician, Osman, came from Zanzibar. He offered the Protestant missionary, Krapf, a site for a mission station. In Mazinde, the economic capital situated in the valley below the highlands, a new type of multi-ethnic culture emerged. Unlike Vuga, the traditional Shambaa capital, Mazinde was a new type of town reflecting the changes which long-distance trade had brought to the kingdom. The population included not only Shambaa but also many Zigua. Its architecture was of the coastal Zanzibar type.

The Shambaa kingdom declined before Kimweri's death. During his extreme old age district governors became more and more independent. His son Semboja, Governor of Mazinde, became overpowerful, because he kept a large portion of the state revenues obtained from the collection of customs and tolls to build up a well-equipped private army. Semboja refused to recognize his father's choice of successor, the young Shekulwavu, and the Shambaa kingdom fell apart in a series of civil wars between 1868 and 1890.

The Pare

The history of nineteenth century Upare shows the divisive rather than the unifying effects of trade on an East African community. In 1800 north Upare constituted a centralized state called Ugweno, although south Upare was divided into at least six very small states. Until the 1860s the Chasu-speakers of Upare mainly exported iron to the Chagga (who made spears for ivory-hunting) and sold food to coastal caravans. In the 1860s there was a great change in this trading pattern, and a consequent change in the political pattern. There was an increase in the slave trade and intense rivalry among Pare rulers for control of the trade. Coastal traders began to supply guns to Pare leaders. Even subordinate rulers like village headmen began to ignore the authority above them, acting independently to enrich themselves and strengthen their power. By the 1880s Ugweno was divided into twelve tiny states while south Upare was more politically fragmented than it had been in 1800. Coastal traders were happy to see this fragmentation since it allowed them greater economic power—as Mashombo, ruler of Mbaga in south Upare found to his cost. He became rich from ivory trading and powerful by possession of a ritual pot for witch-finding. But he was prevented from uniting a large part of Upare by the economic interests of coastal traders, and powerful local leaders of the Pare, who had acquired guns from Shambaa and Zigua middlemen.

The Chagga states

The impact of increased trade can be clearly seen with the Chagga. In the nineteenth century, several Chagga rulers created larger states by conquering and uniting neighbouring clans. Impulses towards aggrandizement were fuelled by the wealth and benefits obtained from trade, but no single ruler managed to unite the Chagga nation. Kibosho, the most powerful of the Chagga states, was created in the middle of the century by the ivory trader, Tatua, who had a large supply of guns. Lokila, Tatua's successor in the 1860s, became very active in the slave trade, raiding Chagga and non-Chagga neighbours for slaves to sell to coast traders; these raids also brought in large numbers of cattle to Kibosho. Sina, Lokila's successor in the 1870s and 1880s, greatly expanded Kibosho. By means of the wealth acquired from trade, he built up a large army stationed at his massive stone fort. His soldiers fought with guns, bought from coast traders, and short stabbing spears, made by captured blacksmiths who were kept in chains to prevent them escaping and making weapons for Sina's enemies. Sina developed a more advanced system of government than his predecessors, and used central government inspectors to check on the actions of local clan-heads. Sina was overthrown in the 1880s when Rindi, ruler of the rival state of Moshi, allied with the Germans against him.

The Kamba

The Kamba of the Athi River basin inhabit the land that slopes gradually from the Kikuyu highlands to the Nyika desert near the coast. Their history provides an example of the rise of a lineage-based trading community which did not create a unified political system.

The rise of the Kamba long-distance trade in the first half of the nineteenth century was due to several factors. At the beginning of the century the Kamba were semi-nomadic and expert hunters, using bows and poisoned arrows rather than guns. Their hunting-parties began to take over the transportation part of the ivory trade from the Nyika middlemen. Kamba hunter-traders worked as far north as Mount Kenya, westwards into the Rift Valley, and southwards as far as Uzigua. They came to monopolize the ivory trade in the Mombasa hinterland. The Kamba also exported their local industrial products over a wide area of East Africa. They were particularly skilled in ironwork, using local ore to make arrow-heads, chains and collars. The Kamba emerged as traders between the coast and other communities to the west, especially the Kikuyu, to whom they sold coastal goods such as beads, wire and cloth in exchange for livestock and ivory. In order to carry on trade some Kamba began to settle outside their homeland. Bands of hunter-traders settled throughout large areas of north-eastern Tanzania. Others settled at the coast, especially at Rabai near Mombasa from 1836, and received Kamba ivory from the interior. The Kamba copied neither the Maasai spear nor their system of age-set regiments, nor did they take up the use of firearms like the Swahili–Arabs. The Kamba military system, with its reliance on the bow and arrow, perhaps surprisingly enabled the Kamba to withstand Maasai and Galla raids and to defend their caravans crossing the Nyika. Kamba skill in the use of these weapons, gained from large-scale ivory-hunting, more than compensated for any lack of new military methods and technology.

The sort of organization which the Kamba used to carry on trading operations is a matter for conjecture. We do know, however, that the Kamba trading co-operatives—whoever they were composed of—were led by *asili*. The Kamba had no chief as such who would wield political power, but it was usual for asili, or outstanding individuals, to rise to positions of leadership through their abilities, personalities or wealth. Amongst the nineteenth century asili was Kivoi wa Mwendwa of Kitui, a diviner and reputed rain-maker who organized many trading caravans under his armed followers. He owned many slaves whom he armed with guns, and he was so powerful that he even levied tribute on some of his Maasai neighbours. However, despite his great wealth Kivoi never became the ruler of any section of the Kamba.

Kamba trade to the coast declined after 1850, largely because of the decline of the elephant population in Ukambani, and because of greater competition from Swahili–Arab traders. Before 1850 the Swahili–Arabs had avoided the Maasai, but the Maasai civil wars—which greatly weakened Maasai power—encouraged the Swahili–Arabs to move on from Kilimanjaro towards Mount Kenya. The result was that the Kamba lost much of their ivory trade with the Kikuyu. They also lost their middleman position with the coastal populations and the Kikuyu. The decline of their ivory trade caused the Kamba to increase their hitherto limited involvement in the slave trade. However, the Kamba slave-raids on the Mount Kenya peoples encountered fierce resistance and led merely to Kamba military defeats. Conditions within Ukambani also undermined Kamba trade. The continuing lack of firm political leadership in the area meant that as the century progressed there were often feuds between different groups of Kamba.

The decline of Kamba trade after 1850 mainly affected the Kitui Kamba. The western, or Machakos Kamba, began to profit from new opportunities provided by the Swahili–Arab arrival. The Machakos Kamba sold ivory, cattle and provisions to the Swahili–Arabs. This particular expansion of Machakos trade did not, however, compensate for the loss of Kitui trade. All parts of Ukambani experienced a relative decline of production, especially in iron goods, since these were supplied direct to the Kikuyu and Maasai by the coastal traders. In fact, the demand for Kamba iron goods collapsed. The Swahili–Arabs wanted only raw materials (ivory) and foodstuffs from the Machakos Kamba. Thus, the pattern of economic dependency, whereby Africans offered labour, raw materials and foodstuffs in exchange for manufactures from economically developed countries, was established in Ukambani in the late pre-colonial period. The arrival of the British in the late 1880s developed this economic pattern in Ukambani even further.

Interlacustrine states: Bunyoro and Buganda

Bunyoro

The Empire of Bunyoro-Kitara in western Uganda had declined steadily from about 1650. This decline continued in the nineteenth century when the southern tributary state of Toro won its independence in the 1830s. However, Omukamas (Kings) Kamurasi (1852–69) and Kabalega (1870–97), successfully exploited the opportunities provided by the expansion of long-distance trade, to revive the ancient kingdom.

Omukama Kamurasi gained his throne through an alliance with the Lang'i, Nilotic neighbours of Bunyoro. He contributed to Bunyoro's revival by admitting to his kingdom Arab traders from Khartoum in the north and Swahili–Arab traders from the southeast.

Bunyoro was already flourishing as a base for long-distance trade in the interlacustrine region before the arrival of Muslim traders. Exports included iron goods, such as hoes and spearheads produced from local iron ore deposits, and salt from the large deposits at Kibero on Lake Mobutu. The Kibero salt mines were under state control and the chief source of the king's wealth. Kamurasi used the profits from Kibero as his chief means of obtaining firearms and ammunition from the Muslim traders. Ivory, which was a royal monopoly, was also exchanged directly with the traders. Kamurasi opened the way to a revival of Bunyoro's former military power over its neighbours.

Omukama Kabalega (Kabarega) or Cwa II was born in 1850. He obtained power by winning a war of succession with his elder brother, Kabigumire, who was supported by the royal family and the provincial leaders. Kabalega won because, having been trained as a soldier, he was popular with the army, which supported him; as a prince he had mixed freely with the people and had the common touch, so the mass of people, the *Bairu* or peasant-farmers, supported him; and he hired both Arab ivory traders from Khartoum who had guns, and Lang'i mercenaries, to fight for him.

Once in power, Kabalega ruthlessly consolidated his position by executing many disloyal princes and their supporters. However he also initiated and carried out far-reaching military, administrative and social reforms.

Kabalega created a regular army, the *abarusura*, of ten regiments, each of 1,500 men, who were under the direct command of the king and were largely equipped with guns. The old system where an army was furnished at short notice in times of emergency by local leaders, who rounded up available peasant farmers, was abolished. The local aristocracy were replaced as military leaders by commoners and foreigners, who were appointed and promoted on merit by the king. The army was recruited from adventurers from all parts of Uganda, but most of the new professional soldiers were Bairu, notably the army commander, Rwabudongo.

What were Kabalega's motives in creating a standing army? Clearly he wanted to build up a force independent of the hereditary *saza* (county) chiefs and members of the royal family who had supported Kabigumire and whose loyalty to him was suspect. It was particularly important and urgent to curb the power of the aristocracy in this way because for many years a rival claimant to the omukamaship, Ruyonga, was at large in the north with a rebel band. A loyal army would make it easier to defend the country against invasion from Buganda, and at the same time make it possible to expand Bunyoro. The army certainly succeeded in reducing the power of the aristocracy. The soldiers were unpaid and lawless; the aristocracy suffered from having their lands and homes plundered at will.

Kabalega's administrative reforms were closely tied up with the army reforms. Army generals were made territorial chiefs, so there was overlap between political and military authority. There was much greater centralization and efficiency, because many chiefdoms became appointive rather than hereditary posts. New chiefdoms were created for able commoners who were dependent on the king. The traditional chiefs, while they kept their titles, were ignored and powerless.

The army, aided by many hired Lang'i warbands, expanded Bunyoro for Kabalega, whose motives were to revive the former glory of the empire, to obtain more grazing land for cattle, which were very important in the economy, and to gain control of the Katwe salt deposits in Toro. In 1876 Toro was reconquered. Successful raids were carried out against Nkore, Rwanda and Karagwe, which were forced to pay tribute. In the north, Chope, between

Bunyoro and Lake Kyoga, was reconquered. Tribute was exacted from Nilotic-speaking communities beyond the Nile, such as the Acholi and Alur. In the east, Kabalega's new army defeated the Bugandan army at the Battle of Rwengabi. Some districts of Buganda were occupied and 20,000 Baganda were enslaved. In 1890 the army passed through northern Buganda to raid Busoga and exact tribute from there. It is likely that Bunyoro would have continued to expand under Kabalega after 1890, probably at the expense of Buganda which was ruled by a weak kabaka, Mwanga, if the British had not invaded the region, and taken sides with Bunyoro's enemies.

Inter-marriage was a policy Kabalega used to unite his country. He himself took wives from all localities, and encouraged his chiefs also to marry girls from different groups. Historically, Bunyoro had been divided into three social groups. At the top were the Babito of Luo origin; next were the Bahima pastoralists; finally there were the Bairu, who were Bantu peasant agriculturists.

Buganda

By 1840 Buganda had reached the limit of her pre-colonial expansion and was the strongest state in the East African interior. Her system of government was highly centralized. Buganda's strength, stability and supremacy were due to a number of political, military and economic factors.

The first political reason for Buganda's success was the way the *Kabaka* (King) was chosen. Only two men, the *Katikiro*, or prime minister, and the *Mugema*, an important clan head, made the choice, so there were relatively few succession disputes and civil wars. Generally, able men such as Suna and Mutesa were chosen. Secondly, there was a strong central government. The kabaka appointed chiefs, gave them land in return for loyalty and service, took it back for disloyalty or inefficiency, and controlled distribution of war booty on the same basis. By the nineteenth century very few chiefs held office by hereditary right. Buganda also developed successful methods of ruling its empire outside the Ganda heartland. Most of the tributary states—the Buhaya states of Karagwe, Kiziba, Basubi and Buzibja, Koki, and intermittently Toro—continued to control their internal affairs to a varying degree.

The military reasons for Buganda's success were the existence of a royal bodyguard, several hundred strong, as a kind of standing army; a flourishing import trade in iron spears from Bunyoro, Karagwe and Unyamwezi; and the existence of a navy of war canoes on Lake Victoria. After the arrival of the Swahili–Arabs in 1844, Buganda began to buy firearms in large quantities, but as we saw on page 31, the value of these new weapons was limited.

The economic reasons for Buganda's rise were various. A fertile soil and plentiful rain meant banana and other food crops could grow easily. Women generally tended the food crops which released the men for other occupations such as war and the building of roads to facilitate military movement. There was abundant wealth—bananas, barkcloth, coffee beans, ivory and slaves—which brought a consistently large revenue to the government, enabling it to organize a strong army. Royal control of market-places in and around the capital, and a levy of ten per cent on all transactions contributed most of the revenue, apart from the regular tributes from the subject provinces. Kabakas Suna and Mutesa welcomed coast traders, who brought not only firearms and cloth, but new food crops as well, which contributed to the growth of the economy. Maize reached Buganda in 1862, cassava in 1875 and rice in 1878.

Mutesa I did not attempt to expand Buganda territorially though his power was often felt beyond the tribute-paying area. For example, his navy of sixty canoes made frequent slave raids in the Kavirondo Gulf region at the expense of the Luo. His main concern though, was to enrich and transform Buganda.

Mutesa greatly increased the wealth of Buganda. He expanded the traditional export trade in barkcloth and coffee beans throughout the interlacustrine area. He allowed Swahili–Arab traders to settle in Buganda from 1862, in order to develop the export trade in ivory and slaves and the import trade in guns. Strict royal control over the trading in ivory and guns meant that at first little wealth went to the ordinary Baganda. The situation changed dramatically in the early 1880s when Mutesa was a sick man and unable to prevent his ministers and county chiefs trading with the coastmen on their own account, thus building up their own wealth and power.

Mutesa was a highly intelligent man with a great interest in new ideas. We saw on page 37, his attraction towards Islam. In the late 1870s he welcomed European Christian missionaries, partly for political reasons. It seems that his interest in the missionaries was guided by diplomatic motives. In 1874 Mutesa sent envoys to Gondokoro to meet General Gordon to seek an alliance against Egypt. The talks broke down when Gordon offered Egyptian 'protection' for Buganda, and Mutesa became aware that Gordon wanted to strengthen the Egyptian position in the lakes region. When the explorer Stanley visited Buganda in 1875, Mutesa arranged through him for European Christian missionaries to be sent to Buganda, because he wanted British diplomatic support to counter Egyptian designs on his country. Mutesa's interest in Christian missionaries waned rapidly in 1879 when Egypt ceased to be a threat to Buganda.

Yao traders and states

A study of the Yao people between Lake Malawi and the Indian Ocean shows how enlargement of economic scale, enlargement of the scale of government, and enlargement of scale in religious culture could all coalesce within one community.

Until the 1850s the basic Yao political unit was the village. There was no central power. Then in the 1850s the Yao scattered from their homeland in the southern hinterland of Kilwa in the face of slave raids by neighbouring Makua. The Yao moved farther inland to the eastern shores of Lake Malawi and to the Shire valley south of the lake, where they clashed with the Nyanja people. In their new lands the Yao became the most prominent ivory and slave traders between Malawi and Kilwa, creating several small kingdoms, and coming increasingly under the influence of Islam.

Yao power was built on guns rather than spears, because their proximity to the coast and long trading connections with the Swahili–Arabs secured them regular supplies of powder and ammunition. As Yao traders were able to arm more followers, they were able to offer protection to more and more villages, and to attract people to their capitals. The rise of these new states, built on the expansion in size and influence of villages, was helped by polygamy. For example, one ruler—Mataka I Nyambi—had six hundred wives distributed over eight large villages in and around his capital Mwembe.

Swahili–Arab influence became very strong among the Yao. This was most apparently obvious in styles of architecture and clothing. Livingstone wrote of Mataka I Nyambi and his town Mwembe: 'He gave me a square house to live in, and indeed most of the houses are square, for the Arabs are imitated in everything.' Yao rulers often employed Swahili secretaries, to make it easier to carry on business and diplomatic communication with the coast. Many Yao became Muslims. There was a growing Islamic community at Makanjila's on the south-eastern shore of Lake Malawi. Makanjila himself became a Muslim in 1870. A mosque was built and also a Koranic school, where children learnt Swahili and were instructed in the Koran. There were similar developments at the town controlled by the trader Mponda, and at the southern end of the lake.

The reasons for the spread of Islam are not clear but it has been suggested that the new Yao rulers adopted Islam because it gave them a source of ritual authority, with which to counter the position of the village headmen who carried out rituals connected with ancestor worship. Clearly, Islamic rituals were incompatible with those connected with ancestor worship. The spread of Islam undermined the authority of the village headman.

The Cokwe

The Cokwe of Angola provide an example of a people who seized the new opportunities of the expanding long-distance trade to

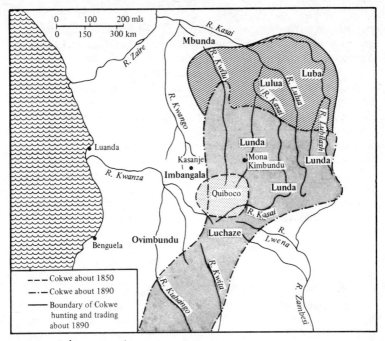

Map 4. Cokwe expansion.

enlarge their area of settlement but who, at the same time, failed to develop new political systems. Their expansion did, in fact, destroy the existing Lunda empire.

In the late eighteenth and early nineteenth centuries the Cokwe established themselves as suppliers of ivory and wax. They were fortunate in that the forests in their homeland of Quiboco swarmed with bees and they lived in an area with abundant elephants. However until the mid-nineteenth century the export of wax and ivory was on a relatively small scale. The attempts by the Portuguese to abolish the slave trade in Angola in the 1830s meant that new products had to be found for export from Luanda and Benguela. Wax and ivory became the substitute products and the Cokwe were in an ideal situation to exploit the new situation.

The decline of the slave trade also had considerable repercussions amongst the Lunda. They had relied on slave exports as the mainstay of their trade. They were not skilled hunters and so began to rely on small Cokwe hunting bands to kill elephants for them. When the Mwata Yamvo decreed that tribute from the governors of the provinces must be paid in ivory the positions of the Cokwe was further strengthened. Any governor who had so far refused to employ them was now forced to do so.

The increased Cokwe wealth also had a profound impact on their population expansion. Cokwe villages had basically consisted of a group of matrilineally related males, usually brothers and nephews. The women in the village came from other clans and often only remained in the village from the time of marriage until they ceased to bear children. A strong demand for slave women had always existed amongst the Cokwe. Women who were integrated into the lineage system in this way were subject to greater control by their husbands and also strengthened the lineage by the addition of children. The wealth created by the wax and ivory trade meant that many more women could be incorporated into the lineage system. By the middle of the century Quiboco was reported to be the most densely populated area in central Africa.

Increasingly in the second half of the century the Cokwe began to play a middleman role in the trade between the coast and the Luba beyond the Kasai. In the last third of the century they also became involved in the rubber trade. Initially they tapped rubber from their own homeland, however, the plants were exploited so inefficiently that by 1875 rubber had disappeared from Quiboco. The Cokwe then followed the precedent they had already set with elephant hunting: they followed the product to the north-east. This time, however, there was a significant difference. Only men had gone to hunt elephants. Now whole villages moved to tap rubber. This was a task which could be done just as efficiently by women and children as by men. The continued population pressure in Quiboco also encouraged such migration. Villages did not move far but advanced just beyond the area of Cokwe settlement. However, increased population pressure then created yet another wave of movement. The Lunda initially did not object to this movement. The new Cokwe settlements were in their uninhabited forests while the Lunda continued in the Savannah areas.

Soon the number of Cokwe in an area increased as more villages arrived. The Cokwe also absorbed large numbers of women from the Lunda, who offered little resistance. The Lunda found that they were treated better and given better food than in their own villages. Children born to Lunda women in Cokwe villages were brought up as Cokwe, assimilation thus taking only one generation. The skill of the Cokwe as traders soon gave them a dominant economic position in their new area of settlement. The Lunda only realized what they had done in allowing Cokwe settlements when it was too late.

While the Cokwe were managing to adapt to the ending of the slave trade and the decline in rubber and ivory production by becoming middlemen, the Lunda empire failed to adapt and went into severe economic decline. At the same time various disputes grew up between the Mwata Yamvo and provincial rulers. Cokwe mercenaries helped to install candidates and then took away their power by capturing their women for slaves and settling on their land.

In 1875 Cokwe mercenaries first crossed the Kasai into the heartland of the Lunda empire. Within ten years Cokwe began to migrate across the Kasai to settle in areas where raiders and mercenaries had previously been. Attempts to resist this movement resulted in a disastrous defeat for the Lunda. By 1887 Cokwe chiefs under the leadership of Mawoka had gained control of the Lunda empire east of the Kasai. Raiding and pillaging took place on a massive scale and the Lunda withdrew to the north and east.

In the 1890s however the Cokwe expansion ceased. A new Mwata Yamvo gathered the defiant Lunda around him; European military officers of the Congo Independent State using Congolese troops pursued the Cokwe; the Mbunda, Pende and Kwese co-operated in the north to inflict a severe defeat on the Cokwe in 1892. The period of massive expansion was over although Cokwe continued to migrate in large numbers into areas which they had already settled.

The Cokwe expansion which resulted from the new opportunities brought by the wax, ivory and rubber trades came about mainly because the Cokwe social system could adapt to the new situation. Women from other societies could be readily incorporated into Cokwe society, thus creating a greater need for migration. At the same time village headmen were able to convert their normal village fission and movement techniques into a system of migration. There was no centralized authority behind the movement nor did a system of centralized government result from the migration.

5
Trading states and peoples: (2) West Africa

Overview

The decline of the Atlantic slave trade and the rise of an alternative trade in 'legitimate' goods, especially vegetable oils, was responsible for considerable economic growth in West Africa. There were remarkable increases both in agricultural production and in the value of overseas trade, especially after 1840.

The Atlantic slave trade did not suddenly end when the British Government unilaterally abolished it for British subjects in 1807. Indeed, the available evidence indicates that the volume quite possibly increased during the period 1807 to 1840, especially to meet the demands of the expanding coffee and sugar plantations in Brazil. It was not until after 1845, when Britain signed a treaty with Portugal and Brazil, giving her the right to stop Brazilian slave-ships, that the Atlantic slave trade began to decline. Even then, it required the abolition of slavery in the USA during the American Civil War (1861–5) and action by the Spanish rulers of Cuba to end slave imports in 1866, to bring an effective end to the Atlantic slave trade.

The rise in the palm oil and groundnut trade from the beginning of the century did not coincide with a decline in the slave trade. The two trades expanded together until about 1840. British imports of palm oil from West Africa rose as follows:

1810: 1,000 tons
1830: 10,000 tons
1842: 20,000 tons
1853: 30,000 tons
1855: 40,000 tons

Exports of groundnuts rose from virtually nothing in the 1840s to 29,000 tons a year in the late 1880s.

The rise of the vegetable oil trade marked a move to a more advanced economy, characterized less by reliance on subsistence

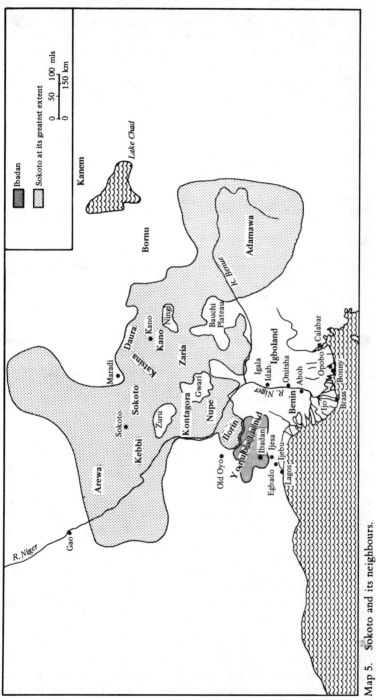

Map 5. Sokoto and its neighbours.

crops and more by the production of cash-crops for export. West African societies did not have to wait until the experience of colonialism before adapting their economies to the growing demand of industrializing countries for palm oil and groundnut oil. The overseas commerce of West Africa in 1850 was valued at approximately £3,500,000 to £4,000,000 a year. By 1900 it had roughly quadrupled to £15,000,000. The trade in vegetable oils was clearly the largest component in this commerce, though other commodities like Senegalese gum and Ghanaian gold were important export commodities.

In spite of the decline of the Atlantic slave trade, the West African economy continued to be exploited by Europe. West Africa became a satellite of the European industrial economy. Many parts of West Africa, particularly the groundnut-producing areas of Senegal and the palm-oil belt from Dahomey to Calabar, became dangerously dependent on a single cash crop for export. The problem with a primary product which is also a raw material for industry is that it may be undersold by a cheaper product from elsewhere. The palm-oil belt suffered from the 1860s onwards when palm-oil prices began to fall from the competition of Australian tallow and American petroleum.

Another aspect of the economic exploitation of West Africa by Europe was the nature of West African imports, consisting almost entirely of European manufactured goods: mainly textiles, iron goods, spirits, salt, tobacco, guns and gunpowder. Most of these imports did not help the development of the economy. Some of them were dangerous to life and health. Others competed with West African industries. There is evidence that in many parts of West Africa, especially in the forest region, local industries suffered from the flood of cheap imports from Europe. Some areas did manage to hold their own against European competition, notably the cotton cloth industry around Kano.

However, not all economic exploitation in nineteenth century West Africa was the fault of Europe. The decline of the Atlantic slave trade led indirectly to an increase of slavery within West Africa. The new palm-oil plantations of Dahomey, Yorubaland and Calabar were developed by exploiting large numbers of slaves, who were also useful as porters to carry the palm-oil to the coast. At Osomari in Igboland on the Niger bank there were 20,000 people in the town and surrounding farms on the eve of the colonial era, but two-thirds of these were slaves. Some West African states, notably some of the Hausa-Fulani emirates, built their economies on plunder, tribute and slavery.

The new palm-oil trade helped the expansion of existing states like Dahomey and the Niger delta states. Dahomey expanded to secure more palm-oil producing territory and more slaves to work in palm-oil plantations. The delta city-states extended their trading empires further into the interior to palm-oil producers' markets. New states arose, like Opobo, which became the most successful palm-oil exporter in the Delta.

In the savanna, Samori Toure's Mandinka empire owed its rise to several factors, but one of them was that Samori was the most successful trader in kola, horses and cattle in the southern part of the western Sudan.

In West Africa, however, unlike eastern Africa, trade was much less important than Islam as a factor in the emergence of new states in the nineteenth century. West Africa's coastal states had been created largely from the stimulus of economic forces, but nearly all of them had been created before 1800. Virtually all the new states that appeared in West Africa after 1800 did so largely as a result of the influence of Islam.

Islamic state-information must not be seen merely as a counter-force to growing European penetration. Islamic reform and state-building in the nineteenth century had its origins in the late eighteenth century Tokolor and Fulani reform movements, before there was any significant European penetration. Equally, state-building *jihads* (holy wars) were not always against non-Muslims. There were also jihads by a Muslim Brotherhood to eliminate the political power of rival brotherhoods. Al-Hajj Umar's jihad that created the Tokolor empire was not only a Muslim jihad against the non-Muslim Bambara states but also a war by the Tijaniyya Brotherhood against the Qadiriyya Brotherhood of Macina.

Al-Hajj Umar and the Tokolor empire

Umar, son of Said Tall, was born in Futa Toro, one of the Muslim Tokolor states in the upper Senegal valley in about 1797. In 1820 he went on a *hajj* (pilgrimage) to Mecca, and returned in 1839. In his nineteen years travelling and studying Al-Hajj Umar witnessed, and was influenced by, the Islamic reform movements stirring the Muslim world in the first half of the nineteenth century. He saw at first hand the Wahhabi struggle against the Turks in Arabia, the efforts of Muhammad Ali to modernize Egypt, and the efforts of reform of Al-Kanami in Bornu, Muhammad Bello in Sokoto and Ahmad Lobbo in Macina. Umar took wives from the families of Al-Kanami and Bello, but he was not well-received in Macina.

On his return to his Tokolor homeland in 1839, Umar began a seven-year mission among the Mandinka, initiating thousands into the Tijaniyya Brotherhood, which he had joined. He thus continued the tradition of Islamic revivalism in the western Sudan that stretched back many centuries, but had been strongly manifested

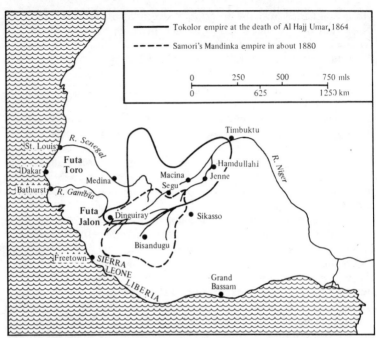

Map 6. The Tokolor and the Mandinka empires.

since the late eighteenth century in Futa Toro and neighbouring Futa Jalon.

The Tijaniyya Brotherhood opposed the Qadiriyya Brotherhood which was many centuries old. The Qadiriyya stressed study and intellectual activity as the way to salvation, and so was favoured by educated ruling aristocracies. It was also ascetic, favouring rigorous prayer and penitences. The Tijaniyya, by contrast, stressed salvation through action, not intellect, and emphasized strict moral behavior rather than formalistic prayers. The best form of action was to convert others. There was no elite, all members being equal. The Tijaniyya naturally attracted men of action—businessmen, the young, members of inferior social classes and women, all of which were groups excluded from Qadiriyya membership. The caste system in Tokolor society, with a superior religious aristocracy, the *torobe*, who were also the political rulers, lording it over freemen as well as slaves, made the Tijaniyya especially relevant to the mass of the people.

From 1839 to 1848 Umar went on preaching tours in the upper Senegal, attempting to convert believers in traditional religion, and to reform non-practising Muslims. He stirred up opposition to the rulers of the Futa states, who belonged to the Qadiriyya. In 1848 the Almami (Muslim ruler) of Futa Jalon expelled Umar who, copying the Prophet Muhammad, organized a *Hegira* (flight) to Dinguiray on the upper Niger. A huge fortress was built, and supporters flocked to him there. With the gifts his followers brought, Umar bought guns from the British in Sierra Leone, and began a jihad to spread Islam by the sword.

Umar built up a standing army of 30,000, composed of infantry with guns and cavalry with lances. From 1852 to 1854 Umar's Tokolor army conquered the Bambara states of Bambuk and Kaarta, which were ruled by traditionalists. Forced conversions were carried out on the Bambara. If a community refused to be converted to Islam, its homes and farms were burnt, many people were killed, and survivors were driven into exile or forced to die of starvation. In 1862 the Bambara state of Segu was added to the new Tokolor empire, and the last Bambara king was executed. Finally, in 1862 Umar's army conquered the reformed Islamic state of Macina, ruled by Fulani of the Qadiriyya. The cities of Hamdullahi, Jenne and Timbuktu were captured and sacked, and Ahmadu III, the King of Macina, was executed. The Tokolor empire was now at its height, and stretched eight hundred miles from east to west. It would no doubt have been much larger had expansion in the west not been prevented by the French in Senegal who repulsed Umar's attacks. Umar was not, however, given time to organize his newly-created empire. In 1864 he was killed in a Macina rebellion led by Ba Lobbo, Ahmadu III's uncle. Al-Tijani, Umar's nephew, reconquered Macina for the Tokolor empire, but Umar had become, in the words of Olatunji Oloruntimehin, a historian of the Tokolor, 'a victim of the violence which his revolution had engendered'.

Umar died before he could complete his task, but it is doubtful if, had he lived, he would have been able to achieve his purpose of creating a truly Islamic society. Islam can no more be spread by means of the sword than Christianity, unless it is at a mere surface level. Only a long period of mission work and education was likely to bring about a genuine change of minds and hearts in any number of people. Umar's attempt to spread Islam by force only engendered counter-violence and hostility to Islam. Significantly, under French colonial rule, the Tokolor in general and the Tijaniyya in particular, had considerable success in spreading Islam among their former reluctant subjects—including the Bambara.

Umar was succeeded by his son Ahmadu, who reigned until the French conquest. Ahmadu failed in his attempt to build a reformed Muslim nation-state out of the recently conquered empire. He had to face too many problems, and barely managed to keep the empire together. As the eldest son of Umar's first wife, Ahmadu was a commoner, and lacked the respect given to his younger brothers who were born princes. He had to put up with many jealous brothers and uncles who gave him allegiance in name only. He had to devote his time and energy to suppressing rebellions, such as that by two of his brothers who declared their independence and gained help from the Qadiriyya Fulani of Macina. In Kaarta there were frequent rebellions by the Bambara against forced conversions. Another major problem was the army, which frequently mutinied and oppressed the common people, causing further popular rebellions. Ahmadu reduced the size of the army, thus gaining a short-term advantage, but weakening his long-term capacity to resist French expansion.

The rise of the Mandinka empire was indirectly linked with the career of Umar who had preached widely amongst the Mandinka, thus preparing the way for Samori Toure.

Samori Toure and the creation of the Mandinka empire

Samori Toure was born in 1830, the son of a Mandinka peasant farmer who practised traditional religion. As a young man Samori became a trader and a Muslim. He joined the Dyula, the famous long-distance traders who were mostly of Mandinka origin, and who operated over the western part of the western Sudan. He was also converted to the Tijaniyya Brotherhood, to which many of the Dyula belonged.

The Dyula had already begun the process of Mandinka state-building before Samori joined them. In the early eighteenth century, the Mandinka of the south-western savannah of the western Sudan were organized in many small states. The Mandinka were overwhelmingly traditionalists in religion. The Dyula, a small Muslim commercial minority, specialized in the import of trans-Saharan products from the Maghrib and Europe, and in the gold, cattle, kola and slave trades. Between 1835 and 1850 they carried out a political and religious revolution in several parts of Mandinka country. In 1835 a Dyula trader, Mori Ule, who had been influenced by jihadist ideas in Futa Jalon, carried out a jihad in Toron and Konyan. He was successful, and extended his conquests to several other small Mandinka states. Using new military techniques of cavalry and guns, he took control of new kola trade routes, converted many traditionalists to Islam, and created the Sise kingdom. Mori Ule was killed in battle in 1845, but the new Sise kingdom continued to expand under his son, Sere Burlay, who ruled from 1849 to 1859, but who made the same error as his father in adopting a policy of forced conversion and was killed in a revolt.

Samori's home came within the orbit of the Sise kingdom when his mother was captured by a Sise raiding party in 1853. Samori surrendered himself to Sere Burlay to take his mother's place, and was put into the Sise army. The young man, who had already shown his organizing ability as a trader, now turned his hand to war. Samori quickly rose on merit to be a commander, where he demonstrated a mastery of the new tactics required if guns and cavalry were to be used effectively.

In 1857 Samori broke away from Sise with his unit of soldiers and became an independent mercenary captain. From 1857 to 1867 Samori was a local Mandinka warlord, winning the support both of his traditionalist clansmen, whom he defended from Sise aggression, and of his fellow Dyula traders. He sometimes fought against Sere Brema, the son and declared successor of Sere Burlay, but sometimes in alliance with him. Samori contributed to the political disorder which he used later as an excuse to build a new state.

Between 1867 and 1881, Samori created his own state and empire. His motives were a blend of religion and economics. He believed God had specially chosen him to secure moral order and spread the faith. He also hoped to control more trade routes, and to establish political order in which trade could flourish. He started by conquering Sanankoro in 1867. Thereafter, he gradually absorbed many small Mandinka states and parts of the weakening Sise kingdom. The Sise king, Sere Brema, came to recognize Samori's military superiority, and allied with him, thus gaining a share of the spoils from Samori's imperialism.

In 1873 Samori established a permanent capital at the newly-conquered town of Bisandugu. In 1875 he took Kumban after a long siege, defeating the Sankaran traditionalists with the aid of the Muslims of the city of Kankan. From 1870 to 1878 he overran a large area in the upper Niger valley, from Kouroussa to Siguiri. Samori's imperialism was not, however, entirely dependent on the use of force. He expanded his authority into parts of Futa Jalon and Tokolor territory around Dinguiray by means of diplomatic alliances with his fellow Tijaniyya Brothers of the area. Amongst these was Agibu, who was rebelling against his brother, the Tokolor Emperor Ahmadu. Samori also made astute matrimonial alliances with some groups, such as the Toure of Odienne.

In 1879–81 the Sise revolted against Samori in a last bid to recover their former hegemony. They were decisively defeated, and Samori became the supreme and undisputed ruler of a vast new state. However, after 1881, and in spite of growing French penetration in the north (see Chapter 10), he continued to expand the new Mandinka empire. His army was swollen with former prisoners of war, and they needed employment, so he sent them on campaigns. In 1881–2 he extended his authority to Kangaba and to part of the Bambara country, north of the Niger, which had seceded from the Tokolor empire. In the south, in 1883, he defeated the Kamara who had defied first the Sise and then Samori for twenty years. This victory established the edge of the great coastal forest as Samori's southern frontier.

French expansion in the north, in the headwaters of the Senegal, diverted Samori to the east and west between 1884 and 1888. To the west, he conquered the state of Solimana, capturing Galaba, and reached the British outpost of Sierra Leone. To the east, he occupied Wasulu and Kabasarana, and reached the Bagoe River on the frontier of the powerful state of Kenedugu with its capital at Sikasso.

Samori's failure to defeat Kenedugu and take Sikasso in a long siege, 1887–8, marked both the end of his imperial expansion and the beginning of his ultimate downfall. King Tieba of Kenedugu strongly fortified Sikasso and had ample supplies stored in the city. Samori lost the war of attrition because he was unable to feed his host of soldiers. To add to his misfortunes, he had to face the Great Revolt of 1888–90 in his northern territories, caused partly by his new policy of forced conversions to Islam, but mainly by his intention to requisition the 1888 harvest for his army at Sikasso. He managed to suppress the Great Revolt, at the price of devastation and ruin to a large part of his empire. However, the fact that his conquests had gone on too long and beyond the bounds of necessity, should not detract from Samori's amazing political achievement.

Samori created the third largest state in West Africa after Sokoto and the Tokolor empire. The Mandinka empire covered 115,000 square miles. Samori's achievement rested to a large extent on his military genius. He relied on a skilled and mobile cavalry force, backed up by well-armed infantry. Every soldier had a gun, usually an old musket bought from Sierra Leone. In the 1890s Samori was even able to obtain 6,000 modern rapid-firing rifles for the struggle against the French. The army was a regular standing body of professionals. The nucleus was a special bodyguard for himself and his sons, composed of young captives brought up by Samori from boyhood and therefore completely loyal and well-trained. The rest were either captured enemy soldiers freed in return for service in Samori's army, or conscripted levies. Men were grouped in units on a nation-wide rather than local basis, as part of a deliberate policy to foster national unity. Soldiers were recruited from all classes— aristocracy, traders, artisans and peasants—so the army was also an instrument of social unity. Promotions in the army were based purely on merit and efficiency, and many commoners and non-Mandinka became officers. Samori's expertise as a trader secured for the army the horses and weapons it needed. He also organized artisans to meet the requirements of the army. Many blacksmiths were recruited to repair and even make guns.

Samori's empire was a military as well as a trading state, the army being used as the basis of administration. The centre and the forest border in the south were organized into three provinces under Samori's direct rule, but the outlying areas were organized into five provinces under military commanders. Many of the former local rulers were, however, given functions in the new political order. Samori tended to treat them as allies rather than subjects.

Samori was not an absolute dictator. He created a council of advisers that he regularly consulted, and he also developed an efficient civil service. The council members were given Cabinet or ministerial tasks, such as treasury, justice, religion and relations with Europeans; others were appointed inspectors of the regional military governments. There was, therefore, no distinction between advisory and executive functions.

Religion was a prime factor in Samori's success. Islam was a bond of unity for the Dyula and even for the Mandinka as a whole, whose democratic traditions made the Tijaniyya, with its emphasis on equality, attractive to them. Samori took the title *Almami* in 1884, and thereby cemented the Muslim support that had already played a key role in his rise to power. His refusal to countenance forced conversions to Islam, except for a brief and disastrous period in 1886–7, won him the support of the religious traditionalists. For virtually all of Samori's career, Mandinka society was not divided by any sharp religious conflicts. Economic factors were also crucial in the rise of Samori, as the Dyula devoted their considerable financial resources and commercial skills to Samori's cause, and thereby secured safe trade routes and the abolition of tolls between a host of former small states. The personal factor in Samori's rise must not be forgotten. The charismatic personality of Samori inspired intense loyalty and devotion among his followers as he rose from peasant to emperor.

The Sokoto caliphate

The Fulani Caliphate of Sokoto was founded by the Muslim reformer Usman Dan Fodio in the early years of the nineteenth century. The jihad of Dan Fodio was continued by his son Muhammad Bello and by 1830 the caliphate had taken the frontiers it was to maintain roughly intact, throughout the rest of the century. Most of the caliphate was ruled by Fulani emirs, each responsible for a particular part of the empire, who had replaced the previous Hausa rulers. Although by the death of Bello the jihad had lost much of its impetus the caliphate was compelled to continue its vigilance against non-Muslims throughout the century. There were non-Muslim enclaves at Zuru, Ningi, part of Gwariland and a large part of the Bauchi plateau. The caliphate was also constantly in conflict with Muslim peoples outside the empire. As a result of all this it can be said that throughout much of the century the caliphate displayed the attributes of a state in formation.

It is not possible to give details of all the border skirmishes, wars and rebellions involving the caliph and the emirs of the various regions of the Sokoto caliphate, but a few examples will give some idea of the problems facing the Fulani. Immediately to the north of Sokoto was Maradi. Initially, Maradawa attacks were directed against Sokoto and Katsina but from the 1840s attacks were made on Daura, Kano and Zaria. From about 1844 to 1851 attacks on the northern part of the caliphate were intensified and until 1877 Maradawa raids as far as Kano became commonplace. There was then a brief period of rapprochement but raids began again in the 1890s and continued until the British conquest of the caliphate.

In Kebbi the caliph faced a different problem when this area of the empire went into rebellion. Yaqub Nabame, a prince of the ruling house, was released from eighteen years' captivity in Sokoto. He almost immediately began a revolt which lasted for twenty years until it became quite clear that the independence of Kebbi, Zaberma and Arewa was an irreversible fact.

To the south of Kano the emirates, which were carved out by the jihad, had been created from non-Muslim and non-Hausa peoples. The integration of these peoples into an Islamic empire was a problem which continued until the period of British conquest. The Gwari waged war against the Kontagora emirate and encouraged unrest amongst Gwari within the emirate. The Bauchi plateau peoples were a constant source of trouble. Although these groups were small and divided amongst themselves they were able to mount annoying raids on the surrounding emirates. The Ningi were a much more serious threat and throughout the century raided into Kano and Zaria. Where the emirates faced problems from non-Muslim peoples they were expected to deal with them without military assistance from the caliph. Sambo, who was Emir of Zaria from 1878–88, was deposed by the caliph partly because he failed to protect his territory from Ningi raids.

On the whole the emirates had to maintain persistent vigilance in the face of pagan and enemy threats. It was extremely difficult for the emirates to deal effectively with these threats because there was virtual parity of military equipment and techniques between the emirates and their enemies. On the other hand the pagan peoples and other enemies were unable to pose a serious threat to the survival of the caliphate because they failed to co-operate and lacked a common purpose. By the last quarter of the century the threat to the caliphate was less serious than at any period earlier in the century.

The caliphate was one of the largest states ever created in West Africa and yet it remained a loose federation of emirates throughout the century. This is partly explained by the way in which the state was formed. Outside the heartland of Sokoto the expansion of the caliphate was the result of successful jihad revolts by independent Muslim leaders and communities. The leaders of these revolts submitted themselves voluntarily to Usman Dan Fodio and his successors. This submission remained one of the strongest bonds of the caliphate.

The manner in which the caliphate was formed had considerable impact on the system of government. No standing army was ever created by the caliph. The emirates had been founded independently and came together voluntarily. It was their job to defend their independence without direct help from Sokoto. The leaders and rulers of the emirates were local leaders and not agents from Sokoto. This did not, of course, mean that the caliph had no powers over the emirs. As we have already seen the Emir of Zaria was deposed in 1888 and there are other instances of emirs being deposed for failing to rule their emirate properly. The caliph had, however, to be careful to act justly and within the terms of the Islamic Sharia (law). In 1893 Tukur was appointed as Emir of Kano but this appointment was regarded as unjust. The caliph was unable to sustain his candidate and after a two-year revolt Yusuf was appointed as emir.

Subservience of the emirs to the caliph was shown in various ways. Tribute had to be paid; each emir was obliged to pay a visit to Sokoto as soon as possible after appointment; troops had to be provided when required. The caliph ensured that the Sharia was followed by the emirs. He attempted to solve disputes between emirates and often co-ordinated action against enemies. The impartiality and integrity of the caliphs helped them maintain the position of esteem first earned by Usman Dan Fodio.

Although the system of central government in the caliphate remained largely unchanged throughout the nineteenth century there were significant new developments within several of the emirates. Standing armies were created and administration, increasingly based on the military, became more centralized.

There was a rapid increase in the number of firearms imported along the Tripoli–Bornu route across the Sahara and up the Niger to Nupe, one of the emirates. The new firearms seem to have had a limited impact on warfare, being used largely to make noise to cause enemy cavalry to panic, but the political and military effects were more important. Regular standing armies, composed of slave musketeer units commanded by slave officers, were created in Nupe under Emir Masaba (1859–73), in Zaria under Emir Abdallah (1873–8), and his successor Muhammad Sambo (1878–88), and in Ilorin after 1878. This military revolution led to a political revolution as emirs relied less on the aristocracy and more on their standing armies as an instrument of government. More direct rule by slave military officers, following the personal instructions of their emirs, began to replace indirect rule through the local traditional feudal rulers.

In economic growth, the caliphate appears to have shared in the general progress in eighteenth century West Africa. The city of Kano became the 'Manchester of West Africa', its cotton cloth products being sold in North Africa at Tripoli, on the West African coast as far as the island of Arguin, and as far south as the Congo basin. Barth, the famous German traveller, estimated that Kano's cloth sales amounted to at least 300,000,000 cowries a year in the 1850s, a figure equivalent to about £40,000. The Kano cloth industry was aided by the existence of three favourable conditions: two locally grown raw materials, cotton and indigo; a large consumer market; and the highly efficient distributive network organized by Hausa traders over a large region. Bida produced glass and a variety of brass and silver goods. Sokoto was noted for its superior iron and its superb quality leather, for which there was a world-wide demand. Barth also found throughout the caliphate a thriving agriculture and a good variety of produce. Guinea-corn, millet, rice, onions, beans, yams, cassava, groundnuts and sweet potatoes were plentiful. Meat and milk were readily obtainable.

The caliphate was fortunate to be at the centre of a number of trade routes. From the south along the Asante–Kano route came slaves and kola nuts; to the north the caravan routes led to Morocco, Algeria, Tunisia, Tripolitania and Cyrenaica from whence came many European products; to the west a route ran to Gao and Timbuktu; and to the east was a route running through Darfur to the Nile and then to Egypt. Along all these routes the Hausa pursued an active import and export trade. Compared with much of the rest of the Sudan the caliphate was a busy and prosperous place.

It was this state with its relative prosperity and its political stability that was ultimately to become part of Britain's African empire. The emirates which had remained largely independent of each other found themselves unable to co-operate against the serious threat of Britain, just as they had often failed to co-operate against less powerful adversaries.

Dahomey

For most of the nineteenth century the Kingdom of Dahomey covered only approximately the southern third of the modern-day Republic of Dahomey. The kingdom had been created by a ruling dynasty known as Fon, or Aja, during the second half of the seventeenth and early part of the eighteenth centuries. This dynasty continued to rule until the end of the nineteenth century. The kingdom declared its independence of Old Oyo in 1818, and developed under the Kings Gezo (1818–58) and Glele (1859–89) into perhaps the most efficient state in Black Africa.

During the reigns of Gezo and Glele Dahomey benefited from a well-organized, centralized administration. Senior civil service posts were filled on merit with able men from the commoner class.

Officials were appointed, transferred and dismissed by the king. They did not hold their positions by hereditary right. The conquered states which formed provinces were completely integrated within Dahomey; there were no vassal kings or separate local laws. The king thus had firm control over the hereditary aristocracy and the outlying areas. The king's council of advisers was transformed into a cabinet of ministers, the most important of whom were the *Mingi*—the Chief Magistrate and Superintendent of Police, the *Meu* or collector of revenue (Finance Minister), the *Tokpe* or Minister of Agriculture, and the *Yevogan* or Foreign Minister, in charge of the administration of the port of Whydah, of overseas trade and of European relations. Women played an important part in the administration. Women officials, known as the *Naye*, were appointed in every province to inspect the work of men officials and to report back to the king.

The civil service proved capable of considerable planning of the economy. Agricultural production was carefully planned so that the royal family, officials and the army would be fed and, at the same time, enough cash crops for export would be grown. Each province had to concentrate upon certain crops: one on beans and maize; another on millet; a third on maize and cassava, and so on. If there was a shortage of a crop, the government would order one or more districts to grow it. Livestock was also carefully controlled. There was a regular census of all livestock, and a strict account was kept of the numbers of animals slaughtered. If sales ran ahead of production, slaughter would be banned for a period. With the decline of the slave trade, Gezo actively encouraged palm-oil production in the 1840s. All palm trees were counted, and a constant check was kept of annual yield. An annual census of people was held, and was the basis of planning. Dahomeyan administrators knew not only the figures for the total population, but also its distribution by province, village, sex and occupation. Originally the human census was designed to aid conscription into the army, but later it was used to help organize taxation. A variety of taxes were levied. There was a tax on agricultural produce, which was paid in kind. One-third of the total production of palm oil was taxed, the tax oil being sold at Whydah in exchange for European guns and powder. A tax on income was levied, as were customs duties and road tolls. Another source of revenue was the rent from royal estates.

Dahomey's government has often been portrayed as an absolute monarchy. There was, however, a great deal of consultation, not only within the council of ministers but also with the Great Council which met at least once a year. This council was composed of twenty to thirty ministers and senior officials, fifty to eighty traders, middle-level administrators and army officers, and several hundred minor officials such as headmen, tax collectors and soldiers who had distinguished themselves in battle. There was considerable freedom of discussion in the council and many small interest groups were represented.

In the 1840s two interest groups emerged that were so large they could almost be described as political parties. The new threat of an alliance of the Egba of Yorubaland and Britain led to a division in Dahomey between the Elephant Party and the Fly Party. The Elephant Party, dominated by the Crown, the high military officials and the Creole slave traders of Whydah, wanted confrontation with the Egba and Britain. The Fly Party, on the other hand, favoured concentration on the palm-oil trade and cultivation of good relations with Britain, the market for palm oil. The Fly Party seems to have been composed of middle level administrators, some wealthy traders, religious leaders, and the women soldiers, who realized how costly war had been to Dahomey, especially after Gezo's attempts to expand into Yoruba palm-oil producing country had met with defeat at Ado in 1844, and Abeokuta, the Egba capital, in 1851. In the 1860s Glele formed a National Party whose policy was to allow Europeans to trade at the coast but not to introduce European culture and Christianity—a successful compromise which brought the Elephant and Fly Parties together.

Dahomey had a standing army of 12,000 regulars and 24,000 militia but it has probably been overrated. It failed ignominiously in Egbaland both under Gezo and under Glele, who made a further unsuccessful attack on Abeokuta in 1864. It did conquer Ketu in the 1880s, but only when that town had already been weakened by an invasion from Ibadan. The women soldiers, or 'Amazons', did not impress the British explorer Sir Richard Burton, a prejudiced but acute observer. He wrote: 'They were mostly elderly and all them were hideous. The officers were decidedly chosen for the size of their bottoms ... They manoeuvre with the precision of a flock of sheep.' However one point in Dahomey's military organization stands out: the army was not, as in many parts of Africa, expected to live off the land. All its equipment and food was supplied by the central government.

Yorubaland

Until the beginning of the nineteenth century, Yorubaland, in what is now the western part of Nigeria, was dominated by the Oyo empire. This was the largest of the Yoruba states and dominated the smaller states such as Egba, Egbado, Ijebu and Ilesa. Oyo was an extremely powerful military state which had built its strength on the proceeds of the slave trade. Its well-trained cavalry easily overwhelmed the infantry of the surrounding states. Towards the end of the eighteenth century the Nupe and the Borgawa to the north obtained their independence from Oyo. This was a serious loss as it cut off the supply of cavalry horses. The Egba became independent in about 1797 and Dahomey ceased to pay tribute in the early years of the nineteenth century. Even more serious for Oyo was the rebellion of Ilorin, which after a series of civil wars and coups became part of the Sokoto caliphate. Attacks by the Fulani from Ilorin seriously disrupted Oyo and the capital Old Oyo was abandoned in about 1835. Many Yoruba fled southwards from the savannah to the forest regions and as a result Ibadan and Abeokuta grew rapidly in size. Around them grew up two powerful Yoruba states, Ibadan and Egba, both of them able to exploit the palm-oil trade with the Europeans. Unfortunately for Ibadan, the Egba and the Ijebu were able to prevent Ibadan from having direct access to the coast. This was one of the major reasons for the constant turmoil and war in Yorubaland in the nineteenth century. The Yoruba wars began after the collapse of Oyo and continued until Britain conquered the area in 1893.

The Yoruba wars became particularly serious after Ibadan had defeated the Fulani at the Battle of Oshogbo in 1839. The defeat of the Fulani jihad meant that the Yoruba now felt free to fight amongst themselves for control of trade routes to the coast, where European traders sold guns and ammunition, vital commodities in a state's defence as well as expansion. Yoruba states fought each other to conquer palm-oil producing lands and palm-oil trade markets and to seize slaves, both to work in palm-oil plantations and to carry palm oil to the coast. The Fon and Aja of Dahomey joined in these Yoruba civil wars hoping to seize palm-oil land and slaves. The two major wars after the defeat of the Fulani were the Ijaye War of 1860–4 and the Sixteen Years' War of 1877–93, both caused essentially by Ibadan's desire to trade directly with the coast instead of through Egba and Ijebu middlemen.

The wars were, on the whole, destructive. Palm-oil production and trade was disrupted and discouraged. The slave trade was encouraged by the social disruption brought by the wars. Some towns were destroyed, such as Ijaye by Ibadan and Ketu by Dahomey. A class of professional soldiers emerged interested in war rather than economic development. The disunity of Yorubaland made British colonization easier than would have been the case had the Yoruba been united.

The most important of the new states created after the collapse of the Oyo empire were Ibadan, founded in 1829; Ijaye and Abeokuta both founded in 1830; and New Oyo, founded by Alafin Atiba a few years after the destruction of Old Oyo city by the Fulani. Ibadan was essentially a military state, and was nicknamed *idi ibon*—the butt of a gun. Young men flocked to it to try their fortunes in war. Military leaders, who rose on merit and achievement, took precedence over civil leaders. Ibadan's great leaders were all soldiers: Oluyole in the early years, Ibikunle in the 1850s, and Latosisa in the 1870s and 1880s. However, a successful Ibadan leader had not only to fight but also to farm and trade. He had to farm to feed his soldiers, and he had to sell palm oil in order to buy guns and ammunition.

Ibadan eventually ruled an 'empire' two hundred miles wide from east to west, and forty to eighty miles deep from north to south. Much of the palm-oil belt was overrun, and many people were enslaved. As these new lands were conquered there was a short-term growth in the economy but, in the long run, Ibadan's militarism mitigated against the peace that was needed before Yorubaland as a whole could undergo lasting economic development.

Abeokuta, the Egba capital, contributed less than Ibadan to enlargement of political scale in Yorubaland, but, under the influence of Sierra Leone Creoles, it attempted to construct a modern form of government. In the late 1830s liberated Egba slaves from Sierra Leone, known as the Saro, began to return to their homeland, settle in Abeokuta, and spread Christianity, literacy and western notions of government. European missionaries who arrived in the 1840s capitalized on the groundwork of the Saro, and became modernizers with printing-presses, cotton-growing and brick-making. The leading Saro was George W. Johnson, 'Reversible' Johnson as he was called by missionaries because of his return to African culture. Johnson arrived in Abeokuta in 1865, already with a clear goal in mind: to create a Christian, modernized state, independent of foreign leadership. He was an example of a Christianized African who remained an African nationalist. In the year he arrived, Johnson created the Egba United Board of Management, a new type of government in which the authority of the traditional leaders would combine with the skills and ideas of the Saro. The President-General of the Board was the *Bashorun*, or Prime Minister. Other senior traditional leaders became members or patrons. Executive posts were held by Saro, with Johnson as Director and Secretary. A considerable degree of modernization was carried out. A postal service was started, a secular school was built, sanitary improvements took place, and Board decisions were publicized by written notices. Customs duties were introduced as a source of revenue for the Board, and accounted for by the use of printed records. Unfortunately Abeokuta's attempt at modernization proved to be abortive. The EUBM had depended heavily on the support it received from Bashorun Shamoye, but after he died in 1868 it could not find an equally influential patron. It became less effective as an instrument of government and finally collapsed in 1874.

The Niger delta

In the Niger delta area of Nigeria the growth of states was clearly helped by the development of trade. The Ijo people founded a number of city states such as Brass, Nembe, Calabar and Bonny.

The creeks of the delta made trade between the states easy. They were able to trade with the peoples, such as the Igbo, to the north of them. As the demand from Europeans for slaves grew the city states of the delta were able to meet much of this demand. Europeans were not allowed into the interior to obtain slaves and the Ijo became more and more prosperous as the middlemen of the slave trade.

The city states were divided into houses. Each house had its own trading and war canoes, the latter being put at the service of the state in time of war. House heads were second in rank to the king, and sat in the council of state. In the eighteenth century only princes became house heads but in the nineteenth century promotion came increasingly to men who were of commoner or even slave origin. Houses realized that they must promote men of ability or they would collapse before their commercial rivals. Besides being efficient trading bodies, the houses were also ideal organizations for absorbing people of different origins, thus giving social cohesion to the delta towns with their mixture of ethnic communities, a mixture brought about by the constant absorption of slaves into the state.

New trade and new men

The House System of the delta city-states was adaptable to the new conditions of the nineteenth century. They were organized as co-operative companies whose main function was trade. Therefore, the Houses did not have to change fundamentally in order to take advantage of the new palm-oil trade. All they had to do was to expand.

The social mobility that was possible in the Houses led to the rise of 'new men'—commoners or ex-slaves—to challenge the authority of traditional rulers in the delta. In Calabar, situated in the Cross River delta, real power passed from the king and house heads to the *Ekpe*, a Secret Society with a hierarchy of grades, *Nyampa*, the highest grade, being supreme. The Nyampa members organized most of the trade with the British, and exercised judicial authority in the state. Slaves also began to assert their influence in politics. The Order of Blood Men, a community of runaway slaves who formed their own state on the Qua River, checked the power of the Nyampa. It was customary to sacrifice many slaves on the death of a king or a Nyampa member, but in 1852 the Blood Men secured the abandonment of this practice by taking up arms on the death of King Archibong, and threatening to destroy the town if any slaves were sacrificed.

Bonny was dominated from 1830 to 1861 by the ex-slave Alali, head of the Anna Pepple House. When King Opobo died in 1830 the heir to the throne, William Dappa Pepple, was a minor. Alali was appointed Regent. In 1836 he was forced to resign by the British Navy because he had imprisoned some British traders in retaliation for the British Navy's seizure of a Spanish slave ship inside Bonny's harbour. Alali now concentrated on trade, and on absorbing smaller Houses into his own. In 1854, when King Dappa Pepple seized a British ship in place of payments owed to him, Alali allied with the British to overthrow him, and became one of a Regency council of four ex-slaves. However, the British brought back the king in 1861 because the British traders found Alali even less prepared to do their bidding. Alali died at this time, probably by taking poison to avoid arrest. His role as an ex-slave challenging royal authority was taken over by his ablest assistant, Jaja.

Jaja

Jaja's full name was Jubo Jubogha, abbreviated by Africans to Jo Jo and by Europeans to Jaja. He was born in Igboland in 1821, and in 1833 sold as a slave to a Bonny trader. He developed into a man of tremendous drive, energy and ability, and was freed for his service as a highly successful trader in the Anna Pepple House in Bonny. In 1863 he was elected head of the House to succeed Alali, on account of his outstanding ability, his mastery of the English language, his excellent relations with the Igbo oil-producers in the interior, and because he was the only trader in the House capable of paying off Alali's huge debts to European firms.

Alali's debts were paid off within two years. Jaja continued, like Alali, to absorb other Houses, and increase Anna Pepple's profits. His success aroused the jealousy of the Manilla Pepple House under the ex-slave Oko Jumbo, who was encouraged by King George Dappa Pepple, who had succeeded his father in 1866. Both Oko Jumbo and George feared Jaja would supplant royal power as Alali had done.

In 1869 civil war broke out in Bonny when the Manilla Pepple House attacked the Anna Pepple House. Jaja was less prepared than his opponents for war and was forced to appeal to the British consul, Charles Livingstone, and the Court of Equity—which settled disputes between Europeans and Africans—to mediate. Oko Jumbo agreed to a truce. However, during the long negotiations between victor and vanquished over how much indemnity Jaja should pay, Jaja quickly settled his House and people in Andony country to the east. What were his motives?

The new settlement of Opobo was carefully placed so as to cut off Bonny from its trading empire on the Imo and Qua Rivers, and ensure Jaja's control of this region. Jaja already benefited from close ties with the Igbo rulers of the Imo River, to whom he was linked by marriage alliances. He was also a priest of *juju*, the traditional religion, and used his ritual authority to tie his palm-oil suppliers more closely to himself. In his new state Jaja became undisputed ruler. In Bonny, for all its social mobility which allowed foreign slaves to become Heads of Houses, Jaja could never become king.

Jaja declared the independence of Opobo, with himself as king, in 1869. Because of his dominant position in Bonny's economy and Opobo's control of routes to the interior, fourteen out of the eighteen most senior of Bonny's Houses moved to Opobo. The British consul discouraged British traders at Bonny from trading with Jaja, but he arranged to trade with British merchants from other Delta states like Brass. This led Bonny to resume the war which continued to 1873, and ended in victory for Jaja as British firms moved to Opobo. Britain recognized Opobo in 1872 and Bonny was forced to do so in 1873.

In the 1870s Bonny declined and Opobo prospered. Jaja became the richest ruler of the Delta. He extended his political control to many parts of the Imo valley, and established trading alliances with the Aro traders of Igboland. In 1884, at the time of the European Partition, he secured a favourable treaty, which allowed him a monopoly of trade, and excluded British traders from passing through his territory to the hinterland.

What was Jaja's significance in African history? He does not qualify as an enlarger of political scale, because by destroying the prosperity and empire of Bonny and founding and developing Opobo, he merely replaced one flourishing economic polity by another. His real significance is that he personifies, perhaps better than any other example in the continent, the rise of new men who successfully responded to the new economic and political conditions of the nineteenth century. Yet Jaja's career also illustrates the struggle of Africans to utilize the benefits of western technology without at the same time surrendering their cultural heritage. As a juju priest, he was utterly opposed to Christianity, and refused to allow missionaries into Opobo. He believed African religion was not incompatible with westernization. He built European-style houses, chartered European ships for direct trade with Europe, and sent his sons to be educated in Britain. He also had a Western school opened—not run by missionaries but by Emma White, a black American woman who had emigrated to Liberia, taken up trading along the west coast, and become Jaja's secretary. Emma was a Christian but not a missionary. Jaja was a traditionalist, but an enlightened one. His example epitomizes the attempts of pre-colonial Africans to modernize, before cultural and psychological dependence on Europe had taken a grip on the African continent.

Itsekiriland

Olomu, son of Asorokun and father of Nana, is often regarded merely as the forerunner of Nana. In reality, Olomu was a great figure in his own right, and Nana's success as 'governor' of the

Itsekiri people of the western delta depended on his father's achievements.

Olomu, born in about 1810 was a typical Niger delta 'new man'. A member of the commoner Ologbotsere family, he emerged as a commercial and political rival to the royal family of the Itsekiri. He was the most successful of the Itsekiri 'new men' who profited from the rise of the palm-oil trade on the Benin River and from the decline in the wealth and authority of the king on the Forcados River. Competition between the royal family and commoner families, like the Ologbotsere, led to civil wars and a political revolution in 1848, when the monarchy's powers were effectively curtailed, though not quite abolished. A compromise was worked out: the Itsekiri would be ruled by a 'Governor of the River' (the Benin River), with the governorship alternating between the old royal family and the Ologbotsere family. Olomu was Governor from 1879 to 1883.

Olomu became the most successful Itsekiri trader by a mixture of force, diplomacy and considerable organizing ability. He maintained a navy of slave sailors armed with guns to defend his trading canoes and to enslave more people, to be employed as traders or sailors. Olomu founded the settlement of Ebrohimi in a strong defensive position in marshes about fifteen miles from the mouth of the Benin River. His main sphere of influence, however, was along the Ethiope and Warri Rivers, deep into Urhoboland among the Abraka, Agbarho and Evrho clans of the Urhobo. He established a friendship with Ovwha, head of the Agbarho clan. In Evrho, trade was assisted by marriage to the local ruler's daughter Memse, Nana's mother. The Urhobo frequently called on Olomu to settle their internal disputes.

Olomu's achievement, however, is detracted from by the legacy of feud with the royal family that he bequeathed to his son. Olomu went to war with Tsanomi of the royal family to force payment of a debt. Ill-feeling was further compounded when Olomu encouraged his son to succeed him, thus breaking the rule of alternation in the Governorship.

Nana, Governor from 1883, followed his father's policies and continued his activities, expanding the oil trade in Urhoboland, largely by marriage alliances, and settling disputes among the Urhobo. He could not, however, resolve his quarrel with the old royal family by any means other than abdication, a measure he would not contemplate. Not surprisingly, the royal family under Dogho actively supported the British invaders against Nana.

Igboland

South-eastern Nigeria was the homeland of the Igbo people, who were, in the nineteenth century, some of the great traders of West

Africa. The Igbo have often been classified as a stateless and disunited society. However, far from being a stateless society they evolved different political systems to suit different environments.

Igbo communities along the Niger and to the west of the river developed centralized states with a 'presidential-monarchy' form of government. On the one hand, they adopted the ideas and practices of the neighbouring non-Igbo states like Benin and Igala, such as the nomenclature, regalia and ceremonials of kingship. But on the other hand, the western Igbo kings were presidents rather than monarchs: that is, in spite of all the monarchical trappings, their actual powers were restricted to the presidency of their *ama ala* (councils of elders) and village assemblies. However, the commonest form of political system in Igboland was the village republic, which was found in the areas east of the Niger in central and eastern Igboland.

Igbo political systems cannot simply be divided into the president-ial states of the west and the village republics of the centre and east. There is a further division, based on the degree of importance of the kinship system in government. Among the central Igbo village republics, government depended essentially on the kinship system. Away from the centre, in the western Igbo states, title systems were as important as the kinship system. The south-eastern Igbo, in close contact with the Ibibio, were influenced by the Ibibio system of secret societies, elements of which they absorbed, and did not rely overmuch on the kinship system in government. The same was true of the north-eastern Igbo, who adopted the age-set system of their non-Igbo neighbours in the Cross River valley.

The Igbo demonstrated their genius for experimentation and adaptation to the challenges of the environment, not just in the political field but in the economic sphere as well. By the middle of the nineteenth century virtually all the original forest had been cleared, and a dense population carried out intensive cultivation of food crops, like yam, and cash crops, like palm oil. In industry, elaborate cotton cloths were woven, iron-working of a highly skilled kind was carried on at Awka, and pottery of an advanced type was manufac-tured over a wide area. With houses, clay walls were constantly rubbed until they shone like stone and developed the hardness of marble, and then they were painted in beautiful coloured patterns. Towns were built with broad and well-planned streets.

The Aro traders and Awka smiths provided economic, political and religious unity in Igboland. The oracle of the god Agbala was maintained at Awka by ironsmiths and that of the god Arochukwu was kept by the traders of the Aro clan. Both oracles were consulted by people from all over Igboland for political and religious functions. The oracles were particularly valuable as courts of appeal which helped to prevent local disputes developing into wars. The Aro also contributed to the enlargement of political scale by using soldiers to attack villages which refused to obey their oracle, and began to assert political authority, though in a loose way, over southern and eastern Igboland. Economically, they linked Igboland more closely with the eastern Niger Delta by expanding the palm-oil trade.

Liberia

Origins

The Black American experiment in nation-building in West Africa provides further evidence of the enlargement of political, economic and religious scale in the pre-colonial period. The creation and subsequent history of Liberia also illustrates graphically the dangers of black colonialism, on the one hand, and excessive economic dependence on the industrialized world on the other.

In 1817 the American Colonization Society was formed by a number of clergymen and slave-owners with the object of settling liberated Black Americans in West Africa. The first settlers sent in by the society arrived in Liberia in 1822. In the course of time only 12,000 came, and they were added to by just 2,000 West African slaves freed by the American Navy. Several hundred Barbadians also settled in 1865 at the invitation of Secretary of State Blyden. Americo–European culture came to dominate Liberia almost inevitably because of the overwhelming number of settlers from North America. The small number of freed African slaves had very little impact on the culture of the country.

Liberia won its independence from the Society in 1847. The black settlers wanted independence partly for nationalist reasons and partly so that Liberia, as a state in international law, could obtain customs duties from foreign traders. The introduction of customs would force foreign traders to operate through certain restricted ports of entry, and thus allow the settlers to develop a middleman trade. Joseph J. Roberts, a Eurafrican of mixed black and white descent and Governor since 1841, was elected the first President of the Republic of Liberia in 1848.

Race politics

Liberia operated a two-party system until 1883. The Republican Party, in power for most of this period, was supported by light-skinned Eurafrican settlers, who believed that because of their part-white descent, they were superior to the other settlers. The Republicans ruled from 1848 to 1869, when the True Whigs came to power, with E. J. Roye as President and the African nationalist philosopher, Edward Wilmot Blyden, as Secretary of State. Frustrated by the Eurafrican administrators, Roye unconstitutionally extended his presidential term from two to four years, and died in a coup carried out by a Republican mob in 1871: Roye was 'arrested' and then shortly afterwards found drowned in Monrovia harbour. Roberts, who inspired the mob that overthrew Roye, returned to the presidency for two more terms (1872–6).

The Eurafricans were, however, a steadily declining proportion of the black settler population as the West African climate took a heavier toll of them than of the other settlers. The True Whigs won the election in 1877 and held power until 1980. Eurafrican racism ceased to be of political importance.

Black colonialism

The new 'pure' black leaders were in some respects no improvement on the Eurafricans. They continued to exploit the indigenous Liberian communities, and practised massive corruption. Few of the Black American settlers realized, as Blyden did, that the success of their experiment would depend on how well they forged a meaningful relationship with the indigenous people.

The settlers alienated the land of the indigenous communities. Occasionally, land was leased for settlement but the owners were later driven away by settler militia. Often it was simply seized and occupied by right of conquest. In this respect the Black American settlers were little different from the white settlers in Algeria and South Africa. In 1855 settlers, supported by the American Navy, drove 2,000 Grebos out of the Cape Palmas region. There were many expeditions of conquest like this one. The indigenous peoples were also commonly subjected to forced labour.

Economic discrimination was also practised since the settlers were taxed lightly and the Kru, Grebo, Vai and other peoples were taxed heavily. In spite of numerous petitions, the Kru port, Setta Kru, was not made an international trading port like the six main settler coastal settlements. There was political discrimination. Until 1884 the indigenous peoples were totally unrepresented in the legislature, and even after 1884 only those few who paid more than a specified very high amount of tax were allowed to vote. The administration was staffed entirely by settlers. There was educational discrimination, as the settler government proposed technical rather than literary education for the Kru. There was social discrimination, as indigenous children were 'apprenticed' as household servants to settlers, and were forced to adopt the names of their masters, abandon their original families, and become assimilated to 'Western' culture.

The black settlers claimed that as Christians they were superior to the local peoples and so failed to utilize the talents of the indigenous peoples such as the Kru and the Vai. The Kru made a great contribution to the development of the ocean trade, working as sailors on European ships where they were renowned for their skill and efficiency. The Vai people were another development-conscious community in Liberia. One of them, Momolu Daolu, created a system of writing in the nineteenth century, and by 1850 a majority of adult Vai males were literate in the Vai script. Unfortunately, unification of the black settlers from America and the indigenous peoples into one nation has not been completed even in the second half of the twentieth century.

In one respect the black settlers of Liberia were influenced by local Africans: like the Creoles of Sierra Leone they developed large extended families. However, they over-staffed the civil service with members of these families, with the result that sixteen leading families came to dominate both the government and the administration, and monopolized almost all vacancies. The financial crisis caused by over-staffing was made worse by the general economic crisis and by the embezzlement and bribery which were all too common.

Economic dependency

Liberia underwent a boom in economic growth between 1830 and 1870, the heyday of her merchant princes. But dependence on exporting primary products led to disastrous economic collapse after 1870.

From 1830 Liberia became a major exporter of palm oil from the Kru coast, camwood—used for dyes—from the St Paul River, of fibres from the raphia palm, and coffee and sugar. Liberian coffee was considered the finest in the world in the mid-nineteenth century. A Liberian merchant shipping fleet, owned by settlers but manned by Kru, was developed to carry Liberian produce to Europe and America. As early as the time of independence, Liberia had a merchant fleet of fifty-eight ocean-going vessels.

Blyden realized the danger of over-dependence on the export of raw materials and the import of manufactured goods. He wished Liberia to become more self-supporting. The force of his realism was seen in the collapse of Liberia's economy during the world trade depression between 1870 and 1900. The advance of European colonization led to the development of new trading patterns which ignored Liberia. Both the British and the French developed palm oil and raphia fibre production in their new colonies. American petroleum reduced the demand for palm oil in the USA. American business abandoned Liberia to concentrate on exploiting Latin America. Brazilian coffee plantations, using the Liberian coffee plant, monopolized the American market, world prices fell, and Liberian plantations were ruined. Liberian sugar failed to compete with Cuban supplies and beet-sugar in Europe. Camwood was no longer required when the Germans developed synthetic dyes. Liberia's shipping fleets had no chance of being economically viable in the face of competition from steam packets from the industrialized countries.

Liberia's economy recovered partially between 1900 and 1914. Germany found that her colonial empire was unable to supply her tropical requirements, so German firms moved into Liberia. By 1914, twenty German firms were established in the country, and two out of three foreign ships calling at Liberian ports were German. A purely fortuitous circumstance kept Liberia functioning in the international economy. However, Liberians involved in export and import business were no longer independent traders, but agents of German firms.

The economic stagnation after 1870 delayed Liberia's effective occupation of the interior and led to loss of territory during the European Partition. In 1883 Sherbro district was taken by the British and added to Sierra Leone, and in 1892 the south-east corner of the country was annexed to the French Ivory Coast. Liberia herself became a semi-colonial state in 1912 when, in order to stave off bankruptcy, she negotiated a loan from American bankers but had to accept the appointment of an American who took charge of customs collection. Liberia's national motto was 'The love of Liberty brought us here'. To some extent, Liberia was a symbol of the black man's desire to be free. It is as well to remember, though, that there were many other free African states before the European Partition. Liberia achieved its symbolic status almost by accident, when it survived the European Partition, something which no other African state except Ethiopia was able to do.

6
North-east Africa before the European Partition

Overview

North-eastern Africa between 1840 and the Partition, like the other regions of Africa, experienced an enlargement of political, economic and religious scale. Ethiopia, which virtually disintegrated between 1755 and 1855, was re-unified by the efforts of Tewodros II, Yohannis IV and Menelik II. Egypt, already a highly centralized subject-state of the Ottoman Empire, occupied the Sudan and created a state there from many smaller ones. The Mahdist revolution in the Sudan failed in its hope of conquering the world, but it was at least able to root itself firmly in the large geographical area previously brought under one government by Egypt. The economies of the north-east African states underwent a similar enlargement of scale, as they steadily became more intimately linked to the European-dominated international economy. Even the Sudan, ravaged by the slave trade, and Ethiopia, wracked by continual wars, seem to have undergone a certain measure of economic growth in the period before the Partition.

Ethiopia

'Ethiopia' and 'Abyssinia'

Abyssinia is an anglicization of *Habasha*, the name the Amhara-Tigre peoples have given themselves. The Tigre inhabit the northern part of the Ethiopian highlands, north of the Takazze River. The Amhara inhabit the central part of the highlands, south of Tigre as far south as Addis Ababa. The Tigre and the Amhara speak different but related languages: Tigrinya and Amharic. They share a common culture based on their religion of Monophysite Christianity, they have similar social institutions, and they have a tradition of political unity within the ancient Ethiopian kingdom. This kingdom has

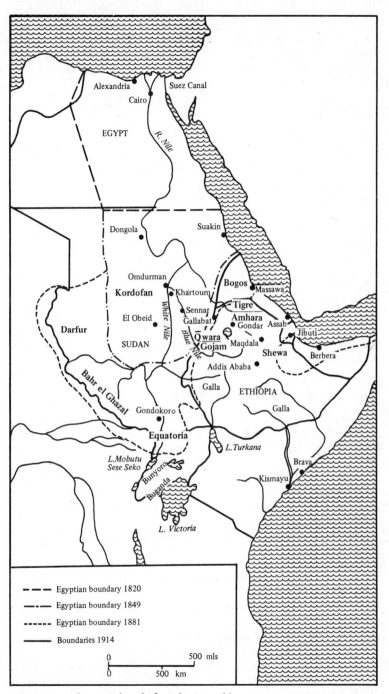

Map 7. North-east Africa before the Scramble.

expanded and contracted throughout history. At its smallest it was only Abyssinia—confined to the Amhara-Tigre areas of the highlands. At its greatest extent it has been Ethiopia, including other peoples such as the Galla, Somali, Arabs, Danakil and Sidama.

Our period opens with Ethiopia in the 'Era of the Princes' (1755–1855). The ancient empire, which had been united for a thousand years, disintegrated in the eighteenth century, when the power of the central monarch collapsed and the various regional kings set themselves up as powerful semi-independent rulers, swearing allegiance to the 'King of kings', as the emperor was known, only for form's sake. The collapse of the empire brought a century of war between provincial leaders and their followers; a break-down of law and order; a severe decline in the economy and the population; and the expansion of the Galla, a predominantly Muslim Cushitic-speaking people, northwards from their well-organized states in the south into the heart of the Amhara-Tigre lands.

Ethiopian tradition did, however, provide some hope for the future. It predicted the appearance of a Messiah-figure as king, by name Tewodros, who would reunite Ethiopia, conquer Jerusalem, Mecca and Medina, put an end to Islam, and bring about a universal peace throughout the world. A man who claimed to be Tewodros arose. His name was Kasa, son of a provincial governor. Kasa became Ethiopia's most successful provincial war-lord, emperor by right of conquest and 'Tewodros' by coronation.

Tewodros II: his rise to power

Tewodros is one of nineteenth-century Africa's greatest figures. He began the process of reuniting and modernizing Ethiopia but ultimately he failed. The country broke up again before the end of his reign; his progressive reforms failed to effect the changes he desired; his unsound foreign policy brought him against the might of Britain, and led to the invasion of his country and to his own death.

Tewodros was born as Kasa, in about 1818. He was the son of the Governor of Qwara province on the western borders of Amhara, where the highlands descend into the Sudanese lowlands. His father died when Kasa was a boy, and his mother was forced to become a seller of koso: flowers used as a medicine for tapeworm. The boy was adopted by his half-brother, Kinfu, the new Governor of Qwara, who had him put in a monastery where he became literate in Amharic, Ge'ez (the ancient language of the Ethiopian Church) and Arabic, and learned in Scripture. He was trained as a soldier, excelling as a marksman and horseman. He developed into commander of Kinfu's army, and won local civil wars for him.

Kasa succeeded his half-brother as governor of Qwara in 1845, having been appointed by Ras Ali II, the Galla regent for Yohannis III, the nominal emperor since 1832. Yohannis had no army of his own and almost no revenue. Ras Ali was the real ruler and controlled most of Amhara, although not Shewa in the south or Qwara in the west. He wanted the increasingly powerful Kasa on his side, and gave him not only the governorship of Qwara but also his daughter in marriage. Kasa, however, was not a loyal vassal and from 1852 he rebelled against Ali and Yohannis and made a determined bid for the throne for himself. His army was swollen by deserters from other governor's armies, who were attracted by the prospect of loot. Although Kasa had some guns and disciplined his forces along Egyptian lines, his army benefited most from certain innovations of his own. He abandoned the traditional, set-piece pattern of Ethiopian warfare of pitched battles in daylight on an open plain, for new and more flexible tactics like surprise night attacks and forced marches with little or no baggage. His charismatic leadership and his personal bravery in the thick of battles won him the intense loyalty and devotion of his soldiers.

In a series of brilliant campaigns from 1852 to 1856 Kasa made himself master of Abyssinia. In 1852 at the Battle of Gur Amba he defeated the army of Biru Goshu, the ruler of Gojjam province, who had been sent against him by Ras Ali. In 1853 he defeated Ali himself in two battles, Taqusa and Ayshal. Ayshal was a decisive battle in Ethiopian history. It was the most vital battle in Kasa's rise to power, and it brought to an end the 'Era of the Princes'.

The western provinces were now under Kasa's control. In order to bring all Abyssinia under his sway, the powerful vassal states of Tigre to the north and Shewa to the south, and the Muslim Wallo Galla between them, had still to be conquered. In 1855 he defeated the governor of Tigre at Deresge. After Deresge, Kasa had himself crowned Emperor Tewodros II by Abuna Salama, the head of the Ethiopian Church. Thus the son of the koso-seller replaced the ancient Solomonian dynasty.

In 1855–6 Tewodros defeated and conquered the Wallo Galla, and carried out a terrible slaughter of their Muslims: he then occupied Shewa, captured the new Shewan king, the eleven-year-old Sahle Mariam (the later Emperor Menelik II), and imprisoned the boy in his fortress capital at Maqdala. Abyssinia had been reunited by military conquest.

Tewodros and Ethiopia

Tewodros was a man with a vision. He came to power hoping to transform his country. However, one of Tewodros' major problems was his inability to carry his people along with him. This problem was made worse by defects in the Emperor's character. He was capable of great generosity and kindness, but equally of great cruelty and violence. He was emotionally unstable. Under the influence of a bout of bad temper he could order terrible atrocities to be committed against prisoners and enemies. For example, when Menelik escaped from Maqdala in 1865 with Galla assistance Tewodros had scores of Galla prisoners put to death. Rebels were treated with relentless severity, with mass slaughter of the men and slavery for their women and children.

Tewodros' first aim was to reunite Ethiopia, as the essential first step for transforming and modernizing the country. He carried out far-reaching administrative reforms. The existing large provinces were broken up into smaller ones under governors appointed by the emperor. Like other nineteenth-century African modernizers, Tewodros created a national standing army. The army was paid, to prevent it from living off the land. Men from different districts were mixed up at random in the new regiments, so that local loyalties would be replaced by national loyalty to the emperor and the nation. In the late 1850s law and order was largely restored, as bandit groups were eliminated. Justice was reformed, when Tewodros decreed that in homicide cases the murderer alone should be executed, and relatives of a murderer should not suffer in any way. Traditional practices like the vendetta and compensation payments were largely replaced by impartial judicial investigation.

Tewodros attempted to carry our reforms in the Church. The Ethiopian Church was in dire need of change. It owned one-third of the country and its lands were free from all taxation. There were a great number of priests, many of whom had sought ordination to escape from manual labour, who were uneducated and who practised concubinage. Tewodros had come to power partly because of his 1854 alliance with Abuna Salama, which won him Church support. Yet Tewodros stunned the Church with his radical reforms. Church property was taken over by the state. Tewodros wanted its wealth, both to pay his army and to modernize the country. Each church was given land sufficient to feed two priests and three deacons, and the excess land was given to farmers. Excess clergy were required to work and pay taxes. Thus the position of the idle *debtera*, or church scribes, was severely weakened.

Tewodros, more than any other nineteenth-century African ruler, except perhaps Samori, perceived the importance of adopting modern technology as part of the response to European penetration. He had learned this lesson when, as a war-lord in Qwara in the 1840s, he had suffered a stinging defeat by a well-armed and well-trained Egyptian force on the Ethiopia–Sudan border. He bought many guns from Europe. Realizing the importance both of artillery and industrialization, he hired European engineers, and persuaded missionary artisans to provide him with the military equipment he needed. Cannon foundries and powder mills were set up, and several huge cannon mortars were built.

However, Tewodros' achievements were more apparent than real. His character deteriorated after the deaths of his beloved wife

Tewabetch in 1858, and of his close friends the British Consul Walter Plowden and the English engineer John Bell in 1860, and the condition of the nation worsened along with the emperor's personality. His administrative reforms failed, because he tried to impose a highly centralized system on the great feudal nobles without due regard to their feelings and without the means to impose his authority effectively. The provincial nobles did not share the emperor's vision of a unified and modernized government. He lacked a bureaucracy on which to build a national administration, and so only a federal system could have worked, with the provincial nobles attached to the Emperor by military and marriage alliance. Yohannis IV and Menelik II learned from Tewodros' failure and slowly but more surely strengthened the central power by diplomacy rather than war.

By constantly marching his army all over the country to suppress the provincial rebels who would not accept the loss of their traditional privileges and powers, Tewodros also turned the ordinary people against him. Imperial soldiers were garrisoned under a system whereby the farmers in each district became responsible for feeding them. This produced a kind of serfdom which alienated the peasantry. The campaigns against rebels soon led to exhaustion of the treasury, which in turn led to an inability to pay the army. There was a return to the old practice of ravaging the country and a high rate of desertion from the army. In the 1860s thousands of soldiers deserted to rebel leaders, notably Menelik of Shewa and the new Kasa of Tigre (later Yohannis IV).

Tewodros had abolished the slave trade on his accession, but the conditions of civil war and rebellion in the 1850s meant that slavery revived and flourished more than ever, since female and child relatives of defeated rebels were distributed as booty to soldiers and governors.

The emperor's attack on the privileges of the Church aroused great wrath among the priests. It turned them against him and towards his political enemies, the provincial nobles. Tewodros' quarrel with the Church alienated the mass of the Amhara-Tigre people. The priests were in much closer contact with the people than the king. Tewodros' religious policies therefore led directly to trouble—which was especially true of his attempts to Christianize Muslims by force.

Tewodros' attempts to industrialize arms production came to nothing. The huge mortars built by the missionary artisans simply rendered his army immobile at Maqdala, and they were deserted by their gunners when the British stormed the fort.

As his reign progressed Tewodros became more and more violent in his reaction to what he felt were insults and opposition. The last years of the reign were taken up with campaigns against one rebel after another. Whole areas of country were devastated, and many captured rebels were horribly mutilated. As the emperor became more repressive so opposition grew. This in turn brought an even more violent reaction from Tewodros. Harshness did not enforce obedience but merely increased disloyalty. As early as two years before his death the emperor controlled only the fort of Maqdala and its surrounding area. Tewodros had thus failed to reunite and modernize Ethiopia, which by his death had broken up once more into warring provinces.

Tewodros and Britain

Tewodros was determined to seek relations with European powers on a basis of equality. He wanted Europe's friendship without its imperialism. He desperately wanted technical aid from Europe. Yet by deliberately treading on the British lion's tail he courted and met disaster.

Tewodros' first contacts with Britain were extremely friendly. He welcomed the Protestant German Missionaries, Krapf and Stern, who worked for British societies and distributed Amharic Bibles. He developed close friendships with two Britons: John Bell, an engineer, who married an Ethiopian, and acted as a kind of secretary for Tewodros, and Walter Plowden, the British consul. When Plowden was killed on a journey to the coast, Tewodros organized a punitive expedition which slaughtered thousands of people. In this campaign Bell saved Tewodros' life and lost his own in the process. The death of Plowden was a tragedy for relations between Ethiopia and Britain, because he was replaced as consul by Cameron, a man less sympathetic towards the Emperor.

Tewodros wrote a letter to Queen Victoria of Britain in November 1862, to arrange for the safe passage of Ethiopian ambassadors he intended to send to England, and suggesting that Britain should give him at least moral support in the war he intended to wage against the Egyptians and Turks in the Sudan and at their base of Massawa on the Eritrean coast. The British Foreign Office not only failed to answer the letter, but even instructed Cameron to go from Ethiopia to the Sudan to investigate its cotton growing potential, and to report on the slave trade there. Egypt, which Tewodros regarded as a prime enemy, ruled the Sudan at the time. The emperor felt that Britain had insulted him and had begun to co-operate with his enemies against him. Fuel was added to the fire when Britain ceased to protect Ethiopian pilgrims visiting the holy places in Jerusalem after the Turks had insisted that Ethiopians were Turkish subjects. On Cameron's return from the Sudan, Tewodros had him arrested, put in chains and tortured. The European missionaries in Ethiopia were also detained and later imprisoned. Tewodros seems to have assumed that Victoria had not replied to his letter because Britain had, from the start, been plotting against Ethiopia in conjunction with Egypt and Turkey.

The arrest of Cameron and the missionaries forced the British government to answer Tewodros' letter, and Queen Victoria signed a conciliatory reply, which was brought to Ethiopia in 1866 by Hormuzd Rassam, the British envoy. Tewodros imprisoned Rassam, too, when he learnt that he was not a permanent ambassador, and demanded Britain send skilled workmen to Ethiopia. Britain sent the workmen but kept them at Massawa, insisting that Tewodros release his prisoners first. Tewodros refused to release them until the workmen arrived. The result was stalemate, which was broken by the British military expedition of 1867–8 under General Napier.

Napier's expedition had one objective: to take Maqdala and rescue the prisoners. It also gave opportunity to test new military technology and methods, such as a specially constructed railway at Zula on the Red Sea coast, new breech-loading rifles, new types of artillery, photographic reproduction of maps, and an early form of searchlight. The British had no problems with supplies of meat, grain, forage and fuel, because they had powerful Ethiopian allies, Kasa prince of Tigre and the Galla around Maqdala. The British army stormed Maqdala in April 1868, although Tewodros had already released the European prisoners unharmed. The Emperor shot himself through the mouth to avoid capture. His soldiers fought on bravely long after all hope had gone.

The British, withdrew from the country after their victory, and the 'Era of the Princes' returned. Kasa of Tigre, however, was rewarded by his allies with a vast store of guns and ammunition, which he used to make himself King of Kings by 1871.

The European powers drew the wrong conclusions from Napier's expedition of 1867–8. They assumed that the British army had destroyed Tewodros' kingdom. In fact, Tewodros had lost it already. The British simply administered the *coup de grâce*, benefiting from Ethiopia's internal political problems. The Italians learnt in 1896 that a united Ethiopia was a vastly different proposition to the weakened empire of the late 1860s.

In the end, Tewodros' failure to reunify and modernize Ethiopia was complete. What cannot be taken away from him, however, was his vision of a united and modern state, and his attempt to give it reality.

Yohannis IV

The decline of the Kasa who became Tewodros was matched by the rise of another Kasa—the leader of Tigre, who was an ally of Britain. Kasa did not immediately become King of Kings: the throne was occupied briefly by Tekle Giyorgis (1868–71) before Kasa won a decisive victory against him at Adwa in 1871. Kasa's 12,000 well-armed and well-trained riflemen defeated cavalry charges by 60,000 men. Kasa was also aided by Ras Alula, the son of a peasant and one of Ethiopia's greatest generals. In 1872 Kasa was crowned at Aksum as Yohannis IV.

Yohannis brought far more of a measure of political unity to Ethiopia than Tewodros. He consolidated his authority over the highlands by diplomacy rather than warfare, and by creating a federation rather than a strongly centralized state. But at least his achievement was within the realm of practical possibility, and proved acceptable to the provincial rulers. In 1878 Yohannis made an agreement with Menelik of Shewa, who agreed to drop his claim to be King of Kings, and pay tribute to Yohannis. In return Yohannis confirmed him as King of Shewa, and betrothed his son Araya Sillas to Menelik's daughter Zewditu. Yohannis would no doubt have liked to reduce Menelik's power, but was unable to do so because of the constant foreign threat. Menelik never fully kept the agreement and continued to trade northwards with the Italians for arms, even when Yohannis was at war with them.

Yohannis cannot be said to have fully united the country. He never really established his authority over Takle Haymanot, King of Gojjam, and had little control over Menelik, who refused to fight with Yohannis against the Mahdist invaders. Paradoxically, it was Menelik, the strongest obstacle to unity from 1865 to 1889, who really united the country in the 1890s.

Yohannis' religious policy was a continuation of Tewodros' policy of intolerant denunciation of certain sects in the Ethiopian Church, and Catholics, Muslims and Traditionalists. These last two groups were ordered to accept Christianity within three and five years respectively. This policy was, of course, impossible to implement effectively, and even where many conversions were made, they were rarely lasting.

Yohannis' major achievement and his real importance in the history of Ethiopia lies in his successful resistance to invasions of Egyptians, the Mahdists and the Italians, although throughout his reign Yohannis was so distracted by these external threats that he was unable to institute widespread reform in his country. By 1872 Egypt had taken control of the Red Sea coast, occupying the port of Berbera. In that year the Egyptians invaded Ethiopian borderlands which were only semi-dependent on the emperor: under the leadership of the Swiss adventurer Munzinger they advanced from Massawa into the highlands and occupied Bogos province in mid-Eritrea. The advance was continued in 1875, when Egypt made a three-pronged attack on Ethiopia. The first expedition left Zeila on the north Somali coast and occupied the town of Harar in the south-eastern foothills of the highlands. Harar remained Egyptian for nearly ten years. A second column under Munzinger marched from Tujurah near Jibuti towards Shewa, but was defeated by the Afar of the coast and so never reached Yohannis' territory. Munzinger was killed. The other column moved inland from Massawa into Tigre and was annihilated by Ras Alula at Gundat. A new expedition under Ratib Pasha, commander-in-chief of the Egyptian army, was heavily defeated by Alula at Gura. Alula won because of his skill at deploying large numbers of men, his brilliant outflanking tactics and his careful use of terrain to overcome superior Egyptian firepower. Thousands of Egyptian breechloading rifles were captured. After the British conquest of Egypt the threat from her receded, and Egyptian forces to the east of Ethiopia were withdrawn.

A new threat soon appeared in the west. The Mahdists of the Sudan launched a jihad against Christian Ethiopia in the years 1885–9. Alula defeated them in 1885 at Kufit but they managed to occupy and sack Gondar under their general Abu Anja. In the face of repeated Mahdist attacks some of the local Ethiopian chiefs wavered in their allegiance; at least one went over to the Mahdists' side. Yohannis almost defeated the Mahdists in 1889 at Metemma on the border, but he was killed by a stray bullet. What had been virtually a victory turned into an Ethiopian rout: the emperor's troops fled as news of his death spread through the army.

Before his death, however, Yohannis had defeated the first Italian attempt to penetrate Ethiopia. In 1869 Italian missionaries bought the Red Sea village of Assab, which became an official Italian colony in 1882. In 1885 the Italians took over Massawa, and abolished the free transit of Ethiopian goods. Their attempts to obtain a foothold in the Highlands led to the destruction of a small Italian force by Alula at Dogali in 1887. However, this did not end Italian designs on Ethiopia. A far more serious Italian threat had to be faced by Menelik, the new emperor.

Egypt

Muhammad Ali, Abbas and Muhammad Sa'id

Egypt had been conquered by the Ottoman Turks in 1517 after their defeat of the Mamluks at the Battle of Cairo. The Mamluks were originally a slave caste of various races, and they had ruled Egypt since 1249. Even after their defeat by the Turks they remained the effective power in the country. However, in 1799 their hold over Egypt was shaken when they were defeated by the French under Napoleon. Although the French withdrew from Egypt in 1801 after their own defeat by the British, they had a profound impact on the country. Their invasion had undermined the Mamluks' position, shown up the weakness of the Ottoman empire and opened the gates to an inflow of western ideas. The Egyptian people, stirred by their religious leaders, became restive under the rule of the foreign Mamluks and Turks. Muhammad Ali, who was an Albanian, identified himself with the discontent of the Egyptians and by 1805 had obtained power in Egypt.

Muhammad Ali who ruled until 1849 laid the foundations of modern Egypt. He was profoundly influenced by the modernizing achievements of the French and believed that Egypt could only develop in partnership with the more technologically advanced west.

The cornerstone of Muhammad Ali's programme of modernization was military reform. This was partly because he feared the designs of the Ottoman Turks on Egypt, and partly because he wished to use Egypt as a base from which to extend his power and influence. Clearly a strong army was needed. However, Muhammad Ali realized that more general modernization would be required to support the reform of the army. He encouraged the spread of western education in Egypt, and sent Egyptian students to Europe to complete their studies. Agriculture was stimulated by a great increase in the area of irrigated land, and a scheme to build a dam across the Nile at Cairo was started. Egypt's first exports of cotton began in the 1820s. Industry was not neglected: a steel and iron foundry was built, ship-building plants were established, textile factories were constructed throughout the country. He stood in the Islamic modernist tradition of the nineteenth century, and opposed the sort of Islamic fundamentalism which responded to growing western pressure by returning to the original, traditional observance of the Koran.

Muhammad Ali was not an Egyptian nationalist. He was an Albanian in the service of his Turkish masters. His own revolt against the Sultan (1839–40) was an attempt, not to secure independence for the province of Egypt, but to make himself the Sultan of the Ottoman empire. Yet in spite of this, Muhammad Ali stimulated Egyptian nationalism. Firstly, his administrative reforms, his efforts to industrialize the country, and his conquest of the Sudan, all helped to give Egypt a clearer identity as a nation-state rather than as a mere province of Turkey, because Egyptians as much as Turks participated in these changes. Secondly, his harsh taxation policy aroused fierce reactions from the mass of the Egyptian population against his autocratic alien Turkish rule.

Abbas, who ruled from 1849 to 1854, reversed Muhammad Ali's policy. He was an Islamic fundamentalist who closed the secular schools opened under Muhammad Ali, and dismissed European advisers. His opposition to western influence was a form of Egyptian nationalism. Muhammad Sa'id (1854–63) had been educated in Europe and, like Muhammad Ali, admired western civilization and was in the Islamic modernist tradition. He lifted all restrictions on private enterprise, restored private ownership of land, abolished monopolies, allowed foreign goods to be imported untaxed, and generally did everything he could to encourage an influx of European businessmen and capital. He granted a concession to the

Frenchman Ferdinand de Lesseps to build the Suez Canal, on which work started in 1859. Thus Muhammad Sa'id went much further than Muhammad Ali in opening up Egypt to European economic penetration. Muhammad Ali had believed that such a canal would soon turn Egypt into a vassal of one of the great European naval powers and had opposed its construction. Muhammad Sa'id also further separated Egypt from Turkey by encouraging the use of Arabic rather than Turkish as the official language.

Ismail (1863–79)

Ismail, the grandson of Muhammad Ali, began his reign in 1863. His aim was to modernize Egypt on the model of France, and to found a great African empire. His attempts to fulfil these aims eventually brought financial chaos and British occupation. Initially Ismail secured greater autonomy for Egypt from the Sultan of Turkey, who bestowed on him the title of *Khedive*, a title which made him a sovereign in his own right, and gave him almost complete independence. How did Ismail use his new power?

Egypt underwent very rapid economic growth under Ismail. Annual revenues increased from just under £5 million in 1864 to £145 million in 1875. Exports rose in the same period from £29 million to £62 million. The customs system was remodelled. Banking facilities were extended with the creation of the Bank of Egypt, and the opening of branches of the Ottoman Bank and the French bank, Credit Lyonnais. Egypt's productive capacity expanded, especially in agriculture, where cotton and sugar cane growing were encouraged. The American Civil War caused a collapse in American cotton production and enabled the Egyptian cotton crop to rise from £5 million to £25 million worth a year. The Suez Canal was completed and opened in 1869. At a less spectacular but no less important level, Egypt benefited from the construction of modern port facilities, new roads, railways, 400 bridges over the Nile, 5,000 miles of telegraph lines and postal services. Cairo was rebuilt with many modern streets and hotels, a theatre and an opera house. Many foreign loans were granted and foreign technical assistance was utilized on a large scale in business, public works, the army, the administration and education. The number of Europeans living in Egypt rose from a few thousand in 1860 to 100,000 in 1876.

Ismail achieved much in the field of education. He developed a national, state-supported school system, under which the number of state schools rose from 185 at the beginning of his reign to 4,817 by the end. By 1875, there were 100,000 pupils in these schools, including girls, and many children of peasants. There were specialized colleges for lawyers, administrators, religious teachers, engineers, school-teachers, and so on. Even the ancient Azhar University, attached to the Azhar Mosque in Cairo, could not escape entirely from the modernist tendencies in education. The cultural revolution in Egypt under Ismail produced a flourishing press, as many newspapers were founded and a class of western-educated journalists emerged. A modernist literary movement developed, using classical Arabic that had remained structurally unchanged since the writing of the Koran, but adapting it to modern needs. Newspapers and magazines which were encouraged by the khedive were eventually to campaign against autocratic royal power—a development which Ismail had not anticipated.

Ismail's successes, however, were heavily outweighed by his failures. There was no significant political reform. The Khedive created a Chamber of Notables, so that he could claim Egypt had adopted the parliamentary institutions of Europe, but the Notables were men who had high property qualifications and the Chamber had no real power. Even so the khedive had to treat it with greater caution than he had expected. There was no real social reform either. The Turkish-speaking governing class did not lose its privileges, although these were extended to many Arabic-speaking Egyptians who were appointed to high posts. The middle-class Christian Copts remained, as before, retail businessmen, tax collectors, and finance officers in the administration. Very few were given high office. The vast mass of the people, the *fellahin* or peasants, continued to remain sorely oppressed, very heavily taxed by the government and frequently in debt to Greek money-lenders. Moreover, Ismail authorized the speedier break up of the traditional land-holding system, which benefited the new class of large private landholders, especially the royal family, at the expense of the fellahin.

Egypt became bankrupt in 1876, largely because of Ismail's extravagant expenditure and his excessive reliance on foreign loans. Luxury spending included £1 million lavished on the entertainment of invited foreign guests and top Egyptian officials at the opening of the Suez Canal. Ismail paid massive bribes—a £3 million lump sum and £750,000 in annual tribute—to the Sultan and his ministers to secure more autonomy. The ending of the American Civil War had also helped to undermine Egyptian finances. When American cotton exports revived the price of Egyptian cotton slumped. The result was that Ismail could no longer pay off the foreign debts which had been incurred.

Egypt's financial position also deteriorated with Ismail's efforts to create a vast African empire which the country could not afford. He greatly expanded the army, and squandered millions of pounds in imperial adventures in the Sudan, in Ethiopia, and in Uganda. By 1875 Ismail was forced to sell Egypt's forty-four per cent share in the Suez Canal to the British Government in order to meet some of his debts. This was at a time when the canal had not begun to return profits to investors. Ismail was forced to obtain loans from European financiers to pay interest on earlier loans.

In 1876 Ismail could no longer pay his own or Egypt's debts, and the country therefore became bankrupt. The British and French governments looking after the interests of British and French creditors in Egypt, appointed a Commission of the Debt and imposed it on the khedive. The European Commissioners attempted to regulate Egyptian finances and thus make it possible for Egypt to repay its debt. The Commission introduced an equitable and efficient system of taxation and cut luxury expenditure. Ismail soon clashed with the Commissioners and dismissed them, whereupon Britain and France put pressure on the Sultan who deposed Ismail and appointed Ismail's eldest son, Tawfiq, to succeed him, and the European Commissioners were brought back. Had Ismail restricted expenditure to worthwhile projects of modernization—such as the development of agriculture, communications and education—and refrained from conspicuous luxury and from imperial adventures abroad, then he might have gone a long way not only towards developing his country, but also to keeping it out of the grip of European economic imperialism.

The Sudan

The area to the south of Egypt at the beginning of the nineteenth century consisted of a number of different societies. Today this area is the modern state of the Sudan. In the north the majority of the population was Muslim and heavily Arabic in character. South of the Sudd, the massive swamp either side of the Nile, were a large number of different ethnic groups, including the Nilotic Shilluk, Dinka and Nuer. They were not united, consisting of different clans which frequently fought amongst themselves. The Bantu Azande were divided into a number of independent kingdoms which also quarrelled with one another. Not since the collapse of the Christian kingdoms of Nubia hundreds of years earlier had the Sudan had a real measure of political independence and unity. Although the Sudan had such a diverse population, during the nineteenth century Muhammad Ali and Ismail gave it a measure of unity, while the Mahdist movement brought it independence, although this was only for a brief period.

Egyptian rule in the Sudan

The Egyptian army that Muhammad Ali sent to the Sudan in 1820 established Egyptian control over the Blue Nile lands as far as the foothills of the Ethiopian highlands, and over the White Nile as far as the great Sudd swamp in the south. The lands south of the Sudd were only brought under Egyptian authority after the penetration of the Sudd in 1839.

Muhammad Ali's government began to develop the Sudan to some extent. Firstly, there was a measure of political development. By uniting under one government many different ethnic communities and political units, he created a larger political unit than had previously existed in the area. He established Egyptian government headquarters of the Sudan at Khartoum, a new town founded in 1824. The rest of the Sudan was divided into provinces, each province having a governor who was responsible to the governor-general at Khartoum, the latter being responsible to the ruler in Cairo. The system of provincial administration begun in the 1820s has been the basis of Sudanese government ever since.

However, Muhammad Ali conquered the Sudan less to develop it than to exploit it. He captured thousands of Sudanese to be used as soldiers for wars in Syria, and for sale in Egypt and other Arabic lands.

Once the southern Sudan came under Egyptian control Egyptian and north Sudanese firms moved rapidly into the area to develop the ivory and slave trades. The Egyptian company of Aqqad gained a monopoly south of Gondokoro and traded as far south as Acholiland in present Uganda. Fortified camps, known as *Zeribas*, were built where the traders and their servants would live while obtaining the ivory. One Zeriba might contain as many as a thousand people, including the armed servants, their wives and other workers. The trade became increasingly violent, because the local communities would accept only cattle in exchange for ivory. So the Egyptian and north Sudanese traders began to raid a clan or chiefdom for cattle and then exchange the cattle for ivory with another clan or chiefdom. Traders often made these attacks just to obtain food.

The slave trade became an important addition to the ivory trade. Often slaves were captured to work in gardens round the Zeribas and so supply the traders with food. However, most of the slaves were exported to Egypt and Arabia. To obtain them the traders took advantage of the enmity between clans or different Azande chiefs. They supplied one group with guns to enable it to raid another for slaves.

The impact of the slave trade on the peoples of the southern Sudan varied according to the group affected. The Dinka and Nuer had a fair amount of protection from the trade because they could easily retreat into inaccessible swamps. The Azande suffered more severely when the traders learnt to exploit the dynastic quarrels of their leaders. Many Azande, including even some of the paramount princes, were enslaved, but Azande society was not totally disrupted. Between the Dinka and Azande, however, lay a belt of weaker communities who were able to offer almost no resistance to slave raiders and were heavily depopulated. These were the Dembo, Jur, and Bongo west of the Nile, and the Bari and Latuka east of the river. The Bari in particular were so exposed to the full impact of the commercial ruthlessness of the slavers that their rudimentary political institutions disintegrated.

When Ismail became khedive he had four aims for the Sudan: to end the slave trade, to expand Egyptian rule further, to introduce European methods of administration, and to develop the economy of the area. All this needed money. His expenditure in the Sudan contributed to the bankruptcy of Egypt and his own deposition.

The main effect of Ismail's rule in the northern Sudan was to improve communications. A system of river steamers was developed on the Nile and a shipyard built at Khartoum. The government also financed service steamers on the Red Sea coast. The postal service was taken over by the government and improved.

However, Ismail was far more interested in the southern than in the northern Sudan. He employed the English explorer Samuel Baker, who had travelled to Lake Mobutu in 1864, to lead an Egyptian expedition to the South. His instructions were to establish Egyptian rule as far as possible and to end the slave trade and 'tribal' wars. Eventually Baker advanced into Bunyoro but was driven out by Kabalega. The expedition achieved very little. Baker had little success in establishing government, legitimate trade or agriculture. The Egyptian administration was weak. Only the stores and ships that Baker had brought with him were going to be of some use to later governors of Equatoria, the name given to the Egyptian province now established in this area. These few results had cost Egypt over £1 million.

When Baker left the Sudan in 1873 Ismail decided to replace him with a British army officer, Charles Gordon. Ismail was eager for Gordon to establish contact with Mutesa in Buganda, open up a trade route from the Sudan to Lake Victoria, divert the ivory trade from Zanzibar to Egypt, and if necessary occupy the Lake kingdoms for Egypt. On reaching Equatoria Gordon attempted to use peaceful methods in pursuit of these aims, but the people were hostile, and Gordon, like Baker before him, found that he had to raid them in order to find supplies for his troops. Gordon suggested to Ismail that a supply route from the East African coast to the Lakes should be established. As a result in 1875 Ismail sent Egyptian troops to occupy the mouth of the Juba River and find a route inland to Buganda. This area, however, was claimed by the Sultan of Zanzibar, who appealed to the British for help against the Egyptians. The British, considering the Sultan a more reliable opponent of the slave trade than Ismail, told the Egyptians to withdraw. Ismail dared not annoy the British, and so the Egyptians left the East African coast in 1876. Egyptian designs on Buganda also came to nothing after H. M. Stanley had publicized Kabaka Mutesa's request for British missionaries. Egypt had lost its chance of gaining control of the Lake kingdoms, and was soon to become too weak to make any further attempts.

In 1876 Gordon resigned, believing he could achieve nothing more as governor in Equatoria. Ismail persuaded him to return to Khartoum as Governor-General of all Sudan in 1877, but he had little success. He was not a capable administrator, he knew little Arabic, and he was a Christian ruling a predominantly Muslim people. The main cause of his failure, however, was due to the bankruptcy of the Egyptian government which could not supply sufficient soldiers for controlling the Sudan or effectively suppressing the slave trade. Gordon was unable to overcome these difficulties and when Ismail was deposed in 1879, Gordon resigned.

The Mahdist Revolution in the Sudan, 1881–5

In June 1881 a Sudanese religious preacher, Muhammad Ahmad ibn Abdallah, despatched letters from his headquarters on Aba Island in the White Nile, informing notables of the Sudan that he was the *Mahdi* (literally 'the guided one'), the divine leader chosen by God at the end of time to fill the earth with justice and equity. In 1885 he captured Khartoum, and virtually all the Sudan was in his hands. How was it that a movement which initially was religious should be able to overthrow Egyptian rule so quickly?

The rise of the Mahdist movement was undoubtedly helped by changed political conditions in Egypt, such as the deposition of Ismail and the rise of Urabi, and the British occupation. Britain was certainly not prepared to spend money on controlling the Sudan. But without the personality and leadership of Muhammad Ahmad the revolution would never have occurred. The Mahdi was able to capitalize on the considerable Sudanese discontent with Egyptian rule and draw together in one revolt people with very different grievances and aims.

Three major groups rallied to the support of the Mahdi and became the *Ansar*, or helpers. First among them were the genuinely religious who believed his claims to be the Mahdi and wanted to build a pure Islamic state. The second group were people who had been threatened economically by the attempts to suppress the slave trade in the Bahr al-Ghazal. Particularly important in this group were the Ja'aliyin and Danaqla. These were both Arabic-speaking peoples whose homeland was north of Khartoum but who had become important traders in the southern Sudan. The decline of Egyptian authority gave them the opportunity to revive the slave trade and their former fortunes. The third group, the Baqqara cattle-keeping nomads of south Kordofan and Darfur, were simply opposed to government of any kind. They strongly objected to the payment of taxes which had resulted from the expansion of Egyptian power in the south, and they formed the bulk of the Mahdist army.

The Mahdist offensive began with a jihad against the province of

Kordofan in 1882 and 1883. The people of the countryside rose in support of the Mahdi, forcing the Egyptian forces to withdraw to their fortified bases, which were captured one by one by the Ansar. When the provincial capital, El Obeid, fell in January 1883, the Egyptians belatedly realized the importance of the Mahdi, whom they had hitherto underestimated. An Egyptian force of 8,000 soldiers under a British officer, Hicks, was sent to crush the Mahdi. Hicks's men were mainly the demoralized survivors of Urabi's army which had been defeated in the British invasion of Egypt. They were further affected by Mahdist propaganda proclamations warning them that 'it is hopeless to fight against the soldiers of God'. Abdallahi's strategy of drawing Hicks's forces deep into waterless scrubland, led to the great Mahdist victory at Shaykan on November 5, 1883, over a demoralized and weakened army. Hicks was killed and only about 250 of his army survived. Shaykan was a decisive battle, because it inspired Sudanese waverers to join the Mahdist side, and convinced the British rulers of Egypt of the desirability of evacuating the Sudan. Moreover, the British Prime Minister Gladstone supported the principle of the Sudanese right to self-determination.

The Mahdists conquered Darfur in December 1883, and Bahr al-Ghazal fell to them in April 1884. The Mahdi's messenger in the Red Sea area, Uthman Diqna, who was of Beja origin, cut the vital line of communication between the port of Suakin and Berber on the Nile, but although Suakin was besieged it never fell to the Mahdi.

In 1884 Gladstone sent ex-Governor-General Gordon to Khartoum to evacuate the Egyptian soldiers and administrators from the Sudan. Instead of carrying out his orders Gordon organized the defence of Khartoum against the Mahdi. This was inadequate: the Mahdists captured Khartoum in January 1885 and Gordon was killed, just two days before the arrival of a British relief force reluctantly sent by Gladstone. Khartoum proved to be the limit of the Mahdi's conquests, for he died, probably of typhus, in June 1885.

The Mahdist state

Before he died, the Mahdi established his capital at Omdurman, on the west bank of the Nile opposite Khartoum. Already during the jihad he had established the basis of an Islamic theocracy. His three chief disciples were equated with the Companions of the Prophet, and he bestowed on each of them the title of *Khalifa*, or Successor. Each khalifa commanded a division of the Mahdist army. The pre-eminent khalifa was Abdallahi, a man of Baqqara origin, who was overall Commander of the Armies and director of the administration. The elaborate Egyptian tax-system was abolished and replaced by the lighter taxes of the Koran. Income, therefore, largely consisted of war booty, but not much of this went into the common treasury. The Mahdi's real interest was not administration but Islam. It was left to Abdallahi to organize a secular and modern administrative system.

Abdallahi's rule (1885–98) marked the transformation of the Mahdist state from a theocracy into a complex and centralized administrative unit. Order was restored over a vast area which had been ravaged by four years of war—an achievement that could only have been secured by the bureaucracy Abdallahi created.

The khalifa created a system of provincial rule. The outer provinces, away from Omdurman and the surrounding area, were normally under the command of military governors who were invariably selected from amongst the Ta'aisha group of the Baqqara. This was the ethnic group from which the khalifa came. The central provinces were the riverain lands. These had neither central treasuries nor military governors and were really fiscal areas rather than full provinces.

Geographically and administratively Omdurman was the heart of the Mahdist state. It was here that the khalifa had his official residence and the administration which centred on him. The two chief officers who assisted him were the Commissioner of the Treasury and the *Qadi*, finance minister and chief justice respectively. The monopoly over military governorships and commands enjoyed by the Baqqara did not extend into the civil administration. Clerical and administrative posts were filled with people from the riverain lands. Between a quarter and a third of these officials had previously served with the Egyptians.

The central treasury never functioned well because of the constant undermining of the commissioners' position. Ibrahim Muhammad 'Adlam, an excellent administrator who was in charge of the treasury, was dismissed and executed in 1890, largely because his methods of obtaining the corn tax were regarded as being too lenient. Various special treasuries were set up. One was created for the khalifa's bodyguard, another was the Khalifa's Privy Treasury. As a result of this the public treasury lost such valuable sources of revenue as the domain land and the booty from war. The economic position was as depressing as the financial. Agriculture was heavily taxed to support an enormous military establishment. Trade with outside areas was not encouraged at all. The coinage became more and more debased during the rule of the khalifa.

In legal matters attempts were made to insist on strict Islamic conduct. Strict regulations were enforced against smoking and drinking; women had to be veiled and were not to go into the markets and public streets. The court in Omdurman seems to have acted as a court of appeal as well as a criminal court dealing with ordinary cases arising in its area.

Abdallahi was successful in defeating attempted coups and revolts. He faced rivalry as the Mahdi's successor from the Mahdi's kinsman,

Khalifa Muhammad Sharif, and his followers, the *ashraf*. The ashraf attempted a coup in 1886, but they were defeated, disarmed and incorporated in the forces loyal to Abdallahi. Thereafter, Abdallahi steadily replaced the ashraf with his own Baqqara kinsmen as provincial and military governors and other high executive officers. In 1887 he defeated a revolt in Darfur under a member of the old royal family, Yusuf Ibrahim. In 1889 there was another Darfur revolt under a messianic figure, Abu Jummayza, who claimed to be the rightful khalifa and ruler. This failed when Abu died of smallpox and his demoralized followers were dispersed. In 1891 there was a revolt by the ashraf supported by the Danaqla and settlers in the Gezira area between the White and Blue Niles. This was ended by the khalifa after careful negotiations. Three weeks later the leaders were rounded up and killed and a huge fine of one-third of their goods was imposed on the Danaqla. The power of the ashraf and the riverain groups was now completely crushed. However, the khalifa remained constantly afraid of conspiracies.

Abdallahi continued the jihad against Ethiopia (Christian) and Egypt (unreformed Islam). Ethiopia was invaded (1887–9), the ancient capital of Gondar was sacked, and the Emperor Yohannis IV was killed. But the Mahdists were unable to occupy Ethiopia because of determined resistance from the Christian population, and they were forced to withdraw. The Mahdist expedition against Egypt in 1889 ended in a crushing defeat for the Sudanese at Tushki, at the hands of the Anglo-Egyptian army.

Abdallahi's position became even more difficult with the failure of the harvest in 1889–90, the resulting famine and epidemics. Three great armies stationed in Darfur, at Gallabat on the Ethiopian border and at Dongola in the north, confounded the problem by their consumption of vast quantities of scarce corn. The transfer of the khalifa's kinsmen of the Ta'aisha to Omdurman made the food problem even more serious. They had been moved to the capital so that Abdallahi would have loyal supporters near him but, of course, they had to be fed. The arrival of thousands of Ta'aisha nomads caused considerable annoyance amongst the Khalifa's more settled supporters.

From 1890 Abdallahi was on the defensive against Anglo-Egyptian imperialism. As he came under increasing pressure his judgement deteriorated. A number of important officials, of whom he became suspicious, were executed. Some support was lost because of this. He withdrew himself more and more from the people. His earlier practice of appearing weekly at Friday prayers ceased and he only went four times a year. A great wall was built around the section of Omdurman where he lived. There can be little doubt that by the time of the British invasion (see Volume 2) Abdallahi's control over the state was not so great as it had been.

7
The Maghrib in the pre-colonial era

The Maghrib is the 'land of the sunset' stretching across North Africa from the borders of Egypt to the Atlantic coast. At the beginning of the nineteenth century two different systems of administration existed in this area. Morocco, under the Alawite dynasty, was independent. Farther to the east were the semi-independent Regencies of Algeria, Tunisia and Libya, which were officially part of the dominions of the Sultan of Turkey. In practice there was a clear division within all these countries between the coastal regions, and the interior where the Berbers remained fiercely independent. The rulers of Morocco, Algeria, Tunisia and Libya found themselves constantly struggling to extend their influence into the interior—a struggle which was almost always unsuccessful.

By 1840 a further political division had come into existence. In 1830 Charles X of France, attempting to save his throne, ordered the invasion of Algeria. The French forces soon defeated the Algerians and France began the process of consolidating her hold on the country. The growth of French influence in Algeria is dealt with in a later chapter: this chapter concerns itself with Morocco, Libya and Tunisia, which remained independent of European rule although European influence was increasingly felt in the nineteenth century. Inevitably the French conquest of Algeria had a considerable influence on the other states of the Maghrib.

Libya

Although Libya escaped European colonization until the early twentieth century it still felt the effects of imperialism. In 1835 the semi-independent Karamanli dynasty in Tripolitania was overthrown by the Turks. By 1842 the whole of Libya had been conquered by Turkey. It was divided into two provinces; in the east Cyrenaica and in the west Tripolitania. In Cyrenaica the governor was directly responsible to Istanbul, but in military matters, the administration of justice, and the collection of customs, Cyrenaica was attached to Tripolitania.

On the whole, little effort was made by the Ottoman Governors to develop the Libyan provinces. Their main concern was to ensure that France did not expand into Libya from her base in Algeria. Only one

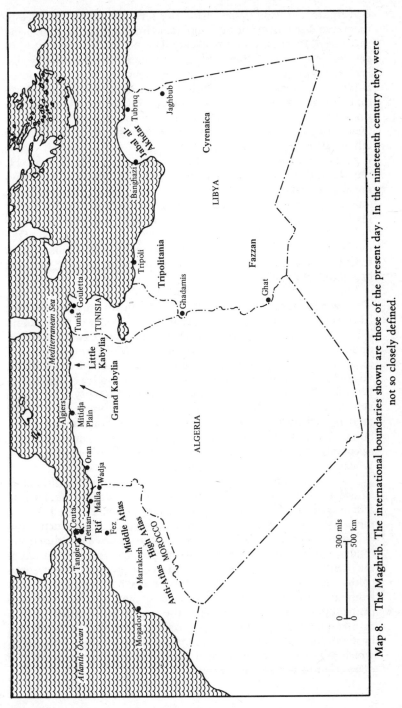

Map 8. The Maghrib. The international boundaries shown are those of the present day. In the nineteenth century they were not so closely defined.

103

Governor, 'Ali Rida Pasha, made any serious attempt at development. He was Governor of Tripolitania from 1867 to 1870. During this period he attempted to develop Tubruq as an important port, dredged the port of Banghazi and began to bore artesian wells. French technicians were used for this work and this inevitably roused British suspicions. Under British pressure the Ottoman Sultan recalled his governor to Istanbul. Although Libya was under Turkish rule effective administration was only established along the coast. In the interior a religious brotherhood, the Sanusiyya, came to play an influential role.

Muhammad Al-Sanusi was born in Algeria in about 1787. He founded the Sanusiyya in Mecca in 1837 with the objective of purifying and spreading Islam. In 1841 he travelled back to North Africa intending to return to Algeria. Finding that the French had occupied his country, he settled in Libya and in 1843 established a *zawiya* (religious centre) on Jabal Al-Akhdar. In 1856 the headquarters of the movement were moved to the desert oasis of Jaghbub. Muhammad's son, Sayyid al-Mahdi, succeeded him as leader of the Sanusiyya brotherhood in 1857.

Muhammad's influence, and that of his son, gradually spread. They were regarded as saints by the Bedouin amongst whom they had settled. As foreigners they were above the rivalry of the Bedouin tribes and so were able to arbitrate in their disputes. Zawiyas were set up in various areas and scholars, trained by Muhammad, administered justice and gave religious instruction to children. Schools, hospitals and poor houses were built in the zawiyas, which also became centres of agricultural and commercial activity. The Sanusi helped to revive the trans-Saharan trade route running from Wadai to Banghazi by founding zawiyas along it. By 1900 there were a hundred and forty-three zawiyas: forty-five were in Cyrenaica, twenty-five in Fazzan, while fifteen were distributed between Wadai, Kanem, Zinder and Timbuktu.

The Turks on the coast and the Sanusis in the interior ultimately agreed to work together. The Sanusis did not accept the Turkish Sultan as the real Caliph but realized that the presence of the Turks on the coast was one of the factors discouraging the French from expanding from Algeria. The Turks in return realized that the strong influence of the Sanusis over the desert peoples, and their hatred of the French, were matters which could not be ignored. The strength of the movement was recognized in 1856 when it was exempted from taxation. In 1879, when Cyrenaica became a completely independent province administratively, the Sanusis assisted the Turks in maintaining law and order and collecting taxes. The Sanusiyya brotherhood had become a unifying factor in Libya, something which was to be demonstrated clearly in 1911 when it led the opposition to the Italian invasion.

Tunisia

Tunisia was, like Libya, part of the Ottoman empire. In practice, however, it remained much more independent of the Ottoman Sultan than Libya. Its rulers, known as *Deys*, struggled to maintain their position against both the Ottomans and against the increasing French influence in the area. Before 1840 the Tunisian government had been forced to make concessions in the face of European pressure. In 1818 the dey agreed that he would never again arm corsair ships, and in 1830 he agreed to allow the European consuls to act in all cases involving European nationals. At the same time the deys felt increasingly the threat of Ottoman power, especially after the overthrow of the Karamanlis in Libya.

Ahmed Dey, who ruled from 1837 to 1855, was an able man who maintained the independence of his country and left it in an apparently strong financial position. Although he resisted the attempts of the Ottoman sultan to take greater control over Tunisia he did try to placate the sultan. Rich gifts were frequently sent to Istanbul and in 1854 Ahmed Dey even sent 4,000 Tunisian troops to fight with Turkey in the Crimea. Equally, while trying to resist the political influence of the sultan, the dey was determined to keep the religious ties with the sultanate. Not only was there great attachment in Tunisia to the Ottoman caliphate, but Ahmed also believed that maintaining religious ties with the sultan would enable him to resist French pressure.

Fear of Ottoman occupation also forced Ahmed to reform his military forces, and he began to expand the army in a way which the country could not really afford. In 1840 he founded a military school at the Bardo to train officers for the army, and ultimately a permanent force of 26,000 men was established.

The burden of expenditure for the army fell on the Tunisian peasant. New taxes were placed on olives and palm trees; excises were increased on agricultural produce, sheep and cattle. A quarter of the price of all sheep and cattle sold was taken by the government. Monopolies on the production and sale of soap, and on the sale of tobacco, salt and leather brought considerable income to the government. However these policies caused a serious decline in agriculture which in turn reduced the government's income. Although Ahmed left 120 million francs in the treasury when he died the economic situation of the country was serious.

Yet to the end of his reign Ahmed's control over the country remained firm. The army continued to support him and he won the goodwill of the religious leaders of his country. He made frequent donations to religious institutions, created new teaching posts at the Zaituna Mosque, and introduced *qadis* (Muslim judges) to the army.

The support of tribal chiefs was won by placing some of them in positions of authority.

During the short reign of Muhammad Dey (1855–9), the weaknesses of the Tunisian economy and the undermining of the dey's authority by European consuls began to show. Muhammad reduced the taxes on agricultural products. This brought an expansion of agriculture but it was not sufficiently large to increase the exports of cereals and olive oil to balance the imports. There was insufficient money to pay European merchants. Under threat from the consuls, Muhammad forced the Tunisians to provide him with a loan.

The Sfez incident showed how powerful the consuls had become. A Jew named Samuel Sfez quarrelled with a Muslim and cursed both him and the Muslim faith. The dey decided that here was an opportunity to obtain revenge on Sfez's employer, a French Jew who was under consular protection. After a trial before the religious judicial council, Sfez was executed. However, the French and British consuls exploited the affair to force concessions from the dey, with France even sending a naval squadron to back up her demands. Muhammad Dey was forced to grant foreigners the right to own land. He also agreed that Muslims and non-Muslims should be equal before the law.

Muhammad's successor, Muhammad Al-Sadiq Dey (1859–82) confirmed the concessions made to the consuls. He also agreed to the promulgation of a constitution by which a supreme council was set up. The first president of the council was Khair al-Din Pasha, a leading reformer, but he resigned when he found that the council had no real power and that the prime minister, Mustafa Khaznadar, continued to rule as autocratically as ever. In 1864 the constitution was suspended and Tunisia continued its slide into economic chaos.

Tunisia's economic affairs for much of this period were dominated by Khaznadar. In 1862, when the treasury was empty and no more loans could be obtained locally, Khaznadar floated a loan in Europe under extremely stringent conditions. He also connived with a European banker to embezzle some of the proceeds of the loan. Effectively, the dey received only a quarter of the nominal value of the loan. In order to service the debt, taxes were increased and in 1864 a tribal rebellion broke out, largely in opposition to the increase in the poll tax. A considerable amount had to be spent in putting down the rebellion. More loans were contracted in order to pay back previous ones and to pay interest, and by 1867 the economy was approaching collapse. After lengthy negotiations an international commission of French, Italian and British representatives was set up to run the Tunisian economy. With the formation of the International Financial Commission Tunisia lost her economic independence.

The executive committee of the International Financial Commission managed to consolidate the Tunisian debt at 125 million francs. The army was reduced from 26,000 to 8,000 and the military academy was closed down. Unfortunately Khaznadar remained prime minister until 1873 and managed to compromise the work of the Commission in a number of ways.

While the financial position of Tunisia improved European influence continued to grow. Italian migration into the country increased. The British consul, Richard Wood, won various concessions for businessmen: a railway line was to be built from Tunis to Bardo and Gouletta, and a gasworks to supply gas for the capital. The London Bank of Tunis was opened in October 1873.

There was some hope of improvement in the Tunisian administration when the reformer Khair al-Din became prime minister in 1873 and remained in the post until 1877. A few important changes were made. The system of tax collection was improved; a regular cleaning operation was mounted in the capital; the Sadiqiyya College with a modern curriculum was founded; some of the dey's worst extravagances were curbed. However Khair al-Din was impotent in the face of attempts by the consuls to increase their power. He resigned in 1877, just four years before France sent troops into the country, having failed to make any radical changes in the system of government in Tunisia.

Morocco

Like Ethiopia's emperors after 1855, Morocco's sultans had two major problems to face in the nineteenth century. One was to uphold central authority within the country itself, and the other was to preserve the country's independence from foreign invaders. Morocco was divided into the *bilad al-makhzan* (the friendly country)—roughly the regions of Fez and Marrakesh, which acknowledged the Sultan's authority and paid taxes to the central government—and the *bilad as-siba* (the unfriendly country), roughly the mountain and desert regions such as the Rif in the north and the Atlas and the oases in the south dominated by provincial nobles or nomads, where the tribesmen refused to pay taxes. We must not think however, that the two parts of the country were constantly in conflict. There was, in fact, considerable cultural and economic interaction. Even those who refused to pay taxes accepted the spiritual authority of the sultan.

Sultan Mawlay Abdul-Rahman (1822–59) was forced to reconsider Morocco's attitude to Europeans by the French invasion of neighbouring Algeria. Until 1830 the Moroccan attitude had been that Europeans should be shunned and that their activities were of no interest to the Moroccan government. The resistance of Amir Abdul-Qadir to French expansion in Algeria roused great enthusiasm in Morocco, and made it difficult for the sultan not to support him. The lack of control over the northern frontier with Algeria allowed Abdul-Qadir to import arms through Moroccan territory. The French made reprisal raids against Morocco, and Mogador and Tangier were bombarded. In 1844 on the Plain of Isly near Wajda the French inflicted a crushing defeat on the sultan, who had sent an army to resist French encroachments.

It was fortunate for Morocco, after her defeat, that the British were opposed to any single European country taking control of Morocco. Britain did not wish to have a powerful country controlling the territory across the straits from Gibraltar. Although France considerably expanded her economic activities in Morocco after the Battle of Isly, the revolution in France in 1848 turned attention away from North Africa to French internal affairs. The British consul began to encourage Mawlay Abdul-Rahman to defy the French. British merchants had long dominated the Moroccan import and export trade and the trouble in France in 1848 enabled them to maintain their control. The 1856 commercial treaty with Britain removed many of the restrictions on European businessmen and abolished the Moroccan government's monopoly over certain major imports and exports. Britain then managed to establish a monopoly of trade in merino wool, iron ore and phosphates.

The defeat by France at Isly not only caused problems for the sultan in his relations with Europe, but it also provoked considerable internal unrest. The tribes of Morocco, even when they were disobeying the sultan, expected him to defend them from the infidel Christians. Clearly he had failed to do this. The result was widespread rebellion which the sultan had difficulty in crushing. Inevitably this further weakened his international standing and undermined his economic position.

Rivalry between European powers also created problems for the sultan. In the mid-1850s Spain became very concerned at the growing British influence in Morocco, believing that the British were trying to exclude all other European powers from the country. Spain accordingly began to make demands on the Moroccan government. Therefore, in 1859 the sultan offered Spain some land around the Spanish-controlled port of Malila, but this was not regarded as a sufficiently large concession. When a group of tribesmen attacked and demolished newly constructed fortifications at the Spanish port of Ceuta, Spain used this as an excuse to land troops in Morocco and occupy Tetuan. The new sultan, Muhammad (1859–73) was thus faced at the onset of his reign with foreign military intervention and the almost inevitable internal rebellions which followed it.

By the Treaty of Tetuan Muhammad was forced to pay a huge indemnity, and to enlarge the Spanish enclaves of Ceuta and Malila. The sultan was only able to pay the indemnity by contracting a loan floated in London. Slowly, Morocco was becoming more and more economically dependent on Europe. During the rest of the reign of Muhammad the size and the activities of the European community in Morocco expanded. It was a community which, because of the concessions granted to European countries, was virtually independent of Moroccan law.

Mawlay Hasan (1873–94) who succeeded Muhammad understood the causes of the decline of his authority at home and abroad. He made serious attempts to reform his country. The eighteen large provinces were broken up into 330 small administrative units under central government control; a new uniform system of taxation was introduced; an attempt was made to reform the army, where tribal contingents were replaced by a fixed levy of recruits from each of the major cities. Some of the judicial authority of the sultan was delegated. Military campaigns were conducted against areas of the country which were virtually independent of the sultan. Unfortunately many of these reforms were not fully implemented. The Moroccan treasury could not afford the weapons needed for army modernization and the discipline of the troops was bad. Students sent to Spain to complete their education were often unable to do so because of inadequate elementary training in Morocco. The fixed rate of exchange for the Moroccan currency, instituted by Mawlay Hasan, was ignored by European merchants.

The failure of the sultan to bring real change is perhaps exemplified best in the Madrid Conference of 1880. The sultan had attempted to end the system of consular protection of foreign nationals by negotiation with the diplomats in Tangier, but this attempt failed. The Madrid Conference was called after the failure of the negotiations in Morocco but only Britain and Spain supported the sultan. The result was that Mawlay Hasan had not only failed to end the system of protection but had given it international recognition by raising the issue at the Conference.

Slowly but steadily, European economic penetration and political influence were preparing the way for the ultimate conquest of Morocco in 1912.

8
The European imperialist overture: (1) explorers and missionaries

Overview

Until quite recently it was common to look on the European explorers of Africa as 'discoverers' of unknown places, and on European missionaries before 1885 as ground-breaking pioneers in the task of Christian evangelization in Africa. However, European expeditions to the interior, whether to explore or to spread the Gospel, were

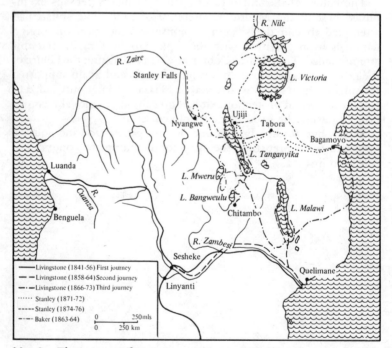

Map 9.   The journeys of Livingstone, Baker and Stanley.

inconceivable without African co-operation. The European explorers relied heavily on Africans and Arabs in a number of ways: principally, the Africans and Arabs guided the white men along their old trade routes—African caravan leaders virtually organized the expeditions for the white men. An example is Sidi Bombay, a Yao who was enslaved at the age of twelve and taken to India, freed there and returned to East Africa to work as a caravan leader for the Sultan of Zanzibar. Sidi served under Speke in his journeys to the source of the Nile in 1857–8 and 1860–2, and later under Stanley and Cameron. Sidi was a brilliant organizer, a skilful interpreter and an astute ambassador in negotiations between his expeditions' leaders and local rulers.

Africans also carried supplies for the explorers, and local rulers provided protection for them. Tippu Tip in eastern Zaire regularly succoured European travellers in difficulties, including Livingstone, Cameron and Stanley.

It should be emphasized that African and Arab traders often undertook great journeys by themselves. Some time between 1800 and 1810 two African traders, unfortunately unknown, crossed the continent from Angola to Mozambique; Arabs completed the crossing from Zanzibar to Benguela in Angola in 1854. Livingstone's transcontinental journey was thus not the first to be made although it was the first made by a white man.

There can be no doubt that, unlike nineteenth century Africans with their rapidly expanding but still relatively limited geographical horizons, the European explorers were able to establish the connections between local African geographical facts and a larger whole. For instance, Speke's discovery that Lake Victoria was the source of the Nile and his establishment of the link between that lake and Egypt was an important addition to all human knowledge. Speke was more than just the first tourist to see Lake Victoria.

It is not generally realized quite how important a role the European explorers played as precursors of the European political scramble for Africa. Not only did they open up the interior to other Europeans in a purely geographical sense, they also stimulated imperialism, be it economic, cultural or political. Most of the explorers favoured colonialism. Livingstone, as early as 1856, proposed a British colony in the heart of Central Africa. Many of the explorers became colonial officials after the scramble, notably Stanley, Johnston, De Brazza, Peters and Wissmann. The colonialist views of explorers were widely expounded in books, journals and newspapers and at public meetings. Stanley's book *In Darkest Africa*, with its openly pro-imperialist message, sold 150,000 copies in the British edition alone.

A missionary–explorer: Livingstone

David Livingstone was born at Blantyre near Glasgow in March 1813. At the age of ten he went to work in a cotton mill. He worked there until 1836 but spent his spare time improving his education by reading and attending evening classes. By 1836 he was sufficiently well qualified to enter university to train as a doctor. He volunteered for work with the London Missionary Society and set sail for South Africa in 1840.

Livingstone initially went to Kuruman, the mission station founded by Robert Moffat. He remained there for a number of years, but all the time wanted to move farther north to areas which had not been evangelized. Ultimately he was given permission to found a station at Mbotsa amongst the Bakgatla where he remained from 1844 to 1845. In the latter year he began work amongst the Bakwena, one of the Tswana peoples. Sechele, the Bakwena chief, showed himself to be receptive to Livingstone's teaching. Eventually he desired to be baptized but there was the familiar problem of polygamy. This was not merely a personal problem but also a political one. Sechele had married the daughters of a number of subordinate chiefs in order to bind them to himself and so encourage greater unity among his people. Ultimately Sechele sent away all but one of his wives and he was baptized in 1848. Later he lapsed into traditional religion for a period but after due repentance was received again as a Christian. This time his conversion was permanent. Surprisingly, although the chief had become a Christian his example was not followed by his people.

While working amongst the Tswana Livingstone's attention was constantly drawn northwards. He made a number of journeys from Kolobeng, his station, seeing Lake Ngami and meeting with Sebetwane, the Kololo king. During these journeys two important ideas developed in his mind. One of them was that the Zambesi might form the highway into the interior of Africa which would make missionary work much easier. The route from South Africa was far too dangerous and inhospitable. The second idea was that if articles of European manufacture were supplied to the interior by means of legitimate commerce then the slave trade would become impossible. Livingstone determined to explore the country to see how feasible these ideas were. Livingstone's first two great journeys can only be understood if his ideas are kept in mind. Although he made geographical observations of great value his primary purpose was always the spread of Christianity and the ending of the slave trade.

Setting out in June 1852, Livingstone reached Linyanti the following year and was welcomed by Sekeletu the new Kololo king. The king provided Livingstone with twenty-seven men and he set off towards the west coast. He moved north-westwards, passed the confluence of the upper Zambesi and Kabompo Rivers, and moved on to the Zaire-Zambesi watershed. He made his way over the hilly plateau towards Luanda seeing everywhere more evidence of the slave trade. He finally staggered into Luanda in May 1854 and then spent four months recovering his health.

Livingstone then set off back to Linyanti and from there continued his journey to the east, becoming the first European to see the Victoria Falls. He then crossed the Tonga plateau and moved into the lower Luangwa valley. Here again he found evidence of the slave trade. Moving on he came to the old Portuguese post of Zumbo, and then journeyed to Tete. He completed his trans-continental journey by sailing down the Zambesi. His travels had taken four years, added greatly to Europe's knowledge of Africa and been accomplished only with the great help of his Kololo porters.

Livingstone's second journey of exploration was made possible by financial assistance from the British government. He studied the navigability of the lower Zambesi and found his hopes of easy access dashed by the Cabora Bassa rapids. Turning to the Shire River he eventually reached Lake Malawi. Once again he was shocked by the ravages of the slave trade. He believed that a small steamer on the river above the Murchison Cataracts would quite effectively stamp out the slave trade. Events were to prove that Livingstone's estimate of the impact of legitimate trade on the slave trade was not quite so great as the explorer had expected. Slave trading proved to be very resilient.

In 1860 Livingstone set off to take his Kololo porters back home. He was greeted by news of the disastrous attempt by the London Missionary Society to set up a mission station at Linyanti. This move had been encouraged by Livingstone and the LMS had sent the Price and Helmore families to start work. However, disease soon took its toll. Of the four adults and seven children who made up the party only Mr Price and two Helmore children survived. Equally disappointing to Livingstone was the failure of the attempt by the Universities Mission to Central Africa to establish work in the Shire Valley (see page 127). Rather unfairly Livingstone branded the mission's withdrawal from the Shire a 'cowardly retreat'. In 1863 Livingstone received notice of the withdrawal of his expedition by the British government and he returned to England arriving in 1864.

Livingstone's last journey was the longest at least in time. It continued from 1866 until his death in 1873. It also had a much more specifically geographical emphasis to it than the earlier journeys. Livingstone wanted to find the source of the Nile; he wished to define more clearly the watershed of Central Africa; if possible he would find the source of the Zaire and trace that river to the sea. During this journey Livingstone travelled along the Rovuma, journeyed again along the Shire and travelled the length of Lake Malawi. He saw the horrors of the slave trade more abundantly than ever before. He was now in country which was the centre of the Arab trade to Zanzibar, the Persian Gulf and the Red Sea. Everywhere there were signs of devastation from slave raiding. In 1867 Livingstone visited Lakes Bangweulu and Mweru. Retracing his steps to Lake Tanganyika he rested at Ujiji then journeyed to the Lualaba. There he witnessed first hand a slave raid in which over three hundred people were shot to death. Returning to Ujiji he was visited by Henry Morton Stanley but refused to travel to the coast with him. Further attempts to chart the source of the Lualaba failed and gradually his health failed. In April 1873 he managed to reach Chitambo and died there on May 1.

It is not the least remarkable part of Livingstone's story that three of his servants carried his body to the coast. Susi, Chuma and Jacob Wainwright knew the risks they were taking. In many areas the carrying of a body would have been regarded as bringing misfortune on the people living there and the three men would have been in danger of their lives. With great bravery they took the body to Bagamoyo and handed it to the acting British consul there, but with gross ingratitude and a total failure to appreciate the service the three Africans had rendered, the consul failed to offer them even a passage to Zanzibar with the body. Fortunately the Church Missionary Society tried to make amends when it paid for Wainwright to be present at Livingstone's funeral in Westminster Abbey.

What were Livingstone's achievements? It has been fashionable over the past few years to sneer at him as a hypocrite and a racialist. He has been labelled as arrogant, neglectful of his wife and family and a mere tourist. There can be little doubt that Livingstone had his faults and did often find it difficult to get along with his fellow Europeans. Nonetheless his achievements were considerable.

During his lifetime he inspired the foundation of the Universities Mission to Central Africa. On his death the United Free Church of Scotland set up its mission at Livingstonia in Malawi. Not to be outdone the Church of Scotland established a mission at Blantyre. Many men were inspired to volunteer for missionary work as a result of Livingstone's example.

Possibly just as important as the establishing of missions were the new concepts which Livingstone brought to missionary work. He was convinced that the missionary had to be more than a preacher going about with a Bible under his arm. He believed that commerce must be encouraged as this would undermine the slave trade and bring Africa into the community of nations. Commerce and Christianity must go hand in hand. But Livingstone can hardly be blamed for the exploitation which often followed in the wake of European commerce.

There is little doubt that Livingstone also helped indirectly to prepare the way for imperialism. Livingstone spread his views by means of his books, such as *Missionary Travels and Researches in South Africa* (1857), which sold tens of thousands of copies, and in his letters, despatches and articles, many of which appeared in newspapers and magazines. He therefore played a major, direct part in forming and preparing public opinion for large-scale British involvement in Africa. Indirectly, he exercised a considerable influence on the events of the Scramble for Africa. Livingstone's death in 1873 activated Stanley's great trans-continental journey from Zanzibar to the mouth of the Zaire between 1874 and 1877, which led to the mapping of the Zaire river, and the active interest of King Leopold II of Belgium and De Brazza of France in the region.

Livingstone had gone to Africa in the days when European knowledge of the continent was sparse. He greatly added to that knowledge. He also went there in the days when Europeans regarded Africans as being much their inferiors. Livingstone realized in his travels that Europe was technologically superior, and he also believed that European civilization was superior to that of Africa. This view he never changed. However, he did try to point out that apart from colour, Africans had the same attributes as Europeans and that both races were equal in God's eyes. It was a view which few were prepared to accept and in the latter part of the century, as the period of colonialism arrived, it was a view that was flatly contradicted by many.

Livingstone has one undeniable and imperishable achievement to his credit: the abolition of the slave trade by Zanzibar. Livingstone's writings and speeches on the horrors he witnessed at first hand in the east and central African interior, more than any other man's activities, stirred British humanitarian interests to put pressure on the British government to enforce abolition of the trade by the Sultan of Zanzibar in 1873, the year of Livingstone's death. Unfortunately the great missionary-explorer was dead before this occurred.

Discoverer-explorers: Heinrich Barth and Samuel Baker

One of the greatest of nineteenth-century European travellers in Africa was the German, Barth. Between 1849 and 1855 he journeyed from Tripoli across the Sahara to the Western Sudan, where he travelled from Timbuktu in the west to Sokoto, Bornu and Lake Chad in the east and Adamawa to the south. His purpose was to survey old trade routes and to make treaties on behalf of the British government which financed him, but the treaties Barth made were not followed up. As a discoverer, his achievements lay less in survey-ing centuries-old Muslim trade routes than in discovering African civilization. In his *Travels and Discoveries* he recorded much of the rich and complex history of the lands he passed through, wrote very detailed and scientific descriptions of the lands he saw and showed a deep understanding of African society.

An example of a discoverer-explorer who completely lacked Barth's priceless quality of empathy was the insensitive Samuel Baker, an English landowner who became bored with running his estates in England and Ceylon and first came to Africa as a big-game hunter, later turning to exploration. When he arrived in Bunyoro in 1864 he was the first European to see the lake (Mobutu) which he named Albert, after Queen Victoria's late husband. But the main effect of Baker's first expedition to Bunyoro was to sow the seeds of misunderstanding between the lake kingdom and Britain.

Baker was not welcomed by the Omukama of Bunyoro, Kamurasi, who at first delayed him at the frontier, then delayed seeing him, next delayed giving him permission to go to the lake, and finally, as Baker was leaving, marooned him temporarily on an island in the Nile. Baker could not have guessed at Kamurasi's motives and actions, since shortly before Baker's arrival Sudanese traders allied to Kamurasi's rival for the throne, Ruyonga, and also claiming to be friends of the explorer Speke (who had left Bunyoro in 1862) carried out a large raid in Bunyoro, killing three hundred people. Baker unfortunately had also claimed to be a friend of Speke. Secondly, Kamurasi could not believe that Baker had come simply to look at a lake and then go away, especially as he had many guns. Kamurasi was convinced that Baker came as a conqueror, and that he had brought Mrs Baker along to provide sons to succeed him. Baker's impatience and angry moods at the delays, and his clearly expressed contempt for Africans in general and for the Banyoro leaders in particular, did nothing to help the cause of mutual under-standing. Baker returned to Bunyoro in 1872, this time as an imperialist.

An imperialist-explorer: Henry Morton Stanley

Henry Morton Stanley first achieved fame when he carried out a newspaper scoop for his paper, the *New York Herald*, by finding Livingstone at Ujiji on Lake Tanganyika after the missionary explorer had been missing in the interior for several years. This first expedition of Stanley's, in 1871–2, was an old-fashioned affair, in the tradition of the fairly peaceful expeditions of the recent past. Not so Stanley's three other journeys into the African interior.

Stanley's second expedition, from 1874 to 1877, across the continent from Zanzibar to the Zaire mouth, his third in 1879–80, when he began work in lower Zaire for King Leopold II of Belgium, and his fourth, the Emin Pasha Relief Expedition of 1887–90, across the continent from west to east were all characterized by his new semi-military methods. Stanley was the first explorer to rely on large, well-equipped, well-armed columns, and ruthless military action against local populations who showed any hostility towards or suspicion of the expedition. The very size of his columns made necessary the intimidation of local peoples, who mistook Stanley and his party for slave traders. Without intimidation it would have been impossible to obtain food. The second expedition, for example, was marked by military action against resisting African societies such as the Bumbire islanders of Lake Victoria and numerous small communities in the Zaire Basin.

The second expedition was the best publicized east–west transcontinental journey made by a European and one of the most significant African journeys of the 1870s. First, Stanley's sojourn in Buganda in 1875 resulted in the sending of European Christian missionaries to Buganda. This in turn was one of the factors leading to British colonial occupation of Uganda and Kenya. Secondly, between 1875 and 1877 Stanley charted the main stream of the Zaire River. This not only opened up to Europe the general possibility of exploiting the economic potential of the Zaire Basin, but led directly to the actual beginnings of Leopold's imperial activities in Zaire. Stanley was to become one of Leopold's agents in Zaire between 1879 and 1885.

In his attitude to Christianity Stanley was a materialist and a realist. He understood that Mutesa, the Kabaka of Buganda, was impressed with Christianity not because of spiritual interest but because of admiration for the white man's technological and military power. He believed that if European Christian missionaries were to be successful in Africa they needed to be linked with European commercial and military power, and specifically with colonial occupation, which would enable Africans to associate the white man's religion with the material benefits of contact with him.

Stanley's last expedition, to rescue Emin Pasha, was an anti-climax after his second journey and his imperialist work in Zaire. It was as futile and as unnecessary as his first expedition to find Livingstone. Livingstone did not need to be found—he well knew where he was. Nor did Emin need to be rescued. Emin, the Governor of that remnant of Egyptian Equatoria not overrun by the Mahdists, was quite capable, with his force of 'loyal' Sudanese under Selim Bey, of defending his base at Kavalli's on Lake Mobutu from the Mahdists, who were preoccupied with Egypt and Ethiopia. In fact, the men of Stanley's relief expedition arrived at Kavalli's in such a state of destitution and sickness that Emin could be said to have rescued his rescuers. When Stanley and his men were fit again, Stanley insisted that Emin Pasha accompany him to Zanzibar. Emin, a renowned ornithologist, simply wanted Stanley to take back to London his collection of several thousand stuffed tropical African birds and give them to a museum. To Emin's disgust, Stanley left the birds behind and took Emin instead, though Selim Bey and most of the Sudanese soldiers stayed.

The European background to Christian missionary activity

The late eighteenth century witnessed a religious revival in Europe which emphasized the duty of the individual Christian to convert his fellows. This revived interest in conversion brought about a resurgence of European Christian missionary activity in non-Christian lands and especially in Africa. The 'Dark Continent' was erroneously considered to be lacking in religion and, therefore, a land where Christianity could be written on a blank slate. The missionaries also genuinely believed they had a spiritual duty to convert the Africans. One may question the attitudes of the missionaries to African religion and to African culture in general, but one cannot deny their sincerity and courage, for many of them gave their lives in order to spread their faith.

The modern European missionary movement really began in 1795, when the London Missionary Society (LMS) was founded. The LMS stimulated the creation of a similar Anglican organization, the Church Missionary Society (CMS), which in time drew many Protestant recruits from the European continent. Fifty years later the LMS further stimulated Anglican missionary activity, when the LMS missionary Livingstone directly inspired the Anglican Universities Mission to Central Africa (UMCA) in the late 1850s. For their finances the new Protestant missionary organizations did not rely on state assistance but on local associations in Europe. To a large extent, the missionary societies depended on the rise of a literate and church-going Christian middle class in a rapidly industrializing Europe.

Protestant evangelization in Africa alarmed the Catholic Church and stimulated the Catholic missionary movement. The French-based Association for the Propagation of the Faith set up an organization for local collections in four hundred Catholic dioceses in Europe and America, and provided many of the funds of the new Catholic missionary societies, such as the Holy Ghost Fathers and the White Fathers.

Whether Protestant or Catholic, the nineteenth-century European missionaries, with hardly an exception, accepted the equation of the advance of Christianity with the progress of western capitalism. They believed that the introduction of capitalism to Africa would end African poverty. They looked on European commerce as a weapon against both the slave trade and traditional African society, both of which would need to be destroyed—or at least seriously weakened—if mission work were to have a hope of real success. They felt that if African traditional society were subjected to alien influence in at least one form—legitimate commerce—then it would more readily absorb an alien religion like Christianity. The missionaries also hoped to spread European culture throughout much of Africa. Like most other Europeans of the time they assumed the superiority of European culture to African, and believed that the spread of European culture and Christianity would inevitably go hand in hand.

The African response to the arrival of Christian missions

In some African societies the rulers allowed missionaries to work, gave them positive encouragement, and many people were converted to Christianity. In other societies the rulers allowed the missionaries to settle in their lands for non-religious reasons, but often placed effective barriers to the work of evangelization. In others, missionaries were banned from even entering the country. It is difficult to generalize about this varied response to the missionaries, a response that differed from community to community and even within communities. However, some common factors do emerge.

First, some rulers welcomed missionaries because they accepted the gospel message. Such men included Khama of the Ngwato and the rulers of Bonny, including the king, George Dappa Pepple, and the leading House head, Oko Jumbo. Such Christian rulers led Christian revolutions in their own states. Some rulers like Mutesa of Buganda and Lewanika of Bulozi welcomed missionaries as part of a policy of diplomatic alignment with European military and political power. They allowed some of their subjects to be converted to the 'white man's religion', though they stood aloof from it themselves. Still other African leaders associated with the missionaries for economic benefit, especially guns, which they rarely got. Some rulers found missionaries useful as honorary secretaries, in the way Mirambo used the British missionary Southon.

More often than not, African rulers kept the missionaries out of their areas. Generally, they feared that the white man would disturb the traditional way of life on which their authority depended. In both Dahomey and Jaja's Opobo the missionaries were banned because it was felt that they claimed spiritual superiority over the local ruler, who was also the traditional religious leader. Such claims made them political as well as religious leaders in the eyes of the rulers. Converts were seen as disloyal to the ruler.

The converts in pre-colonial times were generally 'marginal men' in African society. They were often slaves or freed slaves, or refugees. In West Africa most missionaries were Africans from the freed slave population of Sierra Leone and their converts were generally Yoruba war refugees or Niger delta slaves. In East Africa the converts were mainly freed and runaway slaves who came to live in mission villages at or near the coast. In Malawi, converts were often beleaguered peoples in weak communities who turned to the missionaries as alternative 'chiefs', who would protect them against powerful enemies. In a few rare cases converts were made among groups of standing in society, such as the court pages of Buganda, but as we shall see, there were peculiar local conditions in Buganda which account for this. It was normal for Africans before the colonial era to reject Christianity, and perhaps polygamy was the strongest reason for this rejection. Many Africans thought that the white man's religion was no more than a trick to make them give up their wives. For an African man, the number of his wives was an indication of his wealth. On a less personal level, rulers of comparatively large states, like Moshweshwe and Mutesa, could not embrace a religion that required them to abandon wives who represented alliances with, and helped to ensure the loyalty of, the localities.

Various other factors also discouraged Africans from accepting Christianity. One was the division which they saw between various Christian groups. The division between Catholics and Protestants was particularly noticeable. Surprisingly in Buganda—where these divisions were to lead to civil war—the progress of the gospel did not appear to be hindered. In much of Africa Christianity made less progress than Islam. The reason for this was probably that Christianity demanded a much greater theological understanding and commitment before converts were accepted than did Islam. Converts to Islam initially needed only to accept a number of very basic propositions. Their deeper understanding came after their acceptance of Islam. Islam also had the advantage that it did not demand an end to polygamy.

However, despite the difficulties and problems, the groundwork for the later rapid expansion of Christianity had been laid in many areas before the European Scramble for Africa.

Christian missions in West Africa

Christianity spread more rapidly in West Africa than in any other region of the continent in the half century before the Scramble. By 1900 there were, in West Africa, 29 missions, 518 foreign missionaries, 2,538 African missionaries, nearly 2,000 churches and mission stations and nearly 250,000 Christians. Nearly all Christian activity was heavily concentrated along narrow strips of coast under close British political or commercial domination.

In Sierra Leone the great majority of the freed slaves and their descendants embraced Christianity, and, on the whole, they did so enthusiastically. Their own gods had abandoned them and failed to protect them in their homeland. The historian of Sierra Leone, Christopher Fyfe, has described how they came up from the hold of the slaveship like Jonah from the whale, cut off from their old life, ready to be re-born into a new. They felt grateful to the white man for freeing them and readily adopted his religion. In particular, they were thankful to the English and joined the Church of England in vast numbers. Sierra Leone became more strongly Anglican than even England itself. The colony was administered on the parish basis, each parish supervised by a clergyman, and the CMS provided not only churches but schools in each parish. Sierra Leone was, to a large extent, a theocratic society.

The Creoles of Sierra Leone played the major role in Christianizing the lower Niger and parts of Yorubaland, where nearly all of them had their origins. Two of the greatest black Sierra Leonian missionaries were Bishop Samuel Ajayi Crowther and Bishop James (Holy) Johnson.

Crowther was born in about 1808 in Yorubaland. He was captured in a slave raid, sold to Portuguese traders and freed in mid-Atlantic by a British warship in 1821. He was baptized in 1825, and in 1827 joined the new CMS training institute at Fourah Bay, where he trained as a school-teacher. In 1841 he went on the British government's Niger expedition, and wrote his famous *Journal* about it. In 1843 he was ordained as an Anglican minister, and in 1845 went to Abeokuta in Yorubaland as a missionary. Between 1854 and 1857 he went on two more voyages up the Niger, helping to establish missions at Igbebe, at the Niger–Benue confluence, and at Onitsha. He made a deep study of several African languages, translated some books of the Bible into Yoruba, and published Yoruba, Igbo and Nupe grammars. In 1864 Crowther was consecrated Bishop of an immense Diocese covering West Africa from the Equator to the Senegal River, with the exception of Lagos, the Gold Coast and Sierra Leone. He continued to hold this post until his death in 1891. Crowther was the first black African Protestant bishop. His appointment was the high point of the mid-nineteenth century era of 'Ethiopianism' in the Anglican Church: that is, the idea that self-governing black African churches should be evolved. Ethiopianism was the policy of the Reverend Henry Venn, Secretary of the Church Missionary Society from 1842 to 1872. It was a policy which lost momentum after the retirement of Venn. The new CMS leaders still believed in self-governing African churches but felt that these were many years away.

Venn had hoped that Crowther would oversee the work of the CMS both on the Niger and in Yorubaland and Crowther was involved in missions to both areas. However, the Niger Mission took most of his time and attention. Throughout his period of office he faced problems of communications, of discipline and misunderstanding but it was a period when Christianity gained a firm hold on the Niger.

When Crowther became bishop there was a flourishing mission station at Onitsha and another at Igbebe. The Onitsha mission gradually expanded to the surrounding areas but the most remarkable expansion was in the Niger delta. A station was founded in Bonny in 1864. In 1868 the mission was invited to Brass where there were mass conversions between 1876 and 1879. Kalabari and Okrika received missions in 1874 and 1879 respectively.

Crowther's missionary technique was to build a mission house a little way from the town. He also emphasized the school as a means of evangelizing. He introduced the Niger Mission to new areas by getting the rulers and elders interested in education. This had to be paid for and became a useful source of income for the mission. Crowther was always more reliant than European missionaries on local finance. This arose from the concept of a self-supporting, self-propagating African Church. Education certainly played a major role in the ready reception given to the mission in many areas.

The Niger Mission inevitably faced problems from traditional religious authorities once Christianity began to spread. In Bonny, where the worship of the monitor lizard was publicly renounced in 1867, there was a revulsion of feeling against Christianity. In November 1875 Joshua Hart became a martyr when he was thrown into the river and battered to death with paddles. There were further persecutions in Bonny in 1881–6 but in 1889 after a short devotional service the 'Juju House' in the town was pulled down. Only forty years earlier King William Pepple had asserted that Bonny people would never consent to their Juju House being destroyed.

As the man responsible for the Niger Mission, Crowther tried to act as a pastor to his agents. Unfortunately he was far too gentle a man to stamp his authority firmly on the Mission. Where his agents had been guilty of some offence against Christian morality and teaching he readily forgave them. If they showed repentance their punishment was usually little more than a brief suspension from duty. Eventually Crowther was severely criticized by white missionaries for his leniency. The European secretaries to the Niger Mission wished to be far more ruthless than Crowther, who believed that charges against a man must be proved before he was dismissed. The Europeans felt that suspicions were sufficient for a man to be dismissed as a missionary. Ultimately Crowther was regarded as being rather like an over-indulgent father protecting his children. Crowther also came to be criticized by newly-arriving white missionaries because they believed he was over-emphasizing education and civilization, and not giving sufficient emphasis to preaching.

Special enquiries were made in 1890 into the activities of Crowther's agents. The result was the division of the Niger Mission into two, the Sudan and Upper Niger Mission and the delta and Lower Niger Mission. Crowther had by then resigned from the committee of the Niger Mission, largely because his authority was being denied by a number of new European missionaries. Europeans were gradually turning from guides to rulers not only in the administration of Nigeria but also in the Church. However, the foundations laid by Crowther formed the base upon which Christianity was built in Nigeria.

Another important African church leader of the nineteenth century was James Johnson, who was born of freed slave parents near Freetown in 1837. He was educated at the CMS Grammar School in Freetown and at Fourah Bay, and in 1863 was ordained in the Anglican Church. From 1863 to 1873, when he was attached to a Freetown parish, he became an associate of Blyden in an African cultural liberation movement. Johnson wanted the Church to liberalize its attitude to African culture and customs, though until the late 1890s he was a strong opponent of any accommodation with polygamy. 'Holy' Johnson, so called because of his unfailing asceticism and passionately Christian personal life, was sent to Lagos in 1873, and thence to the Abeokuta mission in Yorubaland. He made a considerable number of converts amongst the Yoruba. Even when he was withdrawn from the area the numerous new stations which he had set up largely survived because his far-sighted self-support programme had left them on a sound financial footing.

From 1880 to 1900 Johnson was pastor of St Paul's Breadfruit Church, in Lagos. As colonialism spread rapidly at the end of the nineteenth century he became even more strident in his African cultural assertiveness. He advocated the reform of the liturgy to suit local conditions. Like Crowther he was impressed by the 'native airs' in the mission at Otta, in Yorubaland. There, scriptural compositions of the people were being sung to traditional tunes. Johnson hoped that such singing and composition would spread to other mission stations. He encouraged Christian parents to baptize their children with local names. While not wishing to change fundamental Christian teaching, Johnson believed that the Church must recognize those things that were good in local culture and adapt them for use in Christian worship. He did not believe that a man needed to become completely divorced from his culture to become a Christian, although he would have to abandon some parts of that culture. Johnson was often misunderstood by European missionaries, but he was an ardent Anglican, and he never seceded from that Church though many of his colleagues and flock did so. He never openly opposed European political rule in Africa, though he bravely condemned Governor Carter of Lagos's expedition against Ijebu in 1892. Johnson served out his final years, 1900–17, as assistant bishop of the Niger, under a white bishop, and was probably more successful as a missionary than Crowther.

Until the era of European political occupation, Christian converts in West Africa were almost entirely drawn from the lowest level of society—like the first Christians in Asia and Europe. In Bonny and southern Igboland the first converts were invariably slaves. In Onitsha, Asaba and Obosi on the Niger they were usually either slaves or alien strangers who had little or no chance of achieving status in traditional society. It is true that King George Dappa Pepple of Bonny was a sincere Christian, but Bonny's House heads supported the establishment of the Mission there not for religious reasons but because they associated Europeans with literacy—most useful in business correspondence and accounting. Bonny's leaders even provided half the cost of the new mission, but when they realized that missionary teachings undermined Bonny's culture, they turned against Christianity and, as we have seen, began to persecute it. Christianity survived the various persecutions of the pre-colonial period, and in some areas obtained a firm foothold before the period of European rule.

Christian missions in pre-colonial southern Africa

The response of southern and central African rulers to Christian missions before the Scramble was largely dictated, as in West Africa, by local political realities and the usefulness or otherwise of the new faith to them. There were exceptions, like the genuine conversion of Khama of the Ngwato, but in general rulers welcomed missionaries primarily for their value in trade or diplomacy.

French Protestant missionaries of the Paris Evangelical Society came to Lesotho in 1833. Moshweshwe adroitly used them to assert his control over outlying communities by allowing them to build their stations in such areas. He encouraged their leader, Eugene Casalis, to inflate his territorial claims against the claims of rival southern Sotho leaders and used the Frenchmen as diplomatic correspondents who would provide him with knowledge of events in the white world and interpret his interests to the Cape colonial government. When Moshweshwe sought British protection for Lesotho in 1868 missionary influence was important in obtaining this protection (see Chapter 9).

The French made very few converts in Lesotho. Moshweshwe was tolerant towards Christianity, even granting divorces to some of his converted wives. He showed a deep personal interest in the Bible and in Christ as a suffering saviour, but he was never baptized. There was the familiar obstacle of polygamy: he had over a hundred wives and would not abandon them. Moreover, Moshweshwe still saw considerable value in African religion, and in old age he became more concerned than ever before in traditional Sotho spirit worship.

Wesleyan missionaries from England exercised a deep influence over the Seleka-Rolong, Moshweshwe's neighbours at Thaba Nchu near the Modder River. The Wesleyans persuaded the Seleka ruler, Moroka, who needed better land, to settle at Thaba Nchu with his followers on land which the mission had acquired. The Seleka were Christianized to a much greater degree than any other southern Sotho group. However, in their positive reaction to Christianity they were untypical of southern Sotho response as a whole.

The Tswana are renowned for an early and ready acceptance of Christianity, but the Christian revolution in Botswana was largely confined to Khama's people, the Bamangwato. Missions among other Tswana communities either failed or experienced very little success. Robert Moffat, who set up a mission among the southern Tswana at Kuruman in 1821, had made less than forty converts by 1840. In the late nineteenth century the number of converts at Kuruman fell with the decline of the settlement, as increasing aridity drove many of its people and their cattle to new lands elsewhere.

Khama was born in 1838, the eldest son of Sekhoma, ruler of the Ngwato, a northern Tswana group. Khama grew up a skilled and fearless soldier. In 1862 he was baptized as a Christian thus challenging the beliefs and customs of his own people. His commitment to Christianity was made in the face of great opposition by his father and other elders; Khama jeopardized his future political career and his position as Sekhoma's heir. However, in 1863 the Ndebele attacked the Ngwato and Khama led his people in successful defence of their land and possessions. His victory won back for Khama the favour of the people. Clearly, his becoming a Christian had not brought down upon the Ngwato the displeasure of the ancestors. After 1863, a steady annual trickle of Ngwato converts was made by the British Protestant missionary John Mackenzie, though, as in other Tswana states, there were no large-scale conversions. Khama's Christian faith was not emulated by the majority of his people, merely tolerated because he was their best soldier.

Khama became ruler of the Ngwato in 1872 by a military coup in which he drove out Macheng, who had usurped Sekhoma's position. His aim in seizing power was to ensure religious liberty and the free expression of Christianity, which had been suppressed by Sekhoma and Macheng. In the civil war of 1873–5 Khama managed to defeat an incongruous alliance of his anti-Christian father Sekhoma and his Christian brother Khamane, who was opposed to Khama's policy of toleration towards religious traditionalists. Thereafter, Khama ruled the Ngwato without being seriously challenged for another forty-eight years, until his death in 1923. He was a dictator, but a benevolent and popular one. He may have sent his opponents into exile, including his brothers and his son, but he also abolished the payment of tribute by conquered peoples, he imported corn and distributed it freely during famine, and he modernized the economy by introducing wagons and ploughs and other benefits of western technology.

As a Christian ruler, Khama made a considerable impact on the Ngwato. He abolished the national circumcision ceremonies, which could only be performed by the chief, simply by refusing to carry them out. He replaced rain-making ceremonies by Christian prayer services, ordered all the Ngwato to observe the Sabbath at Shoshong, and banned the import and manufacture of liquor. Yet Khama did not indiscriminately destroy the culture of his people. In marriage matters, he blended the traditional and the new. As a Christian he was opposed to polygamy and refused to take a second wife. This meant it was impossible for him to carry on the traditional practice of establishing close relations with his sub-chiefs by marrying their daughters. Instead, he used a variation of traditional practice in order to cement such relations: he married his daughters to sons of his sub-chiefs.

Khama became an ally of Britain during the Scramble for Africa. He had for long been a close associate of the LMS missionary John Mackenzie in attempting to Christianize Ngwato country, and was ready to heed Mackenzie's advice in 1885 to accept British rule. Mackenzie genuinely wanted Britain to protect the Ngwato from occupation by the Transvaal Boers, but he also realized that British occupation would break the power of traditional rulers in other Tswana states and so make it easier to spread Christianity in them.

In contrast to the success of missions amongst the Tswana, missions amongst the Ndebele were failures. The lack of success has generally been blamed on Ndebele militarism and its incompatibility with a Christian way of life, and on the autocracy of Ndebele kings. However, another factor was equally important: the presence among the Ndebele of a rival concept of the High God which competed with the Christian concept. The Ndebele had adopted from the subject Kalanga, the High God cult of Mwari (the Shona word for God) together with its associated spirit possession cults based on the 'Jukwa' water spirits.

In Bulozi, where the Kololo were overthrown in 1864, the Lozi ruler Lewanika welcomed missionaries for diplomatic reasons, and to increase his association with the white man's technological power. Lewanika had been impressed by the guns sold to him by the white trader, George Westbeech, and he therefore welcomed the setting up of a mission station by the French Protestant missionary, Coillard, in 1886. Coillard started a school and Lewanika, who had little interest in the Gospel, sent his sons to school to learn the white man's skills. Later, during the Scramble, Lewanika, like Khama, was to ally with the white man whom he hoped would aid him in his struggles against both the Ndebele and internal rebels.

Christian missions in pre-colonial Malawi

Malawi has often been held up as a success story for Christian missions in pre-colonial Africa, though a more realistic picture would show a few small islands of Christian progress in a vast sea of traditionalism.

The first attempt to Christianize Malawi was the Universities Mission to Central Africa expedition in 1861–3. The UMCA was an Anglican body inspired by Livingstone's speeches in Britain. The expedition was a disaster. River communications proved to be extremely difficult, due to bars at the mouth of the Zambesi, cataracts on the Shire and the shallowness of the Shire in many places. Malaria and dysentery took their toll of the missionaries. Four out of seven of them died, including Bishop Charles Mackenzie, and the new bishop, Tozer, sensibly withdrew the survivors from the Shire valley to work in Zanzibar.

Missions among the Yao began in the 1870s. In 1875 the Free Church of Scotland established the Livingstonia Mission among the Amachinga Yao at the southern end of Lake Malawi. The Amachinga, who professed Islam and practised the slave trade, were not interested in Christianity. In 1881 the mission was transferred to the northern end of Lake Malawi. A station was established at Bandawe in Tongaland, where it had much greater success. Many Tonga were attracted to Christianity for political reasons. They believed that the mission would be able to give them protection against the Ngoni. The Ngoni of the area under King Mbelwa (Mombera), had recently suffered a military defeat at the hands of Chewa chief Mwase Kasungu. Mbelwa's was the first of the Malawian Ngoni states to receive a serious check to its military expansion, and he was not unwilling to allow in missionaries whom he saw as the representatives of a technologically superior culture. Mbelwa also realized the economic advantages of trading with the missionaries, selling them food in exchange for their calico, a valuable new form of material wealth. In the 1890s Mbelwa's Ngoni rapidly took to mission education, just as the Tonga had done in the 1880s.

The Livingstonia Mission's two leaders were Dr Robert Laws and William Elmslie, but they depended a great deal in the early days on a remarkable African missionary, William Koyi. A Gaika from South Africa who could speak Zulu, Koyi was trained at Lovedale Missionary Institute in Cape Colony. He served at Livingstonia from 1878 until his death from fever in 1886, and succeeded as a missionary through a combination of Christian humility and courage. He was especially influential because of his ability to communicate with the Ngoni in the Nguni language. There is no doubt that he defused a number of potentially dangerous situations.

In 1876 the Blantyre Mission of the Church of Scotland was established, on a healthy highland site, in the lands of the Amangoche Yao. It had much greater success than the Livingstonia Mission amongst the Amachinga. The Amangoche welcomed the Scottish missionaries as allies against the Maseko Ngoni who were raiding them. A kind of mission state was set up at Blantyre, where the missionaries arbitrated in disputes between Amangoche leaders, ran irrigated plantations of coffee, tea, sugar and tobacco, and operated a benevolent form of despotism for their agricultural workers and the pupils in their schools. Blantyre epitomized the outsize mission villages that sprang up in Malawi and at the East African coast in the 1870s as centres of attraction for runaway slaves and refugees from the slave trade. Like some of the stations set up by the Holy Ghost Fathers and the White Fathers it became a fully-fledged economic and political unit, governed directly by the Mission, and almost entirely divorced from the outside world. Like many other mission villages, its influence beyond the immediate vicinity was negligible. However, in Malawi, just as in Nigeria, the groundwork had been done for the great advance of Christianity after the colonial conquest of the county.

Christian missions in pre-colonial East Africa

The coast

Sultan Said of Zanzibar allowed European missionaries into his territories as part of his policy of maintaining good relations with the European governments with which he had made commercial treaties. However, the missionaries made few converts at the heavily Islamized coast. Krapf, who arrived in Kenya in 1844, and Rebmann and Erhardt who arrived in 1846, were all Germans working for the

British-based Church Missionary Society. They were the first Europeans to see snow-capped mountains near the Equator. Krapf translated the New Testament into Swahili and compiled grammars in several African languages. Other missions also failed to make more than a few converts, but performed valuable social work.

The Holy Ghost Fathers (French Catholic) set up a mission station at Bagamoyo in 1868. It developed into a settlement for freed slaves and abandoned children. Many mission stations were freed slave settlements. They included the CMS mission at Freretown, Mombasa, started in 1875, and the UMCA stations set up among the Yao between 1875 and 1880. These freed slave settlements originated from the British naval patrol against the East African slave trade. Many African slaves were freed from dhows in the Indian Ocean and landed at Bombay in British India. When the slave trade was abolished in Zanzibar in 1873 many 'Bombay Africans', as they were called, were encouraged to settle in freed slave settlements in East Africa. The missionary societies planned to make the freed slaves Christians and to use them to evangelize in African communities.

The achievements of the Bombay Africans were very limited on the Muslim-dominated east coast. Even in the interior among their own people they could achieve little. Many had lost the use of their mother tongues, and were too effectively detribalized to convert their own people. A few were fairly successful. William Jones, who was well-educated and was eventually ordained a priest, was responsible for starting mission work among the Taita to the north-east of Kilimanjaro. His tactfulness, as one African dealing with others, enabled initial Taita hostility to be overcome. Charles Suleiman, another talented evangelist, made most of the converts in and around the UMCA village at Masasi in the early 1880s.

Buganda

The Christian faith shone brightest in the pre-colonial period in Buganda after 1878, where several dozen African martyrs died for their belief in Jesus.

Christian missionaries first went to Buganda as a result of Stanley's visit there in 1875. Stanley, impressed by Kabaka Mutesa's intelligence and organizing ability, described him in letters to Britain as the light which would lighten the darkness of the interior of East Africa. Mutesa accepted Stanley's suggestion that missionaries come from Europe to Buganda. In 1875–6 Mutesa was worried by the advance of Egypt under the Governor of Equatoria, Gordon. Mutesa clearly wanted European missionaries because he associated religion with government and believed missionaries would be representatives of European governments in his diplomatic struggle with Egypt. Mutesa appears to have looked forward with expectation to the military, political and economic power that missionaries would bring him. There is also evidence that Mutesa welcomed Christian missionaries for reasons other than military strategy and foreign policy. Within Buganda the kabaka was engaged in a power struggle with the traditionalist priests of the Lubaale cult, and wished to use Christianity to help defeat them. Mutesa wished to break the power of the Lubaale priests who were an effective barrier to his centralizing absolutism. He had welcomed Islam into Buganda earlier as a counter-weight to Lubaale, and he seems to have intended to use Christianity in the same way. Islam had deeply influenced Mutesa and he may also have invited missionaries to Buganda because of his intellectual interest in this second world religion.

Between 1866 and 1875 Buganda was a semi-Islamic state. Mutesa observed Ramadan and many court chiefs and pages became Muslims. Mutesa was attracted to Islam, to the doctrine of an active God totally unlike the impersonal and disinterested Ganda High God Katonda, to eternal life and the forgiveness of sins, and the recording of the tenets of the faith in a book. Mutesa never became a Muslim himself. The traditional Ganda horror of mutilating any part of the body and thus preventing a vigorous life after death effectively discouraged Mutesa and many other Islamic sympathizers in Buganda from being circumcised.

The first missionaries to arrive were from the Church Missionary Society (British Protestants) in 1877, led by Alexander Mackay. The White Fathers (French Catholics) arrived in 1878, under Father Simon Lourdel. The Protestants and Catholics displayed the most unchristian lack of charity towards each other, and Mutesa and his people regarded Protestantism and Catholicism as two different religions, one for the Ingleza and one for the Fransa. In 1879 Mutesa almost became a Christian and even sent Ganda ambassadors to Queen Victoria, on a trip organized by CMS missionaries. However, the *Katikiro* (prime minister) Mukasa pointed out that the kabaka must remain independent of the three rival foreign religious groups: Muslims, Catholics and Protestants. The katikiro told the kabaka, 'If you join any of these foreign religions there will be no peace in this country.' Even if Mukasa's advice had not given Mutesa sufficient reason to pause, the issue of polygamy—of what to do with about two hundred wives—would have done so. Moreover, the kabaka found the disputes between Catholics and Protestants confusing.

By 1881 Mutesa had lost interest in both Christianity and the Christian missionaries. The Egyptian threat had receded in 1879, when Gordon evacuated his southernmost forts at Mruli and Foweira. At the end of 1879 and early in 1880, when Mutesa was sick, he returned to the Ganda gods and several hundred people were sacrificed in intercession for the return of Mutesa to good health. Between 1881 and his death in 1884 Mutesa revived his earlier interest in Islam. In 1882 the White Fathers left Buganda because they feared a Zanzibari coup, and because they were in despair both at the ban on movement outside the capital and at the strength of polygamy in Buganda.

The absence of the White Fathers between 1882 and 1884 was a blessing in disguise to Christianity in Buganda. African converts, left under their own leadership, continued the work of evangelization with not only fervour but a growing self-reliance and responsibility. Men like Joseph Mukasa Balikuddembe emerged as inspiring Catholic leaders during Father Lourdel's absence. Lourdel's temporary withdrawal also led to an abandonment of the narrow and rather futile policy of trying to Christianize Buganda by first converting the kabaka. From 1882, a new policy of spreading the Gospel widely to all in the capital who would care to listen to it was adopted. By the end of Mutesa's reign in 1884 there were several hundred Christian converts in Buganda.

What attracted the Baganda to Jesus? Firstly there was the idealism of youth amongst the court pages. The Christian teaching of the equality and dignity of man, the message of a personal Saviour and the compelling personality of Christ himself were all a marked contrast to the cynicism and uncertainty of life in the royal court. While political and military factors had enabled Christianity to obtain a foothold in Buganda, the hope of the Gospel message inspired its expansion in the country. Secondly, the pages were attracted by the printed word, and became avid readers. Thirdly, they were impressed by the missionaries' medical skill, which they associated with Jesus' healing activities.

A number of other factors made it possible for the missionaries to make converts in Buganda, one of them being the openness of Ganda society. During Mutesa's reign the power of the kabaka increased and that of the hereditary provincial chiefs declined, as the kabaka appointed *batongole* chiefs alongside clan chiefs. Young men and boys flocked to court for the patronage of the kabaka, hoping in time to be favoured with special royal appointments to office. Ganda society became increasingly dominated by personal ambition, by competition, by individualism and achievement, and less and less by heredity and family. Avenues for personal scope and choice began to be opened up, and one of them led to individuals taking personal decisions to embrace a new, worldwide religious faith.

The accession of Mwanga to the kabakaship in 1884 ushered in the period of Christian martyrdoms in 1885 and 1886. Mwanga was an inexperienced young man, only eighteen years old, when he became kabaka. His character showed evidence of many personal weaknesses. He was easily led, revengeful, unpredictable, addicted to bhang-smoking, and homosexual. His persecution of the Christians was partly inspired by Katikiro Mukasa, who was frightened by the rise of the Christian pages at court, one of whom might usurp his own position. Another influence on Mwanga was provided by the Swahili–Arab traders in Buganda who warned him of the steady advance of white men towards Buganda: the Belgians from the Congo to the west and the Germans who occupied part of the Zanzibar coast in 1885. In 1885 Bishop James Hannington, sent by the CMS, attempted to enter Buganda by the eastern route direct from Kenya, instead of round the south and west of Lake Victoria via Tabora. Mwanga was deeply suspicious of this entry by the forbidden 'back door', fearing that Hannington was the advance guard of European imperialism. The Kabaka arranged for a local Soga chief to have Hannington killed in Busoga. A Catholic chief who protested about Hannington's murder was put to death in November 1885. Worse was to follow. In May 1886, Mwanga summoned the pages and demanded to know which of them were Christians. He was furious that they were resisting his homosexual advances. Over thirty pages admitted to their being Christians and were burned to death at Namugongo, when they refused to recant their faith.

The martyrdom led to an increase in the political influence of the Christians in Buganda. For a start, most of the Christians survived the killings. They were protected by their non-Christian chiefs, friends and relatives, and by the interventions of the Queen Mother and the Katikiro Mukasa who did not want wholesale executions. Soon after Namugongo, Mwanga embarked on a policy of building up a powerful royal party of young chiefs to challenge the authority of the elderly senior chiefs whom Mwanga feared and hated and whom he had antagonized by his policies. Many of the young chiefs were Christians while others were Muslims. Ultimately Mwanga's new policy worked against him. The kabaka came to realize that he could not resist the young chiefs if they united against him, and in 1888 he decided to eliminate his erstwhile friends by killing or expelling all the Christians and Muslims in the country. However the young chiefs, with their powerful armed followings, got their blow in first. Early in 1888 a Christian–Muslim government ruled in uneasy harness until a Muslim coup later in the year expelled the Christians, and imposed a Muslim kabaka, Kalema, on the country.

During the period of Muslim rule, Christian missionaries were expelled, churches and Bibles were burnt and many Ganda Christians were killed. In 1889–90 there was a civil war in which the Christians and Mwanga formed an alliance of convenience and succeeded in overthrowing the Muslims. The Christians needed Mwanga because he had the support of the mass of the people. They won because of the brilliant generalship of the Catholic commander Gabriel Kintu and the Protestant Semei Kakungulu. After the Christian victory nearly all the Zanzibaris in Buganda were killed, and the Ganda Muslims suffered the same sort of persecution that the Christians had suffered earlier. Mwanga was kabaka once again, but his government was Christian, and he found his former absolute powers curtailed. The Protestant leader, Apolo Kagwa, became katikiro (a post he held for thirty-six years) and the other ministries were divided between Protestant and Catholic chiefs. The stage was now set for a Christian political regime to negotiate with a Christian imperialist invader and thereby entrench the primacy of Christian political groups in the government of Buganda.

9
The European imperialist overture: (2) Britain

Overview

During the period 1840–8 Britain pursued a policy of 'paramount influence' in West, East and South Africa. It was an attempt to avoid the growth of responsibilities in Africa. However, in spite of the official view that African possessions were worthless, the period from 1840 to 1885 was one of slow but steady European encroachment on African sovereignty. In many ways this earlier period prepared the way for the Scramble, which was, to a large extent, a logical culmination of preceding European activity in Africa.

The European encroachment between 1840 and 1885 mainly took one of three forms: commercial penetration, political colonization and Christian missionary activity. Sometimes two of these forms operated concurrently. Colonies were sometimes established or expanded for reasons of naval strategy or national prestige rather than for commercial considerations. Britain strengthened her presence in South Africa at this time largely to consolidate her position at the strategically vital Cape of Good Hope, astride the main route from Britain to her colonies of India and Australia. After 1840 France expanded her colonies in Algeria and Senegal principally to fulfil a desire for 'glory'. In the main, however, commerce was the key factor in European encroachment. Britain established colonies in Sierra Leone, the Gold Coast and Lagos largely as part of a policy of replacing the slave trade by the legitimate trade in tropical raw materials. Such materials were in great demand as a result of Britain's industrialization.

The process of European intervention in Africa that had begun with the slave trade and continued with the suppression of the coastal slave trade was intensified with Europe's second industrial revolution between 1879 and 1900, when France and Germany broke into Britain's monopoly of both industrial production and the control of African markets and primary producing sources. French and German rivalry with each other and with Britain rapidly accelerated the pace of European imperialism in Africa. The major difference between Britain and France, her main rival in Africa before 1879, was that whereas British traders led the way in West Africa and the British government reluctantly followed them, in the case of France in Algeria and Senegal trade followed the flag.

Britain in West Africa, 1840–84

Overview

Britain's interest in West Africa was high in the early nineteenth century because of the crusade against the Atlantic slave trade, but by the 1860s the crusade was over, and Britain's interest in West Africa declined. The British government continued to ensure that anti-slave trade treaties with African coastal rulers were observed, but it remained utterly opposed to any extension of territorial responsibilities beyond its existing colonial footholds. Sierra Leone, the Gambia, the Gold Coast forts and Lagos were not considered valuable in themselves. They were regarded as an irritating financial burden to the British government which hoped to disengage from them. However, the policy of paramount influence led inexorably to the government being forced against its will into a larger commitment in West Africa. London might be opposed to colonial expansion on grounds of expense, but the activities of men on the spot—of British traders, missionaries and colonial and consular officials, all of whom were interventionist in one form or another—helped to involve the government against its will in extending the colonies. British traders at first were generally opposed to this because they did not want to pay dues on their exports to maintain colonial administration. However, the push inland of British traders from the 1860s, especially in the Niger delta and the hinterland of Sierra Leone, stirred up African resistance. It became clear that warfare and lawlessness in inland markets could only be put down by the establishment of strong imperial control. Colonial and consular officials, like Glover in Lagos, came to realize that a policy of non-interference in the affairs of the communities surrounding a colony made it impossible to administer a colony effectively. Lagos colony was a financial failure for as long as wars raged in the Yoruba hinterland.

Generally the flag followed trade. In Yorubaland traders followed missionaries and were in turn followed by administrators. On the Niger the missionaries followed the traders before the establishment of colonial rule. Initially, the British government might refuse to give British traders the support of the flag, but it did not inhibit them, and it came to their rescue later when they got into difficulties.

European trade disturbed African government and the African economy. Africans increasingly competed for a share in the trade with Europeans. In a number of cases wars erupted either between different peoples or within an ethnic group as a result of attempts to monopolize direct trade with the Europeans. Britain then found that her policy of paramount influence was inadequate and that trade was being seriously disrupted. She began to spread her influence directly inland in an attempt to stop wars between African states and to keep trade routes open.

The British policy of paramount influence in West Africa between 1800 and 1884 prepared the way for colonialism after 1884. However, it needed French and German intervention in Africa in the mid-1880s to give the final impetus to British expansion into the interior of West Africa.

Britain in The Gambia, 1840–84

Britain's Gambia colony, obtained in 1816, consisted of Bathurst (Banjul) and a small area of land around it. London's reluctance to extend colonial responsibilities in Africa made sense in The Gambia, where expansion would require expensive military pacification of the militant Muslims of the interior. The colony was useful to Britain mainly as a settlement for a few recaptives (freed slaves). Britain did not benefit from the expansion in groundnut production in The Gambia from the early 1830s, even though The Gambia was the first area in West Africa where groundnuts were grown for export. There were two reasons for this. Firstly, the groundnuts were produced in independent states in the interior, not in the colony. Secondly, French traders rather than British traders exploited the new marketing opportunities.

On a number of occasions Britain tried to rid herself of The Gambia which she regarded as an expensive liability. The exchange proposals of the 1860s and 1870s involved the exchange of British Gambia for French Gabon or Ivory Coast. They were blocked by the French government's desire to hold on to Gabon as a naval base and by British traders in Bathurst, whose political leverage proved to be more considerable than their commercial enterprise.

Sierra Leone: the Creole achievement

After Britain abolished the slave trade for British subjects in 1807, the British navy's Preventive Squadron patrolled the West African coast in an attempt to stop the slave trade. Freetown became the squadron's headquarters, and captured slave ships were brought there. Slaves on board were freed and settled in Sierra Leone. Altogether 40,000 free slaves, who were known as *recaptives*, were settled in Sierra Leone.

Governor Macarthy (1814–24) settled the recaptives in villages each of which had a school and a church. He and his successors followed a policy of spreading western education and Christianity among the recaptives who embraced these aspects of British culture with zeal. The original Sierra Leone black settlers and the recaptives were grateful to the British who had liberated them from slavery. They identified themselves with their British rulers but not as a slave identifies with his master. Black Sierra Leoneans felt themselves to be free citizens of the British empire, not a conquered people.

The recaptives intermarried with the original black settlers who had come from England and Canada in the late eighteenth century. By 1850 the Creoles had emerged as a distinct group. The Creoles were essentially blacks with a slight mixture of white blood, but they developed a culture and way of life that was as much European as it was African. They were Christians and monogamists, but they kept the extended family system, as in African societies. Their language, Krio, was the English language Africanized. The Creoles maintained ethnic clubs and societies such as those for descendants of Igbos and Yorubas. Their Christian religion was permeated with practices from African religion, like protracted funerals and communication with the family dead.

The Creole achievement was strongly evident in education. In 1868, twenty-two per cent of the people in the colony had been educated in school. The figures for Prussia were sixteen per cent and only thirteen per cent for England. The British missionary societies deserve credit for their share in this magnificent effort, but they were never able to supply enough schools and maintain enough teachers to meet the demand. There were secondary schools for both boys and girls and a teacher training college, Fourah Bay, was formed in 1827, becoming a university in 1876. Amongst outstanding Creoles were John Thorpe, the first black Sierra Leonean lawyer; William Davies and Africanus Horton, the first black doctors of western medicine; Crowther the first black Protestant bishop; and Samuel Lewis, the first newspaper editor and owner, the first mayor of Freetown, the first African to be granted Cambridge and Oxford degrees, and the first African knight. Creoles made notable contributions to African studies in numerous publications. Horton wrote on tropical medicine and African political science, Crowther on Nigerian linguistics, A. B. C. Sibthorpe on Sierra Leone's history and geography, and Samuel Johnson on the history of the Yoruba.

The educated Creoles excelled in spreading the religion of the Book. In 1861 the Church of England withdrew its missionaries from Sierra Leone and turned the entire work over to Creoles under the Native Pastorate Church. Bishop Crowther led an all-Creole staff in the Niger Mission which partly Christianized the Delta city states and created a self-supporting, self-governing Delta Church. Other Creole missionaries were active among the Igbo and the Yoruba and in The Gambia.

The Creoles were the most active and widespread of the British traders in West Africa, not only in Sierra Leone but all over the forest belt from The Gambia to Cameroon. They pioneered trade in areas untouched or only lightly touched by European traders. They opened up the Sierra Leone hinterland and developed a flourishing trade in groundnuts in the north and palm oil in the south. They bought condemned slave ships and traded along the whole coast. Many Yoruba recaptives returned to Yorubaland and Lagos. A black bourgeoisie arose, living in expensively built mansions in Freetown, Lagos and Bathurst. Each mansion generally contained a marble bust of Queen Victoria—a symbol of Creole wealth and of Creole identification with Britain. Perhaps the most successful Creole trader was Richard Blaize (1854–1904), who left Freetown in 1862 and made his fortune in Lagos. Of Yoruba origin, Blaize started as a retailer mainly in imported cloth, but he expanded his trade to become a wholesaler who imported direct from England, and as an exporter of palm oil, palm kernels and cotton. He started a credit bank and also a newspaper, the *Lagos Times*. In 1896 Blaize's various enterprises were worth £150,000—well over £1 million by today's values.

Finally, Creoles were active in administration. They filled most of the civil service posts, even at higher levels, in Sierra Leone. Many posts in The Gambia, the Gold Coast and Lagos were filled by them, at least until the deliberate de-Africanization policy of the late nineteenth century post-Partition Governors was implemented.

Britain, the Gold Coast and Asante

Britain's policy on the Gold Coast between 1840 and 1874 constantly vacillated. At the beginning of this period Britain controlled the majority of the trading forts along the coast. British aims were to end the slave trade at the coast, to obtain peace in the interior so that British traders could operate there, and to prevent any one African ruler from controlling the coast, because if one did so he would monopolize trade and increase the price of gold and palm oil. These aims were contradictory. Peace could most easily be obtained by letting the Asante of the interior control all the coast, but then the Asante would be able to increase prices. Therefore Britain was forced

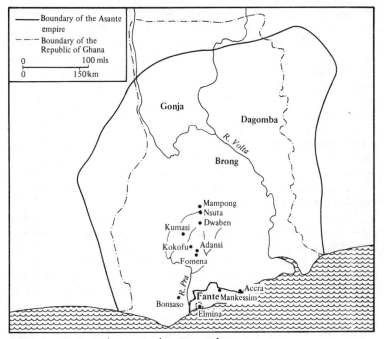

Map 10.   Asante and Fante in the nineteenth century.

to support the coastal Fante people against the Asante. Moreover, British governments were unwilling to maintain the forts if they did not make a profit. Therefore, Britain's policy wavered between withdrawing completely and establishing colonies to ensure her own control of trade.

During the eighteenth century the Asante confederation had expanded its empire into the Fante-inhabited coastal area. In the following century the Asante persisted in their long-standing policy of attempting to trade directly with Europeans on the coast instead of through Fante middlemen. The Asante especially needed guns and powder both to defend their empire and to expand it. The Fante, however, were determined to preserve or win back their independence from the Asante. Nineteenth century Fante country was·

divided into many small states, and this political disunity made it difficult for the Fante to resist Asante attacks. The Fante needed military aid from Britain to help maintain their independence from the Asante. This raised the further problem of how to get help from the British without being dominated by them. This was a problem the Fante never managed to solve.

In the early nineteenth century the Asante had invaded and occupied most of Fante territory. The Asante defeated both the Fante and a small British force at Bonsaso in February 1824. However, stronger British expeditions heavily defeated the Asante in July 1824 and in 1826 and drove the Asante out of their southern vassal states, most of which were Fante. By a treaty of 1831 the Asante were forced to recognize the independence of all vassal states south of the River Pra. George Maclean, the Governor of the Forts from 1829 to 1842, managed to keep the peace between Britain, the Fante and the Asante and to extend British trade among both peoples. The 1844 'Bond' even gave British officials the right to sit as assistants in African courts to hear certain cases in Fanteland, though it did not place the Fante under British jurisdiction. Relations between the British and their trading partners remained peaceful. However, when later British governors forsook Maclean's policy of peaceful and under-standing diplomacy with the Asante, bad relations and military conflict inevitably ensued.

The Asante–British War of 1863–4 was totally unnecessary. It was caused by Governor Richard Pine's failure to understand Asante law and culture. Under Asante law all gold nuggets belonged to the *Asantehene* (King of Asante). Some Asante including a certain Kwesi Gyani stole a nugget in Asante and fled to a British fort. The asantehene, Kwaku Dua I, demanded extradition of the criminals. Pine refused to hand them back. He feared that the asantehene would execute the criminals. Kwaku Dua was an unusually pacific-minded king, but felt that he had no choice but to go to war if he were to uphold his authority over his subjects. He sent his army to invade the coast, but the invasion was a failure. At the beginning of the campaign the Asante managed to defeat the Fante armies and besiege the British forts. However, the Asante were forced to withdraw because of an outbreak of malaria and dysentery among their soldiers. The British then took advantage of this respite to collect an army to attack Asante. The British forces in turn were decimated by malaria and dysentery, and had to be withdrawn.

The loss of many lives and the heavy expenditure on a war that had no sensible cause and no useful result led to questions in the British parliament, and the setting up of a parliamentary committee to study British policy on the Gold Coast and in West Africa generally. In its 1865 Report the committee recommended that, on grounds of expense, Britain should withdraw from West Africa but, that its four West African settlements should first be prepared for early self-government. The committee believed it was necessary: 'to encourage in the natives the exercise of those qualities which may render it possible for us more and more to transfer to them the administration of all Governments...'

The imminent British withdrawal inspired the Fante to form a political confederation to enable them to resist Asante. The moving spirit in the formation of the confederation was James Africanus Horton, a Sierra Leonean British army doctor stationed in the Gold Coast. Horton believed that Africa already possessed nations, such as the Creoles and the Fante, on which modern states could be built. Horton's views considerably influenced the western-educated Fante leaders, many of whom were state rulers, and they in turn convinced the traditional Fante rulers. The Council of Mankessim met in 1868 to make plans for a constitution, but little came of the Mankessim deliberations. A new meeting was held in 1871 and a Constitution was finally worked out and agreed to by thirty-one Fante rulers, though significantly there was no provision for popular representation in this government of the elite. A poll tax was agreed on and collected. Unfortunately, just at the moment when Fante unity and self-government appeared to have been achieved, it was destroyed as a result of a change in British policy, caused by the problem of the Dutch forts on the Gold Coast.

The Dutch lost interest in their forts because they were unprofitable and because the Fante besieged them between 1868 and 1870. The Dutch were traditional allies of the Asante and by besieging the forts the Fante hoped to prevent Asante trade. In 1870–1 the Dutch abandoned their forts and handed them over to the British. The British now occupied all the Gold Coast forts; they could collect all customs duties; they could obtain sufficient income to pay for their government at the Gold Coast. The British were now much more prepared to stay on the coast. Britain no longer supported the idea of an independent and powerful Fante state which might threaten the British position in the area. In 1871 Britain arrested the leaders of the Fante confederation, and put pressure on many Fante leaders to abandon co-operation with it. People stopped paying poll tax. The confederation could not withstand such pressure and quickly collapsed. Britain thus destroyed an experiment in self-government of the type that its parliament, only a few years previously, had strongly advocated.

The British takeover of the Dutch forts also led to the Asante–British War of 1873–4. The Dutch had handed over the fort of Elmina to Britain, but they had no right to do so because Elmina belonged to Asante who rented it to the Dutch for twenty ounces of gold per year. Britain rejected the Asante demand to hand back Elmina, largely because the Dutch had produced a forged document indicating that the Asante had no claim over the fort. Britain believed this document to be true and saw no reason to listen to the demands of the asantehene. The bellicose Asantehene Kofi Karikari sent his army to recover Elmina. As in 1863, disease—this time, smallpox and dysentery—so weakened the Asante army that, after a number of early successes, it withdrew to Asante. Unlike 1863, this time the British counter-attack was carried into Asante. The British General Sir Garnet Wolseley assembled a force of several hundred European troops reinforced by the West Indian Regiment, Hausa police from Lagos, Fante allies and even Opobo men sent by Jaja, grateful for recent British recognition of his new state. The Asante skilfully retreated in the face of the British invasion but made a last stand at Amoafo, just outside Kumasi. Their old muzzle-loading Dane guns were no match for the new British breech-loading rifles, and the Asante were heavily defeated. The British captured and burnt Kumasi, but then withdrew to the coast.

The results of the 1873–4 war were decisive for the history of modern Ghana. Asante imperial and military power was effectively destroyed, and Britain made a decisive new interventionist commitment by establishing the Gold Coast Colony. At the 1874 Treaty of Fomena, Asante was forced to recognize the independence of the coastal states, to give up her claim to Elmina, and to agree to pay an indemnity of gold to Britain. After this, the Asante empire collapsed, as not only southern vassal states but northern ones like Dagomba, Gonja and the Brong states also broke away from Kumasi's control. Even members of the Asante confederacy itself, at the heart of the state, quarrelled among themselves. Kofi Karikari was destooled (deposed) for stealing gold from the tombs of dead kings. Some Asante states such as Dwaben, Kokofu, Nsuta, Mampong, and Adansi left the union. Britain did not annex Asante, which would have been difficult to hold without heavy military expenditure. She did, however, extend her rule far inland and the new colony included all the former Asante southern vassal states and all the former Fante confederation. Horton's dreams of early self-government had been irredeemably shattered.

After 1874 the Fante elite quickly adapted to British colonialism. They welcomed protection from Asante. They benefited from indirect rule and many were absorbed in the administration and legislature of the new colonial structure. Their lands were not alienated to white settlers, and the Pax Britannica provided an opportunity for African traders. John Sarbah the Elder (1834–92) is a good example of an educated African who took advantage of colonial rule. Initially a Wesleyan mission agent and schoolteacher, Sarbah later became a politician and a trader as well. He made his breakthrough as a successful businessman in the early 1870s, set up a network of stores and trading stations, re-invested most of his profits in his firm's expansion, and stimulated the palm oil and rubber trades. Sarbah was a regular member of the Gold Coast Legislative Council, where he strongly espoused African causes while at the same time buttressing colonialism by participating in its institutions. In this he was typical of the Gold Coast elite of his time.

Britain in Lagos

British intervention in and around Lagos provided a clear example of the inconsistency of the policy of 'paramount influence'. The policy of gaining a foothold led inexorably to further expansion in order to secure that foothold.

Originally Britain became involved in this Yoruba port by intervening in the rivalry for the kingship. In 1845 Kosoko drove out Akintoye and made himself king. Both Akintoye and Kosoko were slave-traders, but Kosoko as the one in power was now doing most to keep the slave trade going in Lagos. Kosoko became the target of British missionaries and palm-oil traders who persuaded the British government to drive out Kosoko and make Akintoye king. In 1851–2 the British navy duly intervened. Kosoko put up fierce resistance but the issue was decided by British naval artillery. Akintoye as king signed treaties with Britain in which he promised to expel slave traders, protect missions and trade freely with British merchants. Lagos was now very much under the influence of Britain.

In 1861 Britain formally annexed Lagos and made it a colony. French interest in the port made the British determined to forestall them, and to protect the British palm-oil trade and missionary interests. Moreover, the semi-independent ruler of Lagos, Dosunmu, who had succeeded his father Akintoye in 1853, had not effectively suppressed slave trading by the people of Lagos. Now Dosunmu was replaced by a British governor. Of course, British annexation led to a quick end of the slave trade, but the development of the Lagos palm-oil trade that followed caused slavery to increase in the Yoruba interior, as the warrior merchants of Ibadan used slaves as labourers in palm-oil plantations and as porters in trading.

Having occupied Lagos, the British had to pay the cost of administering it. Revenue could only be obtained satisfactorily from customs duties, and sufficient customs could only be obtained if the colony was expanded along the coast, to annex other ports. Governor Glover, during his period of office from 1866 to 1872, expanded the colony to the west to take in Badagry and to the east to absorb Palma and Lekki. However, the Yoruba wars in the hinterland of the ports continued. Trade was constantly interrupted and revenue remained low. The logic of the British position in Lagos required expansion inland to impose a Pax Britannica on all Yorubaland and end the wars in the interior, thus ensuring free and regular trade. French occupation of nearby Dahomey in 1892 provided the stimulus for Governor Carter to invade the interior.

British economic imperialism in the Niger delta, 1840–84

British political intervention in the Niger delta began soon after the abolition of the slave trade by Britain in 1807. The British naval squadron in West Africa not only caught slave ships in the Ocean but made treaties with rulers to prevent slave-trading in the ports. However, rulers frequently evaded their treaty obligations, so a British consul was appointed to see that treaties were kept: John Beecroft was Consul of the Bight of Biafra and Benin from 1849 to 1854. He used the British navy to follow an interventionist policy seeking to ensure that rulers were friendly to British interests. In 1851 Beecroft was responsible for overthrowing Kosoko in Lagos in order to end the slave trade. In 1852 he mediated in Calabar to arrange peace between the traders of the Ekpe Society and the Blood Men, who were freed slaves, because British trade could not flourish during a civil war. In 1854 he used the Royal Navy to depose and deport King William Dappa Pepple of Bonny as a punishment for clashing with British traders. Delta rulers came to look on Beecroft and his successor consuls as governors of a protecting power long before the European Partition of Africa legalized that position.

From 1854 British power began to be felt on the Niger, when the British ship *Pleid* sailed up the river. Its European sailors were given quinine as a prophylactic against malaria and none of them died. At roughly the same time the steamship had been developed. Thereafter, European trade upstream expanded rapidly. Macgregor Laird began trading on the Niger north of the delta in the 1850s. In 1857–9 British trading posts were set up at Aboh, Onitsha and Lokoja. By 1870 four British companies were operating north of the delta, but on the whole British traders were not very successful between 1857 and 1877. There was strong armed resistance by delta and Igbo palm-oil traders to the British traders and there were numerous armed attacks on Laird's steamships and depots. The British Navy had to be called in to escort merchant ships in convoys.

Then in 1876 George Goldie arrived on the Niger. This ruthlessly ambitious Manxman believed that over-competition was making trade unprofitable. He persuaded British companies to unite in order to create a monopoly. They could then raise or lower prices as economic advantage dictated. He created the United African Company, which was renamed the National African Company in 1883 and was the basis of the later Royal Niger Company. Goldie's policy of amalgamation and monopoly received a severe setback when the French began trading on the Niger in the late 1870s.

Goldie's combine increased the prices it paid to African palm-oil producers until it was making no profit, but it killed off French trade and the French left in the early 1880s. Such aggressive competition also destroyed the competition of traders from Lagos and Sierra Leone. Having established a monopoly, Goldie was able to dictate terms and pay very low prices to the African producers. With the departure of the French and the beginning of the European Partition of Africa the way was clear for Goldie to establish British political power on the Niger. Between 1884 and 1886 Goldie made 237 treaties north of the delta on behalf of the National African Company. These treaties were then recognized by Consul Hewett who had signed protection treaties with such delta rulers as Jaja and Nana between 1883 and 1885. These moves were made in order to forestall the French. However, Goldie was concerned not only with ousting the French. He could not compete effectively as a trader with the Niger Igbos, so he declared war on them. In 1879 he arranged for Onitsha to be destroyed by a British naval bombardment. Aboh suffered the same fate in 1883.

The early involvement of the British in the affairs of the delta and the Igbo city states in order to stamp out the slave trade and protect the interests of British traders was eventually to develop into full-scale political interference.

British consuls and traders in East Africa, 1840–1884

As in West Africa, so also in East Africa Britain followed a policy of coastal influence. However, while in West Africa Britain had mainly commercial and no strategic motives, in East Africa the reverse was the case. Britain regarded the Sultan of Zanzibar as an ally who would help to guard the East African flank of the route to India, around the Cape of Good Hope. This strategic motive was one reason why Britain persistently buttressed the shaky Omani regime in East Africa. Another powerful motive was the humanitarian campaign against the East African slave trade. Economic motives were not important in British policy in East Africa. The anti-slavery campaign in East Africa did not coincide with the anti-slavery interests of British businessmen, as it did in West Africa. There were very few British traders on the east coast either before or after the abolition of the slave trade in Zanzibar in 1873.

The British consul at Zanzibar from 1841 to 1883 was subordinate to the Viceroy of India in Bombay, not to the Foreign Office in London—a sure sign that British East African policy was geared to Indian Ocean strategy. Britain feared a possible revival of French imperialism. The French held Réunion and the Comoro Islands, had established footholds in Madagascar, and felt bitter at the loss of Mauritius and the Seychelles to Britain in the Napoleonic wars at the beginning of the century. Britain therefore backed a stronger sultanate to prevent French expansion on to the coast, encouraged Seyyid Said to move his capital from Muscat to Zanzibar, posted a consul to guide him (1841), and helped him win back his authority along the coast. In return, Said encouraged the 'banyan' merchants of British India to settle in Zanzibar and co-operated to act against the slave trade.

The 1822 Moresby Treaty between Britain and Zanzibar stopped the sale of slaves outside Omani territory, and in particular to British India and French Réunion. The 1845 Hamerton Treaty was stronger. Slaves could no longer be sold outside East Africa. Said feared a revolt by the slave traders and complained to the British agent, 'You have put on me a heavier load than I can bear.' However he had not anticipated the ineffectiveness of the Treaty. The British naval squadron employed to hunt slave dhows in the Indian Ocean was too small, the Ocean was too vast and the coastline was too long; in 1872 the East coast slave trade through Zanzibar was at its peak.

In 1870 when Sultan Majid (1856–70) died Britain made Barghash sultan on condition that he intensified the effort against the slave trade, but Barghash broke his promise and asserted his independence of the British consul, Sir John Kirk. The British were able to force Barghash to abolish the slave trade in 1873 only because of a fortuitous event and the adroit use they made of it. A hurricane in 1872 ruined Zanzibar's economy and Barghash was forced to appeal for aid to his powerful ally. Kirk promised aid on condition that the sultan abolish the slave trade. Kirk was backed up by Sir Bartle Frere who was sent from London to put pressure on the sultan. Frere threatened a British naval blockade of Zanzibar and Barghash signed the 1873 treaty which stipulated that no more slaves could be put on board ship in Zanzibar waters, and the Zanzibar slave market should be closed. This decisive act led to slave-trader rebellions in 1875 and 1876 at Mombasa and Kilwa. Barghash had to rely on the British Navy to suppress them. Smuggling of slaves in the years after abolition was on so large a scale that in 1876 the sultan, at Kirk's insistence, proclaimed that slaves could not be moved by land and slave caravans could not approach the coast. These proclamations were enforced by a new Swahili military force set up and led by a British officer, Lieutenant Lloyd Mathews. Gradually, Mathews took on other responsibilities until he was effectively the prime minister of Zanzibar, though he took his orders, not from the sultan, but from the British consul, the real source of authority. By the time of the German incursion in 1884 and the Partition of East Africa, Zanzibar had been reduced to the role of a puppet state of Britain. The British policy of coastal paramountcy was developing into a barely disguised political imperialism.

In contrast to West Africa, British commercial interests were of little significance in the formulation of British policy on the East Coast. The most active British trader on the east coast was William Mackinnon. In the late 1870s he tried to set up a British trading company to pacify and develop the interior. He got the backing of Kirk, but failed to convince the London government. So Mackinnon was left with his British India Steam Navigation Company, carrying the mail from Zanzibar to Aden, more as a public service than for a desire for profits. Mackinnon's road to Lake Malawi was abandoned just a few miles outside Dar es Salaam. Only the German threat to the traditional British dominance in Zanzibar in the 1880s gave Mackinnon a chance to found the Company with which he intended to carry 'civilization' into the interior.

Britain in South Africa

Overview

In the 1830s many of the *Boers* (Dutch farmers) of Cape Colony moved away from British rule there to conquer and settle in independent African lands on the High Veld, and also the large tracts of land deserted after the ravages of the Mfecane. The Great Trek of the Boers not only put the British government in a dilemma but demonstrated some of the fundamental weaknesses of British policy in South Africa. The dilemma was that since the Boers were British subjects the British government had a duty to extend British authority to all areas occupied by them, to control and prevent the Boers causing a racial war in southern Africa that would affect not only the new Boer republics, but which might also become general and spread to British territory as well. Britain also wished to guard against the Boers seizing a port farther north than Durban. If the Boers took an Indian Ocean port they could undermine Britain's fundamental reason for being at the Cape: strategic control of the sea route to India. However, establishing British control over the Boers would necessitate the heavy expense of administering a vast area, not considered to be economically productive. Therefore, British policy towards the Boers vacillated frequently between annexation and leaving the Boers alone. Annexation, and the idea of confederation of the Boer and British states which went with it, was only considered seriously when it was thought that expansion would be cheaper than maintaining the status quo. At times Britain considered that confederation would lessen the possibility of racial wars and therefore the expense of waging them. Yet confederation was never a realistic alternative for one simple reason: the Boer republics were fiercely determined to preserve their independence from a Britain which

148

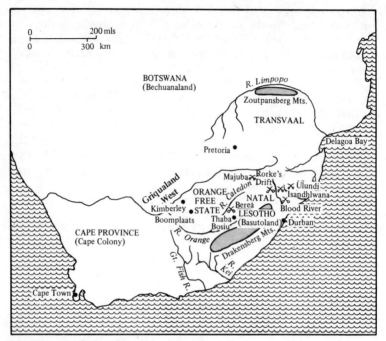

Map 11. Southern Africa before the Scramble.

placed the black man on a legal equality with the white man. This, indeed, had been the fundamental reason for the Great Trek of the Boers away from the Cape.

Yet in spite of the differences in Boer and British legal systems, both of the white communities in South Africa were at root no different in their attitude to African lands. In both the British colonies of Cape Colony and Natal and the Boer republics of the Orange Free State and the Transvaal, white acquisitions of land at the expense of the Bantu- and Khoisan-speaking peoples continued after the Great Trek and right up to the period of unification. Furthermore, the British as much as the Boers were concerned to use the Africans mainly as cheap labour for white farms. In British as well as Boer-ruled states, taxes were imposed on the Africans to ensure a steady flow of black labour to white farms, and the Bantu areas were turned into reserves of labour.

A paradox in white expansion, whether it was undertaken by British or Boers, was that it was often motivated by a desire to overcome a sense of physical insecurity caused by the presence of powerful and more numerous Africans on the frontier. This was the 'frontier mentality'. Paradoxically, it brought whites into contact with more African societies, not fewer, considerably extending the racial frontier and increasing the sense of insecurity.

British rule in Cape Colony

English-speaking South Africans have always claimed to have been more liberal than the Afrikaans-speaking Boers in their attitudes towards Africans. It is a claim not always supported by the facts, although in some cases there can be little doubt that English rule was more liberal than that of the Dutch.

The Cape government's Ordinance 50 of 1828, inspired by London Missionary Society pressure directed by Dr John Philip, gave Coloureds (people of mixed race) and Africans more freedom under the law, especially in master–servant relationships. In 1833 slavery was abolished in the British Empire including Cape Colony, yet the freed slaves continued to occupy a subordinate position in society and the economy. As late as 1891 a third of white children in school attended mission schools with no colour bar. However, once children left school, they were most unequal. Whites took their place in the dominant ruling racial group and educated Blacks and Coloureds found themselves to be misfits—an elite among their own people but firmly excluded from the ruling group and with few opportunities to use their western skills. After 1820 wool farming displaced the declining ivory trade and the economic gap between European and African rapidly increased. As the nineteenth century progressed, white racial attitudes hardened. There was, for example, much more intermarriage between races earlier in the century than there was to be later.

The Cape boasted representative institutions, such as municipal councils established in 1837, an elected parliament in 1852 and self-government from Britain in 1872. In theory there was no racial franchise barrier. As in contemporary England the franchise was dependent on income; therefore some non-white voters got on to the voting roll. However, the franchise was always kept at an income level, by frequent upward revisions, that would ensure an over-whelming white majority. However, in the Boer republics there were no African voters at all.

Although the English may have been more liberal than the Dutch at the Cape their liberalism needs to be kept in proportion. Nothing illustrates this more graphically than the suppression of the independence of the Xhosa of the eastern Cape. The Xhosa fought heroically in a vain bid to retain their land and their independence, first against the Boers and then the British, until their final defeat in 1878. There were nine 'Kaffir Wars' as the Europeans called them, but which are now called the Wars of Dispossession. The white frontier moved steadily eastwards because the Europeans were better armed with guns, were more mobile on their horses, and were members of an organized state. In contrast the Xhosa were ill-armed and divided into many chiefdoms. In these struggles the British received invaluable help from the Mfengu (Fingo), former refugees from the Mfecane, who during the period 1835 to 1856 had been settled by the Cape government on Xhosa lands. The Mfengu acted as auxiliary soldiers and frontier guards for the British.

The failure of the Xhosa in the Axe War of 1846–7 and the war of 1851–3 showed the hopelessness of armed resistance. In 1857 they tried out a new technique of resistance to European expansion. In 1856 a girl named Nongqause prophesied that if the Xhosa destroyed all their cattle and grain and did not sow seed then their dead heroes would rise and a great wind would come and sweep all the whites into the sea. In a nationwide movement in 1857–8, between 150,000 and 200,000 cattle were killed. Needless to say, the hope did not materialize, and scores of Xhosa died from starvation.

Overcrowding in the Ciskei and Transkei of indigenous Xhosa, immigrant Mfengu and Europeans led to a revival of Xhosa armed resistance in 1878. The Gcaleka under Kreli attacked the Mfengu and Europeans, and the Gaika under Sandili joined in. The Cape militia could not cope with the widespread rising, but this final struggle for Xhosa independence was crushed by General Thesiger (later Lord Chelmsford) with British regular troops, artillery and Gatling guns. Monica Wilson in *The Oxford History of South Africa* has emphasized how misunderstandings between Europeans and Africans contributed to the violence on the eastern Cape frontier. Europeans alleged that chiefs had granted land when in fact no chief owned land and could not therefore dispose of it. He could only allow Europeans to *use* it. Similarly Europeans misunderstood polygamy and confused African religion with witchcraft. These misunderstandings were not, however, the cause of conflict. Regardless of how much or how little Europeans understood the Xhosa they were determined to dispossess them of their land, while the Xhosa were just as determined to retain it.

Boer aims and policies

Those Boers who left the Cape Colony on the Great Trek were determined to shake off British rule and to create a community based on their own beliefs. They claimed that the Old Testament proved Africans were an inferior race. They hated the British attempt to force even a limited measure of racial equality on them and to abolish slavery. They were not prepared to accept the African on any basis other than servility. Land hunger also drove the trekboers to the High Veld. Their semi-pastoral way of life and rapid exhaustion of vast areas of grassland had kept them on the move since the earliest days of white settlement at the Cape. Like the Ndebele and the Ngoni, the trekboers were forced by economic factors to seek new lands and create new states to the north.

The new Boer states reflected the trekboers' deep distrust of organized government of any kind. In the Transvaal plans were made in 1849 for a united government and a *Volksraad*, or parliament, but the Transvaal Boers did not get round to appointing a head of state or formulating a constitution until 1860, when the South African Republic was proclaimed. Until then each of four regional groups of settlers was in practice a separate republic. Even after they united in 1860, there was a four-year civil war over who should be president, until peace was made and Pretorius took on the job from 1864 until 1871. The Orange Free State was created not by the Boers but by the British in 1848 and handed over to the Boers in 1854 (see below). Before the discovery of minerals the Boers on the High Veld lived on their herds and flocks, and produced little for exchange. In the almost complete absence of a money economy they were able to maintain only tiny civil services and carry out very limited public works.

The trekboers contrasted sharply with the Cape Dutch who were educated and more liberal and did not join the Trek but stayed in Cape Colony. Indeed most Boers even at the end of the century were Cape Dutch, who never challenged British authority and constituted the majority of the white voters in the Cape electorate.

The Boers, the British and the Africans in Natal, 1838–79

In the late 1830s the trekboers migrated into the land made vacant by Zulu devastations south of Zululand and set up the Boer republic of Natalia. They failed to establish an organized administration or to develop a farming economy of their own. They attempted to enforce land-ownership rights and to extract rent from the Nguni. They also tried to force the Nguni to work for them. The Nguni resisted these pressures and the Boers were not numerous enough to overcome this resistance. By 1845 most of the Natalia Boers had trekked back to the High Veld.

British occupation in 1845 of the area they proclaimed Natal was a response to the earlier Boer occupation, and was motivated by a mixture of philanthropy and strategy. There was philanthropic feeling among British missionaries and anti-slavery groups against the Boer seizure of African lands. The British government had to pay attention to this element in British public opinion, but it also had a strong motive of its own: the Boer threat to Durban. While Durban was 'saved', the fear of the Boers taking an Indian Ocean port farther north in Delagoa Bay was not removed until 1902.

The new British settlers who poured into Natal after 1845 tended to take much the same attitude to Africans as the Boers had done. Their fear of Zulu power led them to adopt and carry out a policy of rigid racial segregation along Boer lines. The government made no attempt to duplicate Cape 'liberalism' in Natal. Official 'native policy' by the British administration tended to buttress the unofficial apartheid established by the white settlers. Theophilus Shepstone, the Natal Secretary for Native Affairs from 1853 to 1875, established a system of separate reserves, or locations, for Africans. He recognized traditional chiefs and codified customary laws, but Shepstone's policy was not a recognition of African rights. Most land went to the whites. Hardly any money was spent on African development, whether in agriculture or education. Shepstone refused to recognize either the capacity of Africans to embrace and use western technology, or their claim to equal status with whites. The failure of Shepstone's vision and policies was shown in the way Natal's economy developed and in the Langalibalele episode.

Shepstone believed that only the white man could develop the economy of Natal. However, the attempt to develop export crop farming with British immigrants failed. The settlers were ignorant of the local soil and climate and of local crop and stock diseases. They suffered from shortages of capital and labour, the Nguni being most reluctant to work for them for the low wages offered. The Natal Land and Colonization Company, which was set up in 1860, realized that the Nguni farmers were quite willing to enter the money economy providing they worked on land without white bosses. The Company made clear profits by renting land to African producers and extracting rent in the form of produce, especially maize. Africans would not work on sugar plantations. Between 1860 and 1865 about 6,000 Indians were brought to Natal on five-year indentures to work on the plantations. Most of them remained becoming artisans, shop-keepers and market gardeners. Thus, African tenant farmers and Indian indentured labour, not white settlers, developed the agricultural potential of Natal in the nineteenth century.

The Langalibalele affair showed that Shepstone—and the white colonial authorities in general—did not understand two vital aspects of African life: the African desire to preserve at least a measure of independence from white encroachment, and the traditional democratic traditions which made it almost impossible for an African leader to force his people to obey and order they opposed. Langalibalele was hereditary chief of the Hlubi, who lived in the Natal Khalamba (Drakensberg). The Hlubi had acquired many guns largely as payment for work on the Kimberley diamond fields. The chief failed to enforce the Natal ordinance against ownership of unregistered firearms. He had no traditional power to force his clansmen to surrender their guns to him, and in any case he supported them. In 1872 he refused to obey summonses to appear before colonial officials for failure to enforce the Ordinance and led a trek of 10,000 Hlubi over the Khalamba towards friendly Basuto clans. Shepstone sent a military expedition which cut off the Hlubi but failed to persuade them to return. Therefore the soldiers exacted punishment by attacking the old men, women and children left behind in caves on the reserve. All the kraals were burnt, 8,000 cattle were seized and two hundred Hlubi were killed. Over five hundred prisoners were handed over to private farmers as virtual slave labour. Langalibalele was eventually betrayed by some Basuto, tried in 1874, and sentenced to life imprisonment on Robben Island. The Anglican Bishop of Natal, John Colenso, bravely condemned the Natal Government and exposed the atrocities, but to no effect. No reforms in the administration were carried out.

The Orange River and Lesotho, 1848–70

In 1848 Britain annexed the area between the Orange and Vaal rivers and named it the Orange River Sovereignty, thus following up the 1845 annexation of Natal. Why did Britain expand into the South African interior in the 1840s? Firstly, many of the trekboers who had settled in this region regarded themselves as British subjects and demanded protection against powerful African rulers, like Moshweshwe of Lesotho, whose lower land they were busy occupying. Secondly, the Khoi-speaking Griqua of the Orange valley, under Adam Kok, were also British subjects, and wanted protection against Boers as well as Bantu. Thirdly, and above all, Britain wanted stable government, not turbulence on the northern frontier of Cape Colony, and believed that extension of the frontier was the easiest way to bring this about.

The 1848 annexation of the Orange River Sovereignty was resisted both by Moshweshwe and by a section of the Boer population led by Pretorius. Moshweshwe fought a war with the Cape from 1850 to 1852. He was initially defeated at Berea in the lowlands but success-fully defended his mountain stronghold, Thaba Bosiu, against attacks from the Cape. One group of British troops, assisted by the Rolong, was defeated. The Cape Governor, Sir George Cathcart, insisted that Moshweshwe pay a fine of 10,000 cattle as a punishment for his victory. Moshweshwe supplied 3,500 cattle but Cathcart insisted that this was not enough and sent troops to collect more. They were driven off while attempting to do this but did manage to capture several thousand cattle. Moshweshwe then scored a diplomatic triumph when he sent a message to Cathcart saying that he hoped the captured cattle would be sufficient compensation and that the Basuto would not be punished further. Cathcart accepted this offer of peace. The Boer resistance was much shorter than that of the Basuto. Pretorius and his followers were heavily defeated at Boomplaats and Pretorius fled to the Transvaal.

As soon as Britain had established effective control north of the Orange River she decided to withdraw. The expense of suppressing armed resistance by Basuto and Boers pointed to the financial wisdom of disengagement. In the 1852 Sand River Convention Britain recognized the independence of the Transvaal Boers, and in the 1854 Bloemfontein Convention she handed over the Orange River Sovereignty to a group of Boers who were willing to accept independence. The Sovereignty was renamed the Free State. Griqualand East was founded in north-eastern Cape Colony as a refugee home for Adam Kok's Griquas because most of Griqualand was given to the Orange Free State.

The first President of the Orange Free State, Josias Hoffman, was forcibly and unconstitutionally deposed by his fellow Boers for adopting a conciliatory policy towards the Basuto. The majority of Free State Boers wanted to extend Boer territory deep into Lesotho, but the Basuto were determined to resist any further encroachment on their already limited grazing lands. The first Free State–Basuto War, in 1858, ended in a Basuto victory when the Boers failed in an assault on Thaba Bosiu. The second war lasted from 1865 to 1868, but this time the Basuto were defeated. Moshweshwe's age—he was now about eighty—was beginning to tell; succession quarrels among his sons hindered united resistance; the Free State was stronger, following a considerable increase in the white population; and the Boers had a regular supply of ammunition whereas the Basuto did not. Moshweshwe, a masterful diplomat to the last, made a decisive choice of the lesser of two evils, and offered his country to the British as a Protectorate in 1868. Sir Philip Wodehouse, the High Commissioner and Governor of Cape Colony, was duly obliging. Wodehouse was able to declare a protectorate over Lesotho in spite of the London government's reluctance on grounds of expense, because the Boers had made the mistake of expelling Moshweshwe's French Protestant missionaries. Missionary circles in Britain put powerful pressure on the British government to put the area under Cape protection. Wodehouse's motives were less concerned with missionary enterprise. Boer victories in Lesotho had led to Basuto refugees invading Cape Colony for food and coming into conflict with African communities under British protection. Extension of protection to Lesotho would stabilize the Cape's north-eastern frontier.

Although Britain restored to Lesotho much of the land taken by the Boers, all land west of the Caledon River was lost. This meant that, deprived of fertile agricultural areas, Lesotho would be condemned to a future as a labour reserve for white South Africa. On the other hand, when Moshweshwe died in 1870 he was happy in the knowledge that the remnant of his land would remain free from white settlement, and the core of his nation had survived.

Griqualand West, federation and the Transvaal, 1867–77

The discovery of diamonds in 1867 in Griqualand on the ill-defined Orange Free State—Cape Colony border transformed South Africa's history. It marked the beginning of the change from an agricultural to an industrial and urban economy. It also led to a revolution in British policy in South Africa by making a federation of British colonies and Boer republics financially acceptable and even economically desirable.

In 1871 Britain annexed Griqualand West ostensibly to establish law and order on the Kimberley diamond fields, and to save the remaining Griqua there from Boer slavery, but in reality to prevent the Boers of the Orange Free State from getting the diamond wealth and hence the means to resist British supremacy in Southern Africa.

The discovery of diamonds brought a vast amount of capital to South Africa which in turn led to railway building and large-scale capitalism. Migrant labour from all over southern Africa flocked to Kimberley. At first, Griqualand West's administration was enlightened. There was no racial bar to the ownership and operation of mines, but in 1875 this liberal policy was abandoned under strong pressure from the white miners, and only whites could henceforth own or operate diamond concessions. Thus was laid the foundation of later South African industrial society: the ownership and management was white and the unskilled labour was black.

British policy in the 1860s favoured federation as desirable in principle, as a means of stopping frontier wars, but in the 1870s the policy was now viable in practice because the Cape could charge customs duties on the goods going to the diamond fields. Confederation was also desirable for strategic reasons. The Boers were threatening to take a port at Delagoa Bay at the expense of the weak Portuguese in Mozambique. In 1875 President Burgers of the Transvaal toured Europe in search of funds to build a railway from Pretoria to Delagoa Bay. It was urgently necessary for London to find an excuse to annex the Transvaal as a step towards a British-dominated confederation.

Britain did not have to look far for excuses. The Boer republics were landlocked and poverty-stricken; the Transvaal was unable to defend itself effectively against Sekhukhune's Bapedi; and there was the danger of a Zulu invasion resulting from a dispute over land. In 1877 Shepstone went to Pretoria and annexed the Transvaal for Britain in the face of only passive resistance by the weakened, bankrupt and demoralized Transvaal Boers. President Burgers even favoured British annexation out of despair at the lack of development in his republic. Unlike the Orange Free State which had developed wool farming on a large scale, by 1877 the Transvaal Boers still had only a subsistence farming and hunting economy. Before the discovery of gold on the Rand in the late 1880s the Transvaal was less viable economically than many African States which were able to produce goods such as hides, skins and ivory, for export and use the profits of this trade to buy firearms with which to resist the Boers.

Britain had, however, completely misread Boer opinion. Burgers' views were not typical. The Orange Free State refused to accept the confederation proposed by the new British High Commissioner, Sir Bartle Frere. Britain bailed out the Transvaal from its national debt, and arranged regular payment of salaried officials, who had not been paid for six months. But Britain exacerbated feelings when she refused to allow the Volksraad, the Transvaal parliament, to meet on the grounds there was no budget to discuss. The Transvaal revolt of 1880–1 indicated the true temper of the Boers.

The main result of the British annexation of the Transvaal from the African point of view was that Britain took over not only the Transvaal but also its disputes with its powerful African neighbours, the Bapedi and the Zulu.

Bapedi resistance to European invasion

The military achievement of the Bapedi in defeating the Boers has been largely overlooked to date, because of concentration by historians on the stirring history of the Zulus at the same time.

The Bapedi are a Sotho-speaking community of northern and eastern Transvaal. They rose as a powerful chiefdom under Thulare, who died in 1820. They successfully defended themselves against the Zulu, the Ndebele and the Swazi by retreating to the highlands, such as the Zoutpansberg and Lulu Mountains, and organizing defensive guerilla warfare. Sekhukhune, who succeeded Sekwati in 1861, absorbed many non-Bapedi in his multi-ethnic state, including Zulu and Swazi refugees. He also took in many new subjects as the Transvaal Boers tried to collect taxes from Africans, seized their land, prevented them from possessing firearms, ammunition or horses, and expected chiefs to provide manpower for agricultural labour on demand. Sekhukhune's kingdom was independent and therefore a natural magnet for African resistance to the Boers. However, Sekhukhune needed land for his thousands of new subjects, so he took the struggle to the midst of the enemy by occupying Boer farms. In the war of 1876 he defeated the Boers, who failed to storm his mountain stronghold. The Boer commando's discipline collapsed, many of its soldiers deserted, the Boer farmers refused to pay taxes and the Transvaal's army and administration ceased to function.

When Britain occupied the Transvaal in 1877 it arranged a truce with Sekhukhune, but the king resumed the war in 1878 by ordering fresh attacks on Boer farms. In 1879, after the end of the Zulu War, the British were able to divert powerful forces against Sekhukhune. General Wolseley's expedition contained over 3,000 Europeans and 9,000 African allies. Eventually British artillery and dynamite overcame the determined resistance of the Bapedi who had many guns but whose marksmanship was poor. Sekhukhune was captured and detained in Pretoria gaol. He was set free by the revived South African Republic in the Transvaal in 1880, but was not restored to his kingship. He was murdered by followers of his rival Mampuru in 1882. Sekhukhune was thus a victim of external aggression and internal disunity.

The lessons of the Bapedi defeat are of significance to the history of the whole continent in the last quarter of the nineteenth century, because they illustrate in microcosm a fatal weakness in African society at the time which made it comparatively easy for African states to lose their independence. That weakness was political disunity, the failure of African societies to make common cause against the invader even on a regional level. Often one African group would ally with the white invaders against their traditional enemy. The predominantly Nguni Swazi assisted the British against the predominantly Sotho Bapedi, largely because of the traditional enmity between these groups. However, even had there been unity it is doubtful whether African armies would have succeeded in the long term in resisting the much more highly-trained European invaders.

Zulu resistance to British invasion

Britain invaded Zululand in 1879 partly to win the favour of the Transvaal Boers. When Britain took over the Transvaal in 1877 she became involved in a land dispute between the Zulus and Boers. Britain wished to reconcile the Boers to the 1877 annexation and to win their support for a scheme to confederate the white states of South Africa.

Transvaal Boers had for some time before 1877 been infiltrating and settling in Zulu territory in the Blood River region, and claiming that Zulu kings had ceded it to them. Britain recognized the justice of the Zulu position and an 1878 Commission of Inquiry of British officers upheld Zulu land claims against the Boers. However, the Commission's Report was deliberately kept secret by Frere, the British High Commissioner at the Cape, until it was too late to prevent the war he planned against the Zulu kingdom.

At first a Boer–Zulu War seemed much more likely than an Anglo–Zulu War. Sekhukhune's successful resistance in the Transvaal encouraged Cetshwayo, the Zulu king, to mobilize his army on the Transvaal border. The custom of 'washing the spears' in the blood of an enemy had not yet been carried out for Cetshwayo who had become king in 1872. The Zulu army wanted war with the Transvaal in order to 'wash its spears', resolve the land dispute, obtain revenge for the Zulu defeat at the Battle of Blood River in 1838, and replace the Zulu cattle lost in the drought of 1877. Yet Cetshwayo was not prepared to fight the Boers unless they started the war and he certainly did not want war with Britain with whom he consistently attempted to maintain peaceful relations.

Neither the Zulus nor the Boers provoked war. Frere wanted war with the Zulus in order to crush once and for all the general threat of a Zulu standing army on Natal's borders, and prevent a Zulu assault on the weakened Boers. He believed that this would attract the Boers into a confederation. Frere also felt bound to protect the Transvaal Boers who were now British subjects, especially as they were white men. He feared a massacre of Boers by Zulus and the dramatic loss of prestige to the white man in general in southern Africa that would ensue from such an event. Frere defied the British Government in London in forcing war on the Zulus, and sent Cetshwayo an ultimatum that the king could not reasonably have met. The ultimatum included heavy fines of cattle as punishment for a trivial Zulu–Natal border incident, acceptance of a British Resident in Zululand to guide Zulu policy and disbandment of the Zulu army. Cetshwayo attempted to comply with the first two demands, but his soldiers would not have broken up their regiments even if he had ordered them to. The Zulus were thus pushed into a war which Bishop Colenso openly declared was unjust and unprovoked on their side.

Once the British forces under Lord Chelmsford, fresh from their victory over the Xhosa in 1877–8, marched into Zululand in January 1879, the London government felt bound to support the men on the spot and prosecute the war until it was won. It was far from being the easy victory that the British expected.

At the Battle of Isandhlwana on January 22, 1879, the Zulu army under its commander-in-chief, Tshingwayo, inflicted the most severe defeat a European army was to suffer in Africa until the Ethiopian victory over the Italians at Adowa in 1896. The British defeat was surprising, for the core of the British force was made up of eight regular battalions armed with the latest Martini-Henry breech-loading rifle, whilst the Zulus, although armed with many rifles, preferred to use their assegais. In some ways the Zulus were lucky to win at Isandhlwana, but at least they took maximum advantage of British errors and their own good fortune. The British camp at Isandhlwana was not laagered, and no trenches were dug, although Chelmsford had been advised by the Boer leaders, Kruger and Joubert, that this must be done every evening without exception.

Before the battle began the Zulu force, marching on Isandhlwana, split up because of a dispute between its commanders. Cetshwayo had remained in his capital at Ulundi, but had given orders for his generals to fight a defensive war, not to invade Natal, and to avoid frontal attacks on British guns. When Tshingwayo ordered a frontal attack on Isandhlwana, General Matyana, who favoured guerilla war and was jealous of the appointment of Tshingwayo over him, marched away with several Zulu regiments to form a separate front of his own. Matyana's feint from the main Zulu force was not, therefore, deliberately intended to draw away Chelmsford and part of the British force from Isandhlwana, but it did have that effect.

While Chelmsford was pursuing Matyana, Tshingwayo led his men against the British camp. Pulleine, the commander, failed to contract the defences but instead moved troops out of the heart of the camp to reinforce the outposts. The perimeter proved to be far too large for the comparatively small number of defenders. For instance, the front of the camp had less than six hundred men to cover a distance of almost a mile. Nevertheless for about an hour, the British appeared to be winning the battle. Two thousand Zulus were shot dead by accurate fire from the Martini-Henrys and the defensive perimeter held, but then the British riflemen began to run out of ready ammunition. There was still plenty of ammunition but most of it remained in the heart of the camp far from the men who needed it. As the British fire became less continuous and even sporadic, the Zulu were able to close in on the perimeter and break it. The tide now turned as the Zulus destroyed the outnumbered British in hand-to-hand fighting. Short stabbing spears killed 905 of the 960 white defenders as well as 470 black Natalian allies of the British. Clearly the incredible Zulu courage was a major factor in the battle, for it enabled the Zulus to sustain enormous casualties before the tide of battle turned in their favour.

In spite of Isandhlwana, the Zulus lost the war. They learnt the wrong lesson from the battle, because good luck had enabled them to win it with their traditional tactics. The successful British defence of Rorke's Drift in the aftermath of Isandhlwana should have been a warning to them. This time only eighty-four British soldiers behind a tiny defence perimeter, and with plenty of ammunition always available, held off a large Zulu regiment. Three hundred and fifty

Zulus but only 17 British soldiers were killed at Rorke's Drift. When the British renewed their invasion they annihilated a Zulu frontal attack at Kambula, a battle which left 18 British and 2,000 Zulu dead. This time the British made no serious mistakes. They laagered regularly and relied heavily on artillery and Gatling guns. Finally, at Ulundi on July 4, a British square of 5,000 men destroyed the last Zulu frontal assault, after Cetshwayo's soldiers had disobeyed his orders to retreat into the forests and adopt guerilla warfare. Cetshwayo believed this would prolong resistance considerably, but the Zulus had had no experience of defensive warfare and had no desire to try it out. The soldiers returned to their kraals, and Cetshwayo was captured by the British and deported to Capetown.

Zululand was destroyed as an independent state in 1879 but it was not annexed by Britain until 1887. Cetshwayo was deposed and exiled, and Zululand was divided into thirteen small kingdoms each under a British nominee. A British Resident loosely supervised the affairs of disunited Zululand. Britain did not step into the vacuum thus created by the removal of royal political, ritual, judicial and economic power, and the result was anarchy and civil war. Two factions emerged, one of pro-Cetshwayo royalists, and another of the new petty kings appointed by the British. Cetshwayo was restored in 1883, in the hope he would re-establish order, and thus save Britain the expense of direct authority over Zululand. Because a powerful anti-Cetshwayo faction had been allowed to emerge between 1879 and 1883, the King's authority was limited to the centre of his old kingdom. His rival Sibebu was confirmed as the ruler of an independent Mandhlakazi kingdom in the north, and the south was allocated as a reserve for those chiefs and clans who opposed Cetshwayo's restoration. Civil war broke out between supporters of Cetshwayo and supporters of Sibebu. Thousands were killed as Sibebu's forces routed Cetshwayo's. Amongst the dead on Cetshwayo's side were Tshingwayo, the victor of Isandhlwana, and old Mbopa, the ex-prime minister and assassin of Shaka fifty five-years earlier. Cetshwayo was forced to flee to the southern reserve, where he died in 1884, probably of poisoning.

Dinizulu, Cetshwayo's fifteen-year-old son, succeeded his father and won back central Zululand by allying with the Boers of the Transvaal against Sibebu, who was defeated and driven into exile. The Boers were then given 4,000 square miles of Zululand by Dinizulu. This alarmed the British who declared the remnant of Zululand a British Protectorate.

The Anglo–Zulu War inspired the Transvaal Boers not to confederate with Britain but to fight for their independence from Britain. Isandhlwana had shown the Boers that Britain was not invincible. Ulundi had removed the Zulu threat to the Transvaal and rendered Boer links with Britain unnecessary.

Basuto wars of resistance, 1879–81

The Basuto or southern Sotho accumulated a considerable number of guns between 1870 and 1880. On the Kimberley diamond fields they were paid in guns, and the farm workers and railway construction labourers in the Orange Free State were paid in cash and bought guns with the money. Nearly every Sotho man owned a gun as he did a horse, as a symbol of manhood. In 1878 the Cape government, fearing another Xhosa War of Resistance gave notice of its intention to disarm all Africans in the Cape, including Basutoland then under Cape rule. This measure led to two wars of resistance by the Basuto.

The first war in 1879 was led by the remarkable Moorosi, who was born in about 1795 and was chief of the Phuthi people in southern Basutoland. Moorosi was determined not to be disarmed, but he had other grievances against the British. The appointment of a white magistrate for the Phuthi in 1877 had been regarded by Moorosi as a rejection by the British of his supremacy over his people. Moreover, the magistrate, Hamilton Hope, was a very young man, and Moorosi regarded his age as an additional insult. Hope did not help by his zeal in trying to override Phuthi customary law by European concepts of equity. Late in 1879 Moorosi's son, Lehana, was arrested and sentenced to four years' jail on a charge of horse stealing. The old man rescued his son from a local jail and hid him in the mountains, where he was besieged in his fortress by colonial forces. Moorosi's people showed their heroism and courage by holding out in the winter without food, but they lost the war of attrition. Moorosi refused to accept surrender terms which included life imprisonment, and he was killed along with most of his kin in the British assault.

During this war 2,000 Basuto enemies of the Phuthi fought on the British side in the hope of gaining loot, but the real economic gains were made by the British. The Phuthi people were dispossessed and sent to work on white farms in the Cape, while the Phuthi lands were opened up for white settlement.

The second Basuto war of resistance was the Gun War of 1880–1 which affected a wide section of the people of Basutoland. Led by Lerotholi, who was the son of Letsie, Moshweshwe's son and successor as paramount chief, many of the Basuto refused to surrender their guns. They resorted to skilful guerilla resistance, using Griqua and Boer commando techniques. These included firing from cover, then mounting and riding off out of retaliatory range, ambushes, and harassing supply lines. The old Sotho technique of defending fortified hills was also used. In 1881 the Cape gave up the struggle; the Basuto were allowed to keep their guns, and peace was restored.

In 1884 the Cape eagerly gave up Basutoland to the British government which made it a protectorate directly under London's control. The Basuto were no longer subjects of a white settler government. The long-term result was that they regained their independence in 1968.

Transvaal independence

The annexation of the Transvaal by Britain in 1877 sparked off a reaction among the Boers. The *Afrikaner Bond*, an organization founded in 1880 to safeguard Boer interests, spread among Dutch-speakers in the Cape Colony, the Orange Free State and the Transvaal. The Battle of Ulundi ended Transvaal reliance on Britain. When the British safeguarded the lands of the defeated Zulus from Boer expansion in the period of 1879–80, the Transvaal saw no advantage in preserving the British connection. The Transvaal Boers held back from revolt during the British General Election of 1880, when Gladstone, the Liberal leader, supported the idea of Transvaal independence. When Gladstone won the election and became prime minister again he suddenly realized there were Africans in the Transvaal who should not be put under Boer rule, and he refused to grant independence. The Boers, led by Kruger and Joubert, rose in armed revolt in 1880 and defeated a small British force at Majuba Hill. Gladstone gave way. He was not prepared to override the principle of Boer independence by sending a punitive expedition, especially as it would be expensive.

At the Pretoria Convention the Transvaal was given internal autonomy, while foreign relations were to be under British control. Britain thus retained its influence over the Boers and its supremacy in South African politics, even if the idea of confederation was, for the moment, dead. However, the discovery of gold in massive quantities on the Witwatersrand in the Transvaal in 1886 would stimulate British economic imperialism in South Africa and revive the scheme of confederation.

The European
imperialist overture:
(3) Portugal and France

The Portuguese empire in Africa, 1840–90

Overview

Portugal's African policy in the mid-nineteenth century was the three centuries old 'civilizing mission'. However, her real aim was simply to hold on to whatever territory she had in the face of challenges from European powers and African states.

By 1840 Portugal's authority in her African colonies had shrunk to the coastal regions of Guinea-Bissau, Angola and Mozambique. The creation of slave economies in the previous three hundred years had made the Portuguese empire in Africa a classical case of economic growth on an exploitative and extractive pattern. The Portuguese claim that they had built non-racial societies because of European–African intermarriage was a hollow one. The absence of white women in Africa had led to massive concubinage of black women for white men, and slavery was often involved in such unions.

There was, however, some attempt at reform in the Portuguese colonies in the nineteenth century. Between 1821 and 1910 Portugal was a constitutional monarchy mostly ruled by liberal governments. The enlightened regime of the liberal prime minister Sa da Bandeira (1836–40) declared the abolition of slavery in Portuguese possessions, but this and other reforms had little practical effect. Determined resistance from colonists and colonial officials kept the slave trade going in Portuguese Africa. It was eventually abolished in practice only when the British government ordered its Navy to seize Portuguese slave ships, and when in 1850 Brazil abolished slave imports. In 1858 Sa da Bandeira was in office again, and this time he passed a law abolishing slavery gradually over a twenty-year period. Once again, colonials in Angola and Mozambique offered violent and open resistance and the measure was never effectively enforced until the twentieth century.

Guinea

Portuguese Guinea was hardly 'Portuguese' at all. There was no effective Portuguese occupation outside the small capital town of Bissau. Commerce was largely undeveloped, and amounted to only £60,000 in 1863. The limited economic development, which was almost entirely based on the cultivation of groundnuts, was dominated by French traders who took two-thirds of the exports, so the Portuguese hardly benefited. Disputes with Great Power rivals led to the loss of territory. In 1859 Britain occupied Bulama Island to stop unofficial slave trading by Portuguese officials, and handed the area over to Sierra Leone. Later the French took the Casamance River basin with its groundnut farms. Within the context of her possessions in Africa Guinea was of little significance to the Portuguese in the nineteenth century.

Angola

Angola, in the late fifteenth century the scene of a remarkable experiment in Christian evangelization and peaceful and fruitful contact between the white man and the black man, was by 1840 a disgrace to the 'civilizing mission'. Ruthless exploitation of the indigenous inhabitants by Portuguese slave-traders and real-estate agents had effectively ruined the country.

The Portuguese tried to encourage white settlement in Angola, but with little success. It was believed that the presence of white men in the country would be a 'civilizing' influence. However, finding that the number of free settlers was small, the Portuguese sent large numbers of *degradados* (exiled criminals) to the colony. Many of them were men who had been guilty of serious crimes such as murder, assault and rape. Once in Angola such men were virtually free. They worked for the government as administrators and soldiers. Official missions to the interior of the country to protect the slave trade, to collect taxes and to procure forced labour gave the degradado troops a licence to murder and plunder. Africans faced with this type of mission, often moved farther and farther into the interior. Most of the degradados lived in the coastal towns. An attempt was made in 1884 to found an agricultural settlement for them in the interior but this soon failed. Clearly no 'civilizing' mission was possible with such a class of people. In fact, the human refuse which was sent from Lisbon constituted a serious threat to the stability of the urban areas.

Effective Portuguese occupation in Angola was limited to a narrow coastal belt. In 1846 only six white men lived east of it. There-after, some efforts were made to colonize the interior. In 1852 Silva Porto, a prominent white colonist, moved inland and settled on the Bihe Plateau, where he not only farmed but developed trading relations with far away Bulozi in Zambia. In the 1870s a number of white settlers expanded into the Kwanza valley and took up coffee growing. On the whole, however, the Portuguese failed to settle in the interior.

Much more initiative was shown by Africans in the development of the interior. An example is Dom Antonio Andre Fernandes Tor-res, the Christian Mbundu chief of the district of Kabuku Kambilo, an area under nominal Portuguese rule. Dom Antonio gained an increasingly greater share of the control of trade routes between Luanda to the west and the further interior to the east and contri-buted to an Angolan boom in agricultural products such as coffee, groundnuts, palm oil, manioc flour, tobacco and cotton. This boom was a result almost entirely of African enterprise in both agriculture and commerce.

Generally, the African way of life was stronger than the European one in nineteenth century Angola. Many Portuguese traders, especi-ally in the interior were more African than European in their ances-try, in their customs and the arts of daily life. At the political level, Portuguese colonial authority was heavily dependent on the loyalty of African rulers who were in effect allies rather than subjects of the white man. The Portuguese relied on local manpower and indirect rule to maintain their slight administrative control.

Mozambique

By 1840 the Portuguese position in Mozambique had declined so far that not even a loose system of indirect rule was possible. The weakness of metropolitan control from Lisbon was graphically illus-trated in the years 1840–50, only a few years after Bandeira's aboli-tion of the slave trade. In that decade the number of slave exports from Mozambique increased to the record figure of 25,000 a year.

The reservoirs for the Mozambican slave trade were the *prazos*, or crown estates, established by the Portuguese government in the lower Zambesi valley in the seventeenth century, and granted by the government to Portuguese adventurers. The *prazeros* (estate-owners) were European, Afro-European or Goan overlords, generally Africanized, who ruled mini-states which were virtually independent of the Portuguese government. The prazero ruled over the slave population on his prazo, but a free African population lived in the traditional manner on its historic lands alongside the slaves. The prazero generally ruled by consultation with the free chiefs. Even the slaves had considerable political power, which they

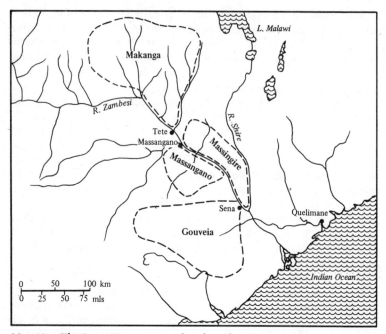

Map 12.   The Supra-Prazos. Note that these frontiers are only approximate, since the boundaries were continually changing.

exercised through their leaders, the *kazambo* and the *chikunda*. Each prazero controlled several slave-regiments, each under the command of a slave chief or *mukazambo*. Each regiment was subdivided into slave squads of ten or twelve men and their families, each squad being headed by a *tsachikunda*. The chikunda were often more loyal to the mukazambo than to the prazero, and frequently demonstrated their willingness to fight for their rights and security. The prazos were, therefore, not an effective instrument of Portuguese control. In several ways they posed a challenge to metropolitan power and even a direct threat to it.

Lisbon relied on the prazos to hold on to territory in Mozambique, but in practice the prazeros had considerable freedom of action within their domains. The prazeros themselves were heavily dependent on their slave captains. The chikunda played a role in collecting taxes for the prazeros from free Africans, but most of the revenue went to the prazeros rather than to the representatives of the metropolitan government. The chikunda were, however, far more than tax collectors. As the principal elephant hunters in south Central Africa, they ensured for the prazos the main source of Mozambique's income—ivory. As military invaders, they helped to destroy the Malawian Undi kingdom. As slave traders, they provided slaves for work on the prazos, and contract labour for export after 1850.

Contract labour was a new form of slavery developed to supply the needs of the French sugar plantation owners in the Indian Ocean islands of Réunion and Comoros for cheap workers. Slaves bought from the prazos, were 'asked' if they were willing to serve as 'voluntary' workers for five years. Legally they were contract workers, but in practice they were slaves. In 1864 the system was abolished by the French Emperor Napoleon III, but it continued illegally until about 1890.

The Portuguese government, alarmed at the increase in slave-trading, at the lack of security for person and property and the general lack of agricultural development, outlawed the prazo system by decrees in 1832, 1838, 1841 and 1854, all of which failed completely to change anything. The government found it needed to use the prazeros to maintain Portuguese authority against African invasions such as those of the Shangane and Ngoni in the 1820s and 1830s. The Nguni invasions nearly destroyed the prazos but they survived because most prazeros paid tribute to the invaders, especially to the Shangane Gaza kingdom.

During the first half of the nineteenth century the prazos went into serious decline. As the demand for slaves rose the prazeros were unable to supply a sufficient number from outside their prazos. Increasingly Africans living on the prazo were sold into slavery. Opposition to this from free Africans continued to grow and revolts became more frequent. Many freemen migrated to distant areas. The stability of the prazos was destroyed largely because the prazeros had ignored the necessity for compromise and co-operation with local indigenous leaders. The growth of absenteeism amongst prazeros also contributed to the decline of the system. Absentee landlords demanded quick profits and did not seriously consider long-term prospects. A prolonged drought from 1823 to 1830 and further droughts in the 1830s further undermined the prazos. By the middle of the nineteenth century, according to an official report, only thirteen out of the fifty-one estates in Tete and seven out of thirty-two in Sena were still occupied and these figures are probably overestimates.

Although the first half of the nineteenth century saw a steady decline in the prazo system the second half witnessed the emergence of four supra-prazo polities: Makanga, Massingire, Massangano and Gouveia's empire. These large multi-ethnic political units in theory maintained Portuguese political power in East Central Africa. In reality, the supra-prazos constituted a form of resistance to Portuguese imperialism and were almost entirely independent of Portuguese control.

The Kingdom of Makanga was the oldest of the four supra-prazos. It was ruled by the Pereira family who formed close contacts with the Undi empire. The rulers contracted marriage alliances with a number of land chiefs. They also attempted to legitimize their position by consulting with the spirit mediums. Gradually the Pereiras adopted the indigenous life style, beliefs, value system and social organization. This tended to increase their legitimacy by blurring the differences between the alien overlords and their indigenous subjects.

The kingdom had a large, well-trained army which allowed it to maintain its independence of the Portuguese and at the same time expand its frontiers. The success of the army was mainly due to its use of European weapons obtained in return for slaves and ivory. The kingdom played a middleman role in trade which it maintained by refusing to allow passage to Africans from the north and Portuguese traders from the south. Although relations with the Portuguese varied considerably the Pereiras were adamant in maintaining their independence.

In Massingire to the south much the same sort of process as had gone on in Makanga took place. Starting as a small prazo of the Portuguese the state was expanded by Fastino de Sousa and his step-son, Mariano vas dos Anjos, who is better known by his African name of Matequenha. A number of Maganja chieftaincies, detribalized Tonga, Sena and chikunda were welded into one state. Matequenha married the daughter of at least one Maganja chief and acknowledged the supremacy of the traditional Mbona rain priests.

Matequenha's relations with the Portuguese varied considerably. When it was in his interests to cultivate friendship with the Portuguese he did so. He assisted the Portuguese against both the Nguni and Massangano. However, Matequenha generally adopted an independent line towards the Portuguese and often raided crown estates. The Portuguese were only able to bring Massingire under their control in 1884 when they called on the help of Gouveia, an even mightier prazero than Matequenha II, who now ruled in place of his father.

While Massingire was being consolidated north of the Zambesi the prazo of Massangano grew up to the south. Once again it was virtually independent of Portuguese control. Several unsuccessful campaigns were launched by the Portuguese against Massangano between 1867 and 1875. The most humiliating defeat came in 1869 when only 107 of 1,000 troops survived a campaign against the prazo. Resistance to the Portuguese continued until the end of the century.

Amongst the greatest of the prazeros of the late nineteenth century was Antonio Manoel da Sousa, better known as Gouveia. A Goan, he built his wealth and power on ivory hunting and trading. He built a string of fortified posts against Gaza, and was granted prazos by the Portuguese government as a reward. He allied with African rulers and married their daughters, thus using polygamy as a diplomatic technique to extend his sphere of influence. Gouveia also won over many Shona leaders by selling guns to them, by mastering Shona languages and by practising Shona customs and manners. He underwent an extensive cultural change which facilitated his political ascendancy. In 1880 he took advantage of a succession crisis in the Barue chiefdom on the death of the chief who was his father-in-law to use force and make himself Regent for his own son, though the boy had no real claim. In 1883 Gouveia became paramount ruler of the Manyika in Mashonaland, and in 1884 aided the Portuguese against Massingire. This co-operation did not imply that he was subordinate to Lisbon. His policies merely coincided with the interests of the Portuguese. He continued to make it plain that he regarded himself as an independent ruler. Gouveia's expansion was halted only by British expansion in Southern Rhodesia. His empire collapsed when the British arrested him and imprisoned him in Capetown. After his release Gouveia tried to rebuild his state but in 1892 he was killed in Barue while trying to recover the Mozambique part of his domains.

Isaacman in his book *Mozambique* has pointed out the similarities between the four supra-prazos of the nineteenth century. The rulers were all given grants of prazos by the Portuguese which stipulated their subordinate position. All relied heavily on the ivory and slave trade. The resulting wealth enabled them to buy European weapons which were used effectively to expand their territories. They all built up their states from peoples who had been weakened by invasions, the slave trade and civil war. They all attempted to obtain some traditional legitimacy and underwent cultural change which strengthened their political position. They all entered into alliance with neighbouring African states and all tried to maintain their independence of the Portuguese. Like many other African states they lost that independence in the aftermath of the Scramble.

France in Africa, 1840–80

Algeria

In 1830 France launched an invasion of Algeria—nominally a Turkish province but in practice completely autonomous. The casus belli was a senseless dispute between Husain, the Dey of Algiers, and the French government over payment for Algerian wheat sold to the French in the 1790s. The real reasons, however, for the French war of conquest were, in the first place, the desire of the unpopular government of King Charles X to gain military glory and popularity by a successful imperial adventure, and secondly the hunger of French commercial circles to exploit Algeria. The conquest of Algiers and its immediate hinterland in 1830 did not save the Bourbon monarchy, which was overthrown shortly after the invasion. French occupation of Algeria was not effective until 1847 when the heroic resistance of Abdul Qadir was finally crushed.

Abdul was born in 1807, son of the 'shaikh' of the Qadiriyya order. In 1832 he declared a jihad against the French, and organized resistance which lasted for fifteen years. After two years of guerilla resistance, Abdul made an agreement with the French. He needed time to consolidate his hold over the divided Berber communities of western Algeria. The French policy until 1840 was 'limited occupation'. They wished to occupy only the main towns and exercise sovereignty over the rest of the country through traditional Muslim rulers. The French recognized Abdul Qadir's role as emir, or sultan, over the territory in the district of Oran outside the three towns controlled by them. The agreement was soon broken by the French but renegotiated in 1837. Peace with Abdul gave the French the opportunity to crush the resistance led by Ahmed Bey of the former Turkish administration. Neither Abdul nor Ahmed realized the necessity of united resistance to the French.

A further factor of disunity played into French hands. This was the quarrel between the Qadiriyya and Tijaniyya brotherhoods. The Tijaniyya refused to recognize Abdul as a ruler when, in the late 1830s, he tried to extend his authority into their lands. Instead, they entered into alliance with the French after Abdul had captured 'Ain Madi', their main centre.

Abdul's policy towards France was of course, unrealistic. Co-existence between a French state in Algeria and a state ruled by Abdul was impossible. He oscillated between a holy war and an accommodation with the French, who were equally inconsistent, since their policy of limited occupation had no clearly defined geographical limits. Abdul and the French clashed over eastern Algeria, which both tried to occupy after the French had taken Constantine in 1837. In 1839 open war broke out once again when Abdul invaded the Mitidja Plain and many European settlers were killed.

Between 1841 and 1847 the new French Governor-General Bugeaud, succeeded in carrying out a policy of total occupation, decisively defeated Abdul, and ensured Algeria would develop as a white colony. Bugeaud used the *razzia*, or punitive expedition, to terrorize the Muslim population and crush resistance. Widespread atrocities stained the honour of the French army as it destroyed Muslim villages, burnt crops, stole cattle, and cut down trees. Many Berbers fought on the French side for loot, and the Tijaniyya supported the French.

Abdul was defeated. In 1843 he retreated to Morocco, where public opinion forced the Sultan Mawlay Abdul-Rahman to ally with him against the French. The Sultan's army was annihilated by the French at the Battle of Isly in 1844, and Mawlay was forced to treat Abdul as an outlaw. However, Abdul was able to gain new followers, both in Algeria and Morocco, and fight on until 1847. He obtained the support of communities in the Rif mountains of north-ern Morocco and Sultan Mawlay, now afraid that Abdul would carve out a state for himself there, co-operated with the French to trap him and force his surrender to the French. Abdul was impris-oned in France for five years, and when released in 1852 settled in Damascus.

Between 1848 and 1864 there were local rebellions in various parts of Algeria, but none on the scale of Abdul's resistance or the rising of 1871-2. The Algerian Muslim rising of 1871 was inspired by several factors. The French defeat in the Franco-Prussian War of 1870-1 encouraged Algerians to rise up against a weakened foe. A second factor was even more important. The French Government granted political concessions to the European settlers in Algeria, giving them the right to elect six deputies to the French parliament and reducing French army control over them. The Muslims feared the advent of a settler-controlled civilian administration and wished to forestall it. Thirdly, during a series of famines and epidemics in the late 1860s the French administration had given very little help to the Algerian people and this had caused considerable resentment.

The 1871 rising began when Muhammad Mukrani, a chief in the mountains of Kabylia, started a tribal rebellion. This developed into a wider rising which came to involve about one-third of Algerians. It was suppressed by the razzia, and the results were indeed devastat-ing. A huge war indemnity was imposed on Kabylia most of which was spent on further settler colonization. Many more Muslim lands were seized for white settlers. In fact, the Muslims were so thoroughly crushed that Algeria was unable to mount a major rebel-lion for another fifty years, although the Tuareg Berbers of the desert did manage to resist the imposition of French rule until the twentieth century.

The Muslims were held down by force during the period after the 1871 rebellion. A special law known as the *Code de l'indigenat* was prepared in the period 1871 to 1873 and put formally into operation in 1881. Under this law administrators could impose penalties with-out a trial on Muslims for forty-one different offences; civil adminis-trators could jail Muslims without trial and order collective penalties and the confiscation of property. Muslims wishing to leave their districts had to obtain the permission of the authorities. Originally intended to last for seven years the Code remained in operation until 1927.

The Algerian people felt the impact of French colonialism most directly in the loss of land. By 1846 there were as many as 109,000 settlers in Algeria, but the coming of settlers and alienation of tribal lands was accelerated after the defeat of Abdul Qadir. By 1871 the settlers numbered nearly half a million. Many French peasant families were settled on small farms, but at the same time large estates owned by a capitalist class of big landowners were developed.

172

growing vines and cereals and using not only Algerian Muslim but also Spanish and Maltese labour.

The Algerians were impoverished by French occupation and the creation of a settler economy. Suppression of armed resistance led to the destruction of thousands of homes and farms. Alienation of land to settlers led to a decline in the production of food crops and in the raising of cattle and sheep, at a time when the Muslim population was increasing. After 1871 many Muslim farmers were forced by poverty and the need to feed their families to become share-croppers, cultivating land owned by the Europeans and retaining a fifth of the produce for their own use.

Algerians were denied elementary political rights. An 1865 law pronounced Algerian Muslims and Jews to be French subjects entitled to serve in the army and civil service. They could also obtain French citizenship if they agreed to be governed by the French civil law instead of their own religious laws. By 1870 only 194 Algerian Muslims and 398 Jews had become citizens by agreeing to be governed by French civil law. French cultural arrogance was compounded by religious bigotry when restrictions were placed on the right of Algerian Muslims to make the *haj* or pilgrimage to Mecca. French fear of the creation of an educated Algerian class that would challenge French control is seen in the deliberate neglect of Muslim education. Muslims were refused a French academic education and were offered only technical education in crafts and agriculture.

What benefits did Algerian Muslims reap from French colonialism in the nineteenth century? The Arab Bureau of the government taught Muslim peasants how to cultivate new crops and to fight malaria, but these measures could not offset the loss of lands. Although about 20,000 Muslims became prosperous landowners, owning between fifty and five-hundred hectares each, this attempt to create a capitalist Muslim class was at the expense of the peasantry whose burdens it increased. In public works many new roads, railways, ports and dams were built, but the *colons* benefited most from them.

The period between 1871 and 1914 saw a growing division of Algerian society into two extremes: a European settler minority elite, and an economically depressed Arab Muslim proletariat. The settlers regarded themselves as the guardians of European culture in Algeria and opposed any attempt to improve the lot of the Muslim majority.

Senegal

French government policy in West Africa from 1850 to 1880 varied from formal empire in Senegal to informal empire based on commercial influence at the Dahomey coast. In Senegal, Governor Faidherbe, who ruled from 1854 to 1861 and from 1863 to 1865, laid the foundation of France's West African empire thirty years before the European Partition. He united the scattered and precarious French coastal trading settlements known as the Four Communes as part of a larger colony about a third of the size of modern Senegal. Faidherbe opposed the French policy of informal empire which was similar to Britain's West African policy in this period. He wanted Senegal to develop like Algeria, where European commerce had not flourished before effective European occupation of the interior.

French motives for expansion in Senegal in the 1850s were closely related to the policies of the new political regime in France: Emperor Napoleon III's Bonapartist dictatorship. Faidherbe was required by his Emperor to win new lands for the glory of France and the regime. Indeed France embarked on imperial expansion for purposes of national prestige in many areas of the world in the 1850s, notably in Indo-China. This was in notable contrast to British imperial policy in the period.

Another factor was military: France's fear of the expansion of the military, Muslim Tokolor empire of Al-Hajj Umar from upper Senegal to the lower Senegal valley and into the immediate hinterland of the Four Communes of Gorée, St Louis, Dakar and Rufisque. Economic motives for French expansion were also important to a regime in Paris that was determined to speed up the industrial revolution in France. Senegal was to provide not only new markets for French manufactured goods but also groundnuts for French industry. Groundnut oil was essential as a raw material for making soap, candles, cooking oil and lubricants for machinery. Groundnuts had been grown in Senegal from the early 1840s, but in the independent African states in the hinterland of the French ports, especially in the Wolof and Serer areas south of the Senegal River. It was this groundnut-producing region that Faidherbe intended to conquer. Like many of his countrymen, Faidherbe was a passionate believer in France's civilizing mission: to spread the ideas of the French Revolution of 1789 to other peoples. He was a strong advocate of the equality of races and the spread of education.

Faidherbe's military conquests extended French rule three hundred miles inland to Fort Medine on the banks of the upper Senegal, at the edge of the Tokolor empire, and as far south as the state of Sine-Saloum on the north bank of the Gambia River. By treaty with enemies of Umar or by conquest he occupied the whole of the lower Senegal valley. Faidherbe halted Umar's westward expansion when French troops held out at the siege of Fort Medine in 1857 against Tokolor troops and thereby diverted Umar's ambitions eastwards to the Niger. But in checking the Tokolor threat Faidherbe raised a new one to France. In 1861 he deposed the *Damel* (ruler) Macodou of Cayor, and thereby stirred up fierce armed resistance by the Cayor leader, Lat Dior Diop, for a quarter of a century.

Faidherbe's conquests enabled French trading companies from Bordeaux and Marseilles to take advantage of the initiative of African farmers producing groundnuts in the interior. A considerable two-way traffic developed as African producers and traders brought the product to the coastal ports or to the new trading depots which Frenchmen began to set up in the interior. Groundnut production rapidly expanded, supplying large-scale exports to France where the oil was refined. Dakar grew as the main port for groundnut exports. Imports began to match exports as products from France and France's other colonies in the tropics poured into Senegal. Imports of flour, rice, sugar, alcohol, metal goods, cloth, arms and jewellery, together with groundnut exports, enabled the colony's revenue to treble between 1850 and 1870. A booming economy and abundant finance made it possible for Faidherbe to modernize the capital, St Louis, by the construction of many new streets and buildings, and to build a telegraph line from St Louis to Dakar. They also made it necessary to set up the Bank of Senegal.

The change-over to a groundnut economy considerably stimulated economic growth in Senegal and even wider afield as migrant labour from as far away as modern Mali began to trek regularly to the groundnut farms of western Senegal. It could be argued that the new economic pattern placed Senegal firmly in the grip of international economic imperialism, as French merchants reaped huge rewards in their role as middlemen in the groundnut trade, as Senegal became a one-crop economy, and as the upper Niger region began to rely on the export of its manpower as a main source of wealth. On the other hand, the groundnut economy was a great stimulus to the economic growth that was necessary for the Senegalese manufacturing industry to develop at a later time.

Another of Faidherbe's achievements was in the field of education, of considerable importance if the French policy of assimilation was to be achieved. This policy was meant to turn the African subjects of France into black Frenchmen who spoke the French language and accepted French culture and beliefs. The Governor established a number of state schools, including a school for chiefs' sons and lay schools for Muslims, who objected to Catholic mission schools. Small technical schools were created. Secondary education scholarships in France were awarded to promising students. Thus Faidherbe accelerated the policy of assimilation in Senegal, by increasing the opportunities for Africans to embrace French culture and educational facilities, as part of the *mission civilisatrice*. Assimilation in the sphere of culture was racist in the sense that it denied the value of African culture, but it was the opposite of racist in another sense: it did not deny African intelligence and the capacity of the African to master western knowledge. Faidherbe was ahead of his time among Europeans in believing that an African's intellectual ability was equal to a European's.

Assimilation took other forms apart from the extension of French education. There was political assimilation to the metropolitan country through the representation of the Senegal Communes in the Chamber of Deputies in Paris, and the establishment of elected municipal councils in the communes. There was also the personal assimilation of Senegalese, especially those living in the four communes, by giving them the status of French citizens. However, the policy of assimilation had only very limited success in the nineteenth century (or indeed in the twentieth). French educational facilities were made available only to a small minority, and no real assimilation was possible without widespread French education. Even black Africans in the Four Communes who were French citizens did not adopt French culture to any significant degree. Many were Muslims, strong in their faith and customs. Others such as freed slaves who worked as labourers or servants for Eurafrican masters, were working class and had had no opportunities to learn French culture. By 1865 the colony had 15,000 French citizens, but most of them were illiterate and mostly Muslim or traditionalist in religion. In the conquered interior, Africans were French subjects, not citizens, and did not enjoy citizens' rights. They could not leave the 'protected areas' where they lived, they had no right of meeting or association, and they suffered from the *corvée*, or forced labour, on the maintenance of roads.

In the Four Communes the African majority failed to use their power in elections until the election of Blaise Diagne in 1914. In the nineteenth century they allowed the white French and Eurafrican merchants, who employed most of them, to dominate Senegal's politics. As a largely unorganized working class, the black Senegalese citizens were not roused to use their political privileges until it became necessary to defend them, when some white politicians proposed, in the early twentieth century, to disfranchise them. In any case, the growth of elective institutions in the communes in the 1870s and 1880s was due less to assimilationist policy than to the influence and agitation of Bordeaux firms in the French parliament. The Bordeaux merchants wanted their local European and Eurafrican agents in Senegal to obtain local political control and local self-government in order to resist or prevent the imposition of high taxes by the Governor. Assimilation, then was limited to the coast, and a failure even there. However, if it had succeeded, one basic fact would not have been altered: the Governor's power was absolute and he was advised, not directed, by the free citizens of Senegal.

Dahomey

French policy towards the Popo kingdoms of the Dahomey coast oscillated between exerting a purely commercial influence and

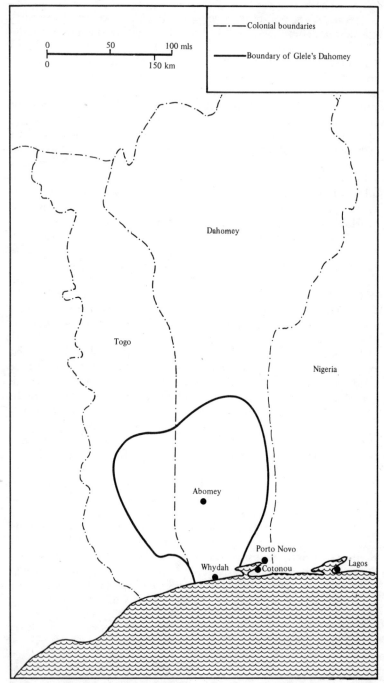

Map 13.   Dahomey under King Glele.

establishing colonial protectorates. The French had traded in slaves on the Dahomey coast in the eighteenth century, but the trade changed to palm oil in the 1840s when the Marseilles trader, Victor Regis, established himself in Porto Novo. In 1851 Regis made a commercial agreement with King Gezo of Dahomey, but soon had to face stiff competition from British palm-oil traders backed up by the British Navy. In 1861 Britain made Lagos a colony in order to suppress the slave trade and encourage palm-oil trade there. But the British had to pay for the expense of administrating Lagos at a time when palm-oil exports from Yorubaland were disrupted by the Ijaye War (see Chapter 5). Therefore, they wanted Dahomey to divert her palm oil from Porto Novo to Lagos. The Royal Navy duly bombarded Porto Novo on the pretext that the slave trade was still being carried on there. The bombardment merely caused King Sodji of Porto Novo to ask the French to make his town a French protectorate, which Regis accepted in 1863. However, the French government in Paris wanted friendly relations with Britain because of its bad relations with Russia and Prussia at this time. When Sodji died in 1864 the French abandoned their protectorate but Anglo–French trade rivalry continued.

In 1868 Regis made a treaty with King Glele of Dahomey who ceded Cotonou to the French for trading purposes. In 1878 the French made a new trade treaty with Dahomey as a response to the British blockade of Dahomey's main port of Whydah in 1877. Then in 1883 a new French Protectorate was established over Porto Novo. Acute commercial rivalry had developed between Britain and France. Each thought the other wanted to establish protectorates to guarantee trade for her own traders, and decided to establish them to forestall the rival Great Power. The stage had been set for the European Scramble for Africa.

Bibliography

This bibliography makes no pretence of being comprehensive. A number of useful books are recommended and most of them have much more comprehensive bibliographies which can be used by a reader wishing to study some aspect of the history of Africa at a greater depth.

ABUN-NASR, J. M. — *A History of the Maghrib*, Cambridge University Press (2nd Edition), 1975.

AJAYI, J. F. A. and CROWDER, M. (Eds) — *A History of West Africa, Vol II*, Longman, 1974.

CURTIN, P., FEIERMANN, S., THOMPSON, L., VANSINA, J. — *African History*, Longman, 1978.

ANENE, J. C. and BROWN, G. N. (Eds) — *Africa in the Nineteenth and Twentieth Centuries*, Ibadan University Press and Nelson, 1966.

AYANDELE, E. A. — *The Missionary Impact on Modern Nigeria*, Longman, 1966.

BENDER, G. J. — *Angola Under the Portuguese*, Heinemann Educational Books, 1978.

BOAHEN, A. A. — *Ghana: Evolution and Change in the Nineteenth and Twentieth Centuries*, Longman, 1975.

CROWDER, M. — *Senegal: A Study in French Assimilation Policy*, Oxford University Press, 1962.

CROWDER, M. — *The Story of Nigeria*, Faber, 1962.

CROWDER, M. — *West Africa Under Colonial Rule*, Hutchinson, 1968.

DAVENPORT, T. R. H. — *South Africa: A Modern History*, Macmillan, 1977.

DE KIEWIET, C. W. — *A History of South Africa*, Oxford University Press, 1941.

DENOON, D. — *Southern Africa since 1800*, Longman 1972.

DUFFY, J. — *Portugal in Africa*, Penguin, 1963.

FYFE, C. — *A History of Sierra Leone*, Oxford University Press, 1962.

GRAY, R. and BIRMINGHAM, D. (Eds) — *Pre-Colonial African Trade*, Oxford University Press, 1970.

GREENFIELD, R. — *Ethiopia. A New Polical History*, Pall Mall, 1967.

GROVES, C. P. — *The Planting of Christianity in Africa*, *Vols II and III*, Lutterworth Press, 1955 and 1958.

HARGREAVES, J. D.	*Prelude to the Partition of West Africa*, Macmillan, 1963.
HARGREAVES, J. D.	*West Africa: the Former French States*, Prentice Hall, 1967.
HARLOW, V. and CHILVER, E. M. (Eds)	*History of East Africa Vol II*, Oxford University Press, 1965.
HOLT, P. M.	*The Mahdist State in the Sudan*, 1881–98, Oxford University Press, 1958.
HOLT, P. M.	*A Modern History of the Sudan*, Weidenfeld and Nicolson (2nd Edition), 1963.
HOPKINS, A. G.	*An Economic History of West Africa*, Longman, 1973.
ISAACMAN, A. F.	*Mozambique*, University of Wisconsin Press, 1972.
JEAL, T.	*Livingstone*, Putnam, 1973.
JONES, A. H. M. and MONROE, E.	*A History of Ethiopia*, Oxford University Press, 1935.
KIMAMBO, I. N. and TEMU, A. J. (Eds)	*A History of Tanzania*, East African Publishing House, 1969.
KIMBLE, D.	*A Political History of Ghana*, Oxford University Press, 1963.
KIWANUKA, S. M.	*A History of Buganda*, Longman, 1971.
NEWITT, M. D. D.	*Portuguese Settlement on the Zambezi*, Longman, 1963.
OLIVER, R.	*The Missionary Factor in East Africa*, Longman (2nd Edition) 1965.
OLIVER, R. and MATHEW, G. (Eds)	*History of East Africa, Vol I*, Oxford University Press, 1963.
OLIVER, R. and FAGE, J. D. (Eds)	*The Cambridge History of Africa*, Volume 5, Cambridge University Press, 1976.
OMER-COOPER, J. D.	*The Zulu Aftermath*, Longman, 1966.
RANGER, T. O. (Ed.)	*Aspects of Central African History*, Heinemann Educational Books, 1968.
ROBINSON, R. and GALLAGHER, J.	*Africa and the Victorians*, Macmillan, 1961.
ROBERTS, A. (Ed)	*Tanzania Before 1900*, East African Publishing House, 1968.
RUBENSON, S.	*King of Kings: Tewodros of Ethiopia*, Oxford University Press, 1966.
SIMMONS, J.	*Livingstone and Africa*, English Universities Press, 1955.
THOMPSON, L. (Ed.)	*African Societies in Southern Africa*, Heinemann Educational Books, 1969.
TRIMINGHAM, J. S.	*Islam in the Sudan*, Oxford University Press, 1949.

TRIMINGHAM, J. S.   *A History of Islam in West Africa*, Oxford University Press, 1962.

TRIMINGHAM, J. S.   *Islam in East Africa*, Oxford University Press, 1964.

VATIKIOTIS, P. J.   *The Modern History of Egypt*, Weidenfeld and Nicolson, 1969.

WALKER, E. A.   *A History of Southern Africa*, Longman (3rd Edition), 1957.

WARD, W. E. F.   *A History of Ghana*, Allen and Unwin, 1958.

WEBSTER, J. B., BOAHEN, A. A. with TIDY, M.   *The Revolutionary Years: West Africa since 1800*, (Revised Edition) Longman, 1980.

WILLS, A. J.   *An Introduction to the History of Central Africa*, Oxford University Press, (3rd Edition), 1973.

WILSON, M. and THOMPSON, L. (Eds)   *The Oxford History of South Africa*, *Vol. I to 1870*, Oxford University Press, 1969.
Vol II 1870–1966, Oxford University Press, 1971.

Many useful articles can be found in the *Journal of African History* (Cambridge University Press) and in *Tarikh* (Longman).

Index

DATE DUE

GAYLORD			PRINTED IN U.S.A.